PRISONS
IN AMERICA

A Reference Handbook

Other Titles in ABC-CLIO's

CONTEMPORARY
WORLD ISSUES
Series

Affirmative Action, Lynne Eisaguirre
AIDS Crisis in America, Second Edition, Eric K. Lerner and Mary Ellen Hombs
Censorship, Mary E. Hull
Cults in America, James R. Lewis
Feminism, Judith Harlan
Genetic Engineering, Harry LeVine III
Hate Crimes, Donald Altschiller
Human Rights, Second Edition, Nina Redman and Lucille Whalen
MIAs, Jeanne M. Lesinski
Single Parents, Karen L. Kinnear

Books in the Contemporary World Issues series address vital issues in today's society such as terrorism, sexual harassment, homelessness, AIDS, gambling, animal rights, and air pollution. Written by professional writers, scholars, and nonacademic experts, these books are authoritative, clearly written, up-to-date, and objective. They provide a good starting point for research by high school and college students, scholars, and general readers, as well as by legislators, businesspeople, activists, and others.

Each book, carefully organized and easy to use, contains an overview of the subject; a detailed chronology; biographical sketches; facts and data and/or documents and other primary-source material; a directory of organizations and agencies; annotated lists of print and nonprint resources; a glossary; and an index.

Readers of books in the Contemporary World Issues series will find the information they need in order to better understand the social, political, environmental, and economic issues facing the world today.

P R I S O N S
IN AMERICA

A Reference Handbook

Nicole Hahn Rafter and Debra L. Stanley

**CONTEMPORARY
WORLD ISSUES**

ABC-CLIO

Santa Barbara, California
Denver, Colorado
Oxford, England

Library of Congress Cataloging-in-Publication Data

Rafter, Nicole Hahn–1939
    Prisons in America : a reference handbook / Nicole Hahn Rafter, Debra L. Stanley.
        p. cm.—(Contemporary world issues)
    Includes bibliographical references and index.
    ISBN 1-57607-102-2 (alk. paper)
        1. Prisons—United States   2. Corrections—United States.
    3. Imprisonment—United States.   4. Punishment—United States.
    5. Prisoners—United States.   6. Prisoners—Legal status, laws,
    etc.—United States.   I. Stanley, Debra.   II. Title.   III. Series.
    HV9471.R36   1999
    365'.973—dc21   99-35719
                                                                     CIP

05 04 03 02 01 00 99   10 9 8 7 6 5 4 3 2 1

ABC-CLIO, Inc.
130 Cremona Drive, P.O. Box 1911
Santa Barbara, California 93116–1911

This book is printed on acid-free paper ∞.

Manufactured in the United States of America

Contents

Preface

For over 200 years, imprisonment has held the central place in the punishment of criminals in the United States. Imprisonment is not our most frequently used punishment (offenders are more likely to be sentenced to probation), nor is it as severe as the death penalty. However, incarceration is our punishment of choice for most serious offenders. All citizens ought to know something about the origins of imprisonment, its evolution, key policy issues raised by its current use, and problems likely to be associated with it in the future.

Americans can be said to have invented modern incarceration as a means of criminal punishment. Although Europe provided precedents, theoretical justifications, and even architectural plans for imprisoning offenders, Americans developed the blueprints for the typical prisons of today and devised the disciplinary routines, types of sentences, and programs that prison systems of other countries subsequently adopted or modified. Today the United States continues to lead other nations in such areas as the recognition of gender differences in the treatment of prisoners, the movement to build and operate private prisons, and the construction of "supermax" penal institutions for inmates considered particularly dangerous. What we do affects prison policies around the world.

Americans disagree about the purposes of imprisonment. Some argue that the primary goal should be incapacitation—keeping criminals off the streets. Others strongly believe that prisons should aim first and foremost at deterrence—discouraging future crimes. Still others hold that the main goal of prisons should be rehabilitation, so that offenders will become law-abiding citizens. And many argue that the central purpose of prisons should be to punish or retaliate against those who have broken the law. For the past twenty-five years, the goal of punishment has enjoyed the widest public support; before that, however, rehabilitation was more popular, and even today Americans tend to endorse several (sometimes contradictory) goals for the prison system. To develop effective and efficient prison policies, we need to be able to distinguish among these various goals and understand which can actually be achieved and which are probably beyond reach.

Over the past three decades, the United States has become the lock-'em-up leader of the world. With well over 1 million men and women behind bars in state and federal prisons, we incarcerate a greater number of prisoners than other countries. Aside from Russia, we have the highest rate of incarceration in the world, locking up close to 450 people for each 100,000 people in our general population. With over 1,000 prisons, the United States operates many more penal institutions than other countries, and it spends more annually to operate these institutions— around $30 billion—than many countries spend on all governmental activities combined. Still, many people feel that our prisons are failures—or, worse yet, that they actually increase crime. When we spend so much to lock up so many, why have we apparently achieved so little in terms of overall social benefits?

This book provides a comprehensive overview of the origins and development of our current penal policies, emphasizing fundamental controversies that prisons face today. In addition to laying this groundwork, it offers guidance to students and general readers interested in discovering more about specific events, people, and problems in prison management. Finally, it presents an overview of the labyrinth of agencies and organizations involved in prison management and of the rich but sometimes confusing welter of print and nonprint resources available for further study.

Chapter 1 outlines the origins and evolution of U.S. prisons and the philosophies behind them. It also presents an overview of U.S. prisons today—their goals, size, costs, and most critical administrative problems. Chapter 2 summarizes opposing views of eight of the most controversial issues in current prison policy.

Chapter 3 presents a chronology of the major events and turning points in U.S. prison history, and Chapter 4 provides biographical information on key figures in the evolution of American prisons. Two types of material can be found in Chapter 5: documents basic to understanding prison oversight and information on the operation of prisons today. The documents excerpted in Chapter 5 include the U.S. Constitution, prisoners' rights court cases, and other writings that have had an impact on the regulation of U.S. prisons over time. The information on prison operations includes current data on sentencing, prison system growth and costs, prisoner characteristics, and private prisons. These tables and graphs also illustrate the type and quality of data available on U.S. prisoners and prisons.

The last three chapters are essentially resources for readers who wish to follow specific pathways into the study of American prisons. Chapter 6 lists public and private organizations involved in prison management and reform, along with contact information and brief descriptions of the work they do. Chapter 7, on print resources, describes the major books and government publications on prisons and supplies information on how to obtain them. Chapter 8, on nonprint resources, describes films and Internet sites that are useful in the study of prisons. The book concludes with a glossary defining some key terms in the study of the development and administration of U.S. prisons.

History of American Prisons

1

The American prison system is the largest in the world, and its inmates typically serve longer sentences than those of other western nations. "The" American prison system is in fact not a single entity but rather a vast network of penal institutions, some run by the federal government, others operated by the states. In 1995 there were 112 federal and over 1,000 state confinement facilities.

Recent rapid growth is the most remarkable—and controversial—feature of the U.S. prison system. In June 1998, federal and state penal institutions held an estimated total of 1.2 million prisoners, an increase of nearly 60 percent since 1990. One might ask if that huge increase is merely a result of growth of the total U.S. population. It is not, as one discovers by examining incarceration rates (the number of people in prison per 100,000 people in the general population). In the 1920s the U.S. incarceration rate per 100,000 people was well under 100; by 1997 it was about 445. Nor is this high rate due mainly to huge increases in violent crime. In fact, violent crime rates have been declining in recent years, even as the prison population continues to swell.

In the United States, where responsibility for punishing people found guilty of serious crimes falls mainly on state governments, the great majority of people incarcerated are state prisoners. Most prisoners (state and federal) are male (almost 94 percent), a result of much lower rates of crime among females, especially serious crime. Almost 50 percent of all state and federal prisoners are black, a figure that contrasts markedly with the proportion (around 15 percent) of black people in the general population and has given rise to charges of racism in the justice system.

In addition to the charges of racism, the prison system faces other serious problems. For example, its goals are not clearly defined: Americans disagree over whether prisons should serve mainly to punish criminals, or to rehabilitate them, or to keep criminals out of circulation, or to deter potential criminals from committing crimes. Another serious problem lies in our incarceration rate, which is the second highest (after Russia's) in the world. Moreover, the cost of incarcerating such large numbers is steep. It currently costs $20,000 or more to lock up a single person for a single year; in addition, capital outlays and prison construction drain off other funds that could otherwise be spent on education or health care for the general population.

To explain how the U.S. prison system became so large, expensive, and uncertain in its goals, this chapter provides an overview of the history of American prisons, focusing on developments related to key issues today. First it examines the background and origins of our prison system and then the establishment of the first penitentiaries. Next the chapter details the 1870s birth of the reformatory movement and the new penal philosophy of rehabilitation. The history of U.S. prisons is then traced through the early-twentieth-century Progressive Era up to about 1970, when Americans rejected the rehabilitative ideal and returned to using prisons to incapacitate and punish criminals. The chapter concludes with a summary of the state of U.S. prisons at the end of the twentieth century.

Background and Origins

In colonial America (the period from the first European settlements through the Revolutionary War), there were no state or federal prisons. Towns operated jails, but these local institutions held mainly debtors and people awaiting trial or execution. The various colonies had different laws for dealing with felons (serious offenders), but generally speaking, their criminal laws imposed physical punishments. Colonial punishments included flogging, branding, mutilation (as in the removal of an ear or nose), hangings, public humiliation, and banishments to wilderness areas, but they seldom involved confinement in penal institutions. In short, in the colonial period punishments emphasized the infliction of pain, not the deprivation of liberty.

After the Revolutionary War, citizens of the new country began to rethink issues of crime and punishment. Proud of having achieved liberty from England and stressing the importance of self-government, the leaders of the new United States began to think of deprivation of liberty as a better type of punishment than the old-fashioned physical punishments of the English and Continental traditions. Moreover, they decided that local communities should continue to be responsible for the punishment and correction of misdemeanants (minor offenders), but states should mete out the consequences for felons.

The first steps toward a new approach to punishing felons were taken in Philadelphia, which was the governmental center of the new country and also the region with the highest concentration of Quakers. This religious group emphasizes the value of the individual, holding that each of us has the ability to discover an "inner light" that leads to God. Quakers therefore oppose capital punishment and believe that no one is beyond redemption. As a colony under the leadership of William Penn, Pennsylvania had adopted the Quaker principle of humane treatment as a guideline for criminal punishments, greatly limiting the use of corporal and capital punishments.

Shortly after the Revolutionary War, Philadelphians made the first move toward the creation of the prison of today by expanding their local lockup, the Walnut Street Jail. Like other jails of the colonial period, the Walnut Street Jail had been constructed like a large house, with front and back entrances and large rooms off a central hallway. In 1790 Philadelphians added to this structure a strip of single cells in which serious offenders could be held for long periods, apart from the lesser offenders and also apart from one another. There, the Quakers hoped, felons might reflect on their sins, discover their inner light, repent, and thus emerge reformed. Here, in embryonic form, was the idea later embodied in institutions called "penitentiaries."

As the Quakers experimented with this new approach, they were influenced not only by their religious principles but also by new ideas arriving from Europe about the treatment of criminals. In 1764 an Italian named Cesare Beccaria had caused excitement throughout the western world by publishing a short book, *On Crimes and Punishments,* that argued for replacing the harsh physical punishments of the past with confinement. Incarceration, Beccaria argued, could be adjusted in length of time so that the punishment could fit the crime. This principle of proportionality, according to which the seriousness of the punishment should be matched to the seriousness of the offense, appealed greatly to the leaders of Pennsylvania and other new states, as did the idea of a punishment—deprivation of liberty—that meshed with the values of the new nation.

The innovative thinking reflected in the 1790 addition to the Walnut Street Jail quickly spread to other states, which began around 1800 to build separate prisons for the punishment of felons. However, most of these new institutions followed the plan of the older jails rather than that of the solitary cells added to the jail in Philadelphia—that is, they were designed more like very large houses than the type of institutions we think of today as prisons.

The large-house design of the early prisons soon proved inadequate. It led to the holding of a number of prisoners together in large rooms, a mixing that made it difficult to discipline those confined or to keep them from teaching one another criminal ways. Moreover, constructed like houses, these early prisons tended to be relatively small institutions, built for 50 or 100 prisoners but not easily expandable once the space was filled. Moreover, their floor plans made it difficult to prevent escapes or to separate women and children from the men. Such drawbacks led prison administrators and reformers to seek a better architectural model for confining criminals.

Some of the disadvantages of the early state prisons, from both the convicts' and the keepers' points of view, are made clear by the example of Connecticut's Newgate Prison at Simsbury. Named after an English prison, Newgate was established in 1790 on the site of an old copper mine where prisoners had in fact been held since 1773. Working deep in the earth in mine shafts and caverns, the prisoners—some of them the Tories who opposed the colonists during the Revolutionary War—could not easily escape.

But after the war, the local community became concerned about conditions at the mine. Laboring in cold and clammy conditions, covered with vermin, prisoners became ill and died. Some found ways to escape or turn on their keepers. Nor was it easy to expand the mine shafts as the convict population grew. And so in

1824 Connecticut closed Newgate and moved its inmates to a new, more modern and secure structure at Wethersfield. Around the same time, other states, too, began to abandon their original state prisons and to construct more adequate quarters.

The First Penitentiaries

About 1830, prison managers and reformers arrived at what seemed a superior architectural design: the penitentiary. In contrast to the earliest state prisons, penitentiaries were relatively large institutions surrounded by walls and entered through a fortresslike gate that could be securely locked and bolted. Within the penitentiaries, administrative offices were separate from the prisoners' quarters, and prisoners were held in long rows of single cells. From a central tower or observation post on the walls, a single guard could maintain surveillance of a large portion of the grounds. Moreover, there was room inside the walls to add new rows of cells if the institution became overcrowded.

These penitentiaries cut their inmates off from the free world, isolating them under circumstances in which they could be taught good habits, disciplined when necessary, and, it was hoped, reformed. Reformation would result (or so the thinking went) if the convicts were forbidden to talk with one another, visited by no one but the occasional preacher, and encouraged to read the Bible in their cells. Through reflecting on their sins, they might repent and become honest men and women.

Sentences to the new penitentiaries were "flat" or "definite" sentences; that is, they had no minimum or maximum length but rather were for a set period of time, such as five years. But penitentiary administrators soon realized that they needed some means to encourage good behavior and instill a ray of hope. Thus they asked state legislatures to enact "good time" laws that reduced prisoners' sentences by a specific length of time in return for good behavior. A good-time law that permitted one day of sentence reduction for every five days of good behavior, for instance, could lead to the release of a prisoner with a five-year sentence in four years.

Good-time laws, like the architecture and routines of the first penitentiaries, were designed in part to encourage reformation. However, the central goal of incarceration in early-nineteenth-century penitentiaries was simply punishment. If confinement also kept criminals out of circulation, or deterred free citizens from committing crime, or led some convicts to reform, so much the better. But if not, at least society was able to get revenge, retaliating against criminals to a degree proportionate to the seriousness of their offenses.

At first there were actually two competing types of penitentiaries, one associated with Pennsylvania, the other with New York State. The Pennsylvania system was first realized at the Eastern State Penitentiary in Philadelphia, an institution that, inside its walls, was designed like a wagon wheel, with long corridors of cells radiating off a central area in the middle of the yard. Theoretically, one guard standing in the central area could inspect all the wings at once. Under the Pennsylvania system, prisoners remained in their cells, alone, for the entire length of their sentence, the solitude broken only by an occasional visit from a minister. Each cell had a workbench where the prisoner could make simple products such as shoes; and many of the cells had their own tiny yards, walled open areas outside the cells where convicts could get exercise and fresh air. Although the Pennsylvania system was widely admired in Europe, it was seldom adopted in the United States outside of Philadelphia.

The competing model, sometimes called the Auburn system after the New York State prison where it was first implemented, also held prisoners in separate cells and forbade communication, but it brought them together during the day for silent labor in prison factories. (Because it allowed prisoners to congregate during the day, the Auburn system was sometimes also called the "congregate" plan, a term contrasted with the "segregate" plan of the Pennsylvania penitentiary.) As states decided to build penitentiaries, nearly all of them adopted the Auburn system.

The Auburn system triumphed because of its greater cost effectiveness. States found that it was far cheaper to build and operate congregate than segregate penitentiaries. Cells could be stacked on top of one another in tiers, whereas in the Pennsylvania system, stacking was impossible if prisoners were to have their own yards. Then too, cells could be smaller in the Auburn system, since prisoners did not have to be confined in them twenty-four hours a day for periods of years; and the institutions could earn more money from the sale of factory-made products than from those made through individual labor in cells. Backers of the Auburn system also claimed that the perpetual solitude of the segregate system drove prisoners mad, but in fact, economics counted most and was the consideration that led other states to adopt the congregate model of prison familiar today.

Following the examples of Pennsylvania and New York, other states erected penitentiaries as their convict populations outgrew the original, large-house type of prison. By 1870 nearly every state had a penitentiary for the punishment of male and female felons. Moreover, nearly every state had built a separate institution for juvenile delinquents to prevent the incarceration of children alongside adult criminals.

However, nearly all the penitentiaries had become crowded, so that it was no longer possible to maintain the ideal of one person to a cell or to prevent convicts from communicating. Moreover, by 1870, thanks to improved record-keeping, prison administrators were becoming aware of recidivism or repeat offending; they released convicts only to receive them again a few months later, convicted of a new offense. By 1870, then, the penitentiary system seemed to need an overhaul.

The Reformatory Movement

Interest in devising better methods of punishing felons intensified about 1870, partly because the end of the Civil War enabled northern and midwestern reformers to turn their attention to new causes. In the late 1860s two reformers, Enoch Wines and Theodore Dwight, inspected all the penal institutions in the United States and Canada on behalf of a private group, the Prison Association of New York. What they found distressed them. In their *Report on the Prisons and Reformatories of the United States and Canada* (1867), Wines and Dwight wrote that, "There is not a prison system in the United States . . . which seeks the reformation of its subjects as a primary object."[1] Indeed, most prisons seemed to be schools for crime. Wines and Dwight found no institution making systematic efforts to educate convicts, train them for a trade, or instill religious principles. The most important message of the *Report* was that convict reformation *should* be the key purpose of prisons. Reading between the lines of Wines and Dwight's *Report*, we can see that the goal of incarceration was changing.

The next major step toward overhaul of the prison system occurred in 1870, when reformers from throughout the country met in Cincinnati for a conference on improving the nation's prisons. (The formal title of the conference was the National Congress on Penitentiary and Reformatory Discipline. It became the first annual meeting of the group known today as the American

Correctional Association.) Enoch Wines, an organizer of the conference and later the editor of its *Transactions*,[2] opened the meeting with a speech summarizing his and Dwight's *Report* on the state of prisons. Another report, written by Sir Walter Crofton, formerly director of Irish prisons, described the "Irish system" of prison discipline, an innovative method of encouraging good behavior with the promise of early release. Zebulon R. Brockway, the superintendent of the Detroit House of Correction, delivered a speech arguing for more scientific methods of prison administration, methods that would, he explained, de-emphasize the traditional goal of punishment and work toward the goal of reformation.

At the end of the Cincinnati conference, the delegates unanimously approved a document, the "Declaration of Principles," that became the philosophical foundation of American prison management for the next 100 years. The Declaration of Principles begins by asserting that the fundamental purpose of punishment is to reform the criminal. At the time, this was a truly radical statement. Previously, retribution or revenge had been the primary purpose behind the punishment of offenders, but now the Cincinnati delegates were giving first priority to reformation—what we today would call rehabilitation. Next the Declaration called for a "mark" system of rewards, similar to Sir Walter Crofton's Irish system, that would give convicts incentives to reform.[3]

A third proposal called for sentences that would keep convicts in prison until they had truly reformed. Those who never changed for the better, the Cincinnati delegates maintained, should stay in prison until death. The delegates referred to the proposed new type of sentence as an "indeterminate" sentence. By that, however, they did not mean, as we do today when we speak of indeterminate sentences, a term with a minimum and a maximum, such as seven to ten years. They meant truly open-ended or indefinite sentences of one day to life for everyone committed to prison. And for convicts released on good behavior, they envisioned a system of the type now known as parole, in which state officials would keep former convicts under surveillance as they readjusted to the community. Those who returned to crime could be sent back to prison.

In addition, the Declaration of Principles strongly endorsed religious, vocational, and remedial education for prisoners. It further advocated classifying prisoners by their degrees of reformability, so that the reformable and the unreformable could be separated, and the latter could not teach the former new tricks of the criminal trades. In sum, the Declaration of Principles set forth a new philosophy of prisoner rehabilitation and a practical plan for achieving it.

The Principles were soon put into effect in a new type of penal institution, the reformatory prison for youthful adults. New York and other states began constructing reformatories in the 1870s. Designated for young (e.g., 16 to 30 years of age) first offenders who had not yet hardened into criminal ways, the reformatories held these prisoners not on the indefinite sentences advocated by the 1870 conference delegates, but on indeterminate sentences with minimum and maximum terms. (Indefinite sentencing failed because it did not conform with the principle of proportionality, according to which the punishment should fit the crime.) In return for good behavior and improvement, prisoners could be released on parole before the end of their maximum term.

The reformatories offered religious and vocational training; some also schooled illiterate prisoners. On the theory that a healthy mind requires a healthy body, the men's reformatories scheduled regular times for exercise in the yard. Women's reformatories provided female-specific programs, under the guidance of female staff. As women's reformatories opened, state legislatures wrote new laws enabling courts to sentence to them females who were not felons but merely misdemeanants or violators of city ordinances. Sentences of up to three years (a typical women's reformatory sentence) might have seemed severe to the young women who were sent to reformatories for minor morals offenses, but because this was called rehabilitation and not punishment, and because it was done for their own good, such lengthy sentences seemed reasonable to the lawmakers and judges who imposed them. And so there developed two new branches of the prison system, reformatories for young male felons and for young female minor offenders, both using indeterminate sentences with parole and both based on the ideas approved at the 1870 prison congress.

In recognition of the reformatories' rehabilitative goals, those who ran them were no longer called "principal keepers" or "wardens" (the titles of old-fashioned prison penitentiary managers) but "superintendents." Like Zebulon Brockway, who had become superintendent of the men's reformatory at Elmira, New York, these superintendents often considered themselves to be "scientists," specialists in the new science of penology or prisoner rehabilitation. Terminology shifted for lawbreakers as well.

Hardened offenders were still called "convicts," but the prisoners of the new reformatories were now called "inmates" or, in some cases, "patients."

The Progressive Era and Its Aftermath

Enthusiasm for prison reform and for the application of scientific principles to the treatment of prisoners continued well into the twentieth century, where it formed part of a broader reform movement called the Progressive movement (ca. 1900–1920). Early twentieth-century Progressives worked on a host of projects, from municipal and civil service reform to the "Americanization" of immigrant populations and the establishment of special courts for juvenile delinquents. One concern that drew early-twentieth-century reformers together, undergirding their diverse improvement programs, was that of social control: they worked to strengthen the ability of government to manage its various populations and ensure civic order. This concern with social control spilled over into reforms of the prison system, manifesting itself in development of the so-called medical model of prison management and in a resurgence of interest in indefinite sentencing.

The medical model is actually a theory of crime as well as an approach to prisoner treatment. According to this model or explanation of criminal behavior, people who commit crime do so because they are in some way sick. In the Progressive Era, some advocates of the medical model argued that offenders are physically sick, unhealthy, and therefore unable to compete with normal workers. Others argued that offenders are genetically inferior to law-abiding citizens and thus, through mental subnormality or some other "defect," unable to obey the law. Still others argued that offenders are mentally ill, unbalanced people who need psychotherapy to be restored to normality and law-abiding behaviors.

This medical interpretation of criminal behavior, which was in fact implicit in the 1870 prison congress's calls for more scientific management of convicts and its view of the prison as a moral hospital, appealed greatly to prison administrators of the Progressive Era. It elevated them almost to the status of physicians and invested them with authority to determine when their "patients" were sufficiently cured to be released.

The medical model took strong hold in the early twentieth

century among both prison administrators and the general public. Prisons hired psychologists to administer intelligence tests to inmates in order to determine which were too intellectually weak to follow the dictates of law. Some institutions also hired psychiatrists to diagnose prisoners' mental ailments. Legislatures throughout the country gave prison managers greater discretionary authority to decide who should be released on parole and who should be held until the expiration of the maximum term. In practice few if any prisoners actually received the benefits of psychotherapy. The main effect of the popularity of the medical model was to reinforce the idea that the American prison system should rehabilitate those who broke the law. Another effect was to increase the state's power over prisoners' lives, and now even their mental states.

Confidence in the medical model was bolstered by the popularity of the eugenics movement, an international effort to prevent "inferior" people from reproducing. Although eugenics theory was eventually discredited, it was widely endorsed in turn-of-the-century America, especially by men and women in charge of socially problematic groups such as criminals. Eugenic scientists seemed to have proved that criminality was often an inherited trait, passed through the generations in the "germ plasm." From this pseudoscientific theory eugenicists concluded that the best way to eliminate social problems is to prevent their "carriers" from "breeding."

In several states the eugenics movement led to the sterilization of prisoners and the enactment of statutes establishing special eugenic prisons where criminals with bad "germ plasm" could be held either for life or until they were no longer able to have children. These eugenic institutions were one logical conclusion to be drawn from the medical model of crime control: if one believes that certain criminals are fundamentally defective, it follows that they will never recover and, if released, will be bound to recidivate. At the time, this sort of reasoning made up-to-life sentences seem sensible, at least for some groups of offenders.

In fact there was a renewed interest in completely open-ended or indefinite sentences in the early twentieth century, not only among eugenicists but also among many other Americans concerned with social control. The medical model, with its idea that criminals who were not cured of the disease of crime were bound to relapse, implied that all sentences should be indefinite, with scientific penologists, not judges, being the ones to decide on a prisoner's release date. Although only a few states adopted eugenic sentencing laws, many enacted habitual-offender laws, which stated that on conviction of a third (or fourth) felony, a defendant should be imprisoned for life. Moreover, in the mid–twentieth century some states enacted sexual psychopath laws, which made it possible to hold anyone convicted of a sexual offense and found by a psychiatrist to be "psychopathic" on special one-day-to-life sentences, with release (if any) to be determined by psychiatric experts.

By the 1920s, when the Progressive and eugenics movements began to lose their energy, prison systems were well-formed and in place in nearly every state. In their typical configuration, these systems had a central penitentiary (often a renovated institution dating from the early nineteenth century) for serious adult offenders, male and female. In the Northeast and the Midwest most states also operated two reformatory prisons for young adults, one for males and one for females. Typically the female reformatory would receive mainly misdemeanants and minor first offenders, but increasingly they also received female felons formerly held at the central penitentiary. (No males convicted of misdemeanors and other minor offenses were sent to state prisons; instead, the men's reformatories held youthful felons.) In addition, some populous states had established an institution where criminally insane prisoners and defendants judged too mentally ill to stand trial could be held. There might also be a second high-security prison for male adults, built when the original penitentiary could be expanded no further. Otherwise, however, there were usually no other prisons in a state system until the 1970s began. Within their prisons, states segregated prisoners by race until lawsuits of the 1970s ended that practice.

Prison systems developed somewhat differently in the South and the far West. Southern states built penitentiaries before the Civil War, but these were mainly institutions for white felons. Slaves were punished by their owners on plantations. During the Civil War, southern prisons often held northern prisoners of war, and by the war's end, most of these institutions were in shambles.

Immediately after the Civil War, southern states passed "black codes" and "pig laws," racist legislation that imposed extremely harsh sentences for behaviors (such as stealing a pig) that newly freed and impoverished blacks were particularly likely to engage in. At the same time, southern states approved leasing systems by which a (white) farmer or factory owner could lease state prisoners for a yearly fee. In effect, the lease system reinvented slavery, as black prisoners were returned to the fields to work under overseers, much as they had before the Civil War. Conditions under leasing were even worse for black prisoners than they had been for slaves, because now the plantation owners had no incentive to keep workers healthy and alive. Prisoners' death rates soared.

Gradually southern states replaced their original prisons, but for years the new institutions held mainly white prisoners. These new prisons tended to be located on vast tracts of land. As leasing died out about 1900, southern states in effect became lessors, working black gangs on the prison plantations and holding them at night in crudely built wagons, guarded by white men with rifles and watchdogs. Sometimes the white guards were other prisoners, tough and brutal men appointed to serve as "trusties" or assistants to the regular administrators.

Among the western states, the prison system of California, which was settled early, developed along lines similar to those followed by eastern prison systems. Other western states, however, due to late settlement and sparse populations, often had only one central penitentiary well into the twentieth century. Men, women, mentally disturbed prisoners, and sometimes even children were held at these penitentiaries. However, prisoners usually were segregated by race, with blacks being sent to inferior quarters.

Civil Rights, Prisoners' Rights, and the Crumbling of Walls

The civil rights movement of the 1960s attempted to extend the guarantees of the U.S. Constitution to disenfranchised groups such as racial minorities, women, and prisoners. This struggle was waged on many fronts: at segregated lunch counters in the Deep South; in police departments that refused to hire women and minorities; and in the courts. Under the leadership of Chief Justice Earl Warren from 1953 to 1969, the U.S. Supreme Court decided a number of key civil rights cases that led to greater equality for previously subordinated groups. One such group was prisoners.

Before the Warren Court and civil rights movement, courts had followed the hands-off doctrine, according to which courts should not interfere in prison management. Prisons are operated by the executive branch of government, supporters of the hands-off doctrine reasoned, and therefore the judicial branch should not attempt to tell prison administrators how to run them. Moreover (this reasoning continued), prisoners, because they have broken the law, do not deserve constitutional protections. The civil rights movement challenged these premises; the Warren Court agreed with the challengers; and lower courts had to abandon the hands-off doctrine.

The civil rights movement also fed into the Black Muslim movement, a militant, nationalist effort by black prisoners to take control of their own lives. Starting in the late 1950s and at its most powerful in the 1960s, the Black Muslim movement organized black prisoners and preached a message of black superiority. Incarcerated Muslims insisted that they had a right to observe the dietary requirements of Islam, including its prohibition against the eating of pork (a staple of prison diets). Muslims also insisted on their right to have a copy of their holy book, the Koran, in their cells, just as Christian and Jewish prisoners were allowed to have copies of the Bible.

Prison administrators, the overwhelming majority of whom were white, fiercely resisted Muslim requests. They feared change, but even more, they feared black power. The racial balance of power in prisons was shifting in any case, because populations were becoming predominantly black. Prison guards, many of whom came from rural and predominantly white areas, balked at the Muslims' demands.

With the help of civil rights lawyers, Muslims nevertheless managed to present their complaints in the courts, where they found sympathetic judges. The very fact that this litigation occurred was revolutionary, for it meant that black prisoners could face off as equals against white administrators. Even more empowering were court decisions recognizing Muslim demands and insisting that prison personnel treat Black Muslims as the equals of Christians and Jews.

Imperceptibly, the civil rights and Black Muslim movements flowed into the prisoners' rights movement, a period of litigation from about 1965 to 1980 that resulted in a recognition that the U.S. Constitution applies not just to law-abiding citizens but to prisoners as well, though to a lesser degree. By 1980 inmates had won the right to access to the courts; to living conditions that meet certain minimum standards of cleanliness and safety; to medical attention for serious health problems; to freedom to practice any religion so long as it does not disrupt institutional routines or threaten institutional safety; and to present their side when facing punishment for violating prison rules.

One of the most important results of the civil rights and prisoners' rights movements, as James B. Jacobs points out in his classic study, *Stateville: The Penitentiary in Mass Society*,[4] was a crumbling of prison walls. The walls did not literally crumble, of course, but they became more permeable, and prisons became more open institutions. Media representatives, lawyers, and visitors could now see prisoners as a matter of course, not as a rare privilege granted by an authoritarian administration. Prisoners' mail was no longer routinely censored, and prisoners could read newspapers. Courts assumed temporary oversight of particularly oppressive prisons, clipping the wings of dictatorial wardens. The public could now scrutinize prison conditions and work for their improvement. In all these respects, Jacobs writes, prisons moved from the margins of society toward its center.

Rejection of the Rehabilitative Ideal, 1970–2000

When the federal government began compiling annual statistics on U.S. prisoners in the mid-1920s, there were about 100,000 state and federal prisoners in the entire country, and the number stayed below 200,000 until about 1960. In fact, it even fell during the 1940s, when many young men (the most prison-prone segment of the population) became soldiers and went overseas to fight in World War II. The totals rose a little above 200,000 in the early 1960s, only to dip again with the Vietnam War, which siphoned off the prison-prone population. Then in the early 1970s the prison population began soaring. By the mid-1980s, 400,000 people were incarcerated in U.S. prisons. By 1990 the figure had doubled to 800,000, and in the early 1990s it hit the 1 million mark.

What happened in the 1970s to create this remarkable surge and to necessitate a vast expansion of the U.S. prison system? The rapid inflation of U.S. prison populations was triggered by radical changes in our approaches to sentencing offenders. Just after the Revolutionary War, as we have seen, all prison sentences were flat or definite sentences of a set period (such as five years), with some reductions allowable for good behavior. With the opening of the rehabilitative era about 1870, states and the federal system switched to indeterminate sentences with minimums and maximums (e.g., a five-to-eight year sentence), a type that gives prisoners more incentives for good behavior and prison administrators more flexibility in regulating the size of their populations. In times of overcrowding, for instance, parole boards can grant more early releases.

The rehabilitative philosophy and, with it, indeterminate sentencing prevailed for about 100 years. About 1970, however, leaders in the formulation of prison policy began urging a return to flat or definite sentencing.

Liberals and conservatives alike supported the return to definite sentences. Liberals objected to the indeterminate sentence because it put prisoners at the mercy of parole boards and made it impossible to predict a specific release date. Some people were concerned that racial discrimination might be a factor in parole-granting decisions, a fear reinforced by the fact that most parole board members were middle-class and white, whereas prisoners tended to be lower-class and black. A series of prisoner riots, culminating in a dramatic, four-day standoff at New York's Attica Prison in 1971, brought the media to the prison's gates, where reporters learned that racism and uncertainty about release dates constituted two of the convicts' main grievances.

About the same time, on the other side of the country, California prisoner George Jackson published his dramatic book of letters, *Soledad Brother,* charging U.S. prisons with extreme racism and calling on black prisoners to rebel.[5] Jackson's indeterminate sentence, which gave California authority to hold him for close to life if it so chose for a robbery of about $70, seemed to confirm his charge that the prison system existed to immobilize black men. This suspicion again seemed to be confirmed when, not long after the publication of his book, Jackson was shot dead in the prison yard.

At the same time, conservatives, alarmed by rising crime rates and civil disorder, began objecting to indeterminate sentencing on the ground that it enabled criminals to gain release before serving their entire terms. Studies showed that parole boards were in fact incapable of accurately predicting who would relapse into criminal behavior. Conservatives thus joined liberals in calling for the abolition of parole. Simultaneously, the crime victim, a previously ignored figure in the criminal justice process, started demanding a say in sentencing, launching a victims' rights movement that became another factor in the shift back to determinate sentencing. In particular, victims demanded "truth-in-sentencing" as opposed to indeterminate sentencing, under which a prisoner with a sentence of, say, five to eight years might be released in four years or less with time off for good behavior.

Victims insisted that an eight-year maximum sentence should mean something close to eight years in prison.

Starting in the mid-1970s, ten states rejected indeterminate sentencing in favor of definite sentences, abolishing parole in the process. Other states greatly narrowed court discretion at sentencing while retaining aspects of their traditional parole system. (For example, California has done away with its parole board but still uses parole officers to supervise prisoners released before expiration of sentence on good-behavior time.) The variations are numerous, but the overall effect of definite sentencing is the same: Prisoners now spend more time behind bars.

Whereas some states embraced definite sentencing, others adopted related types of sentencing that have also contributed to the rapid rise in incarceration rates. One of these is mandatory sentencing. A mandatory sentence removes the judge's discretion; if the defendant is found guilty, the judge must impose a specified sentence, no matter what the circumstances. Mandatory sentences can be indeterminate or definite (determinate), but most of them impose prison time. Some states have enacted mandatory sentences of, for example, one year behind bars for people convicted of carrying unregistered handguns. Others have enacted mandatory sentences for drug offenses, sex crimes, and crimes of violence.

Repeat-offender laws are one type of mandatory sentence. Like the earlier habitual-offender laws, repeat-offender laws impose certain sentences on offenders convicted of specific types of crime. For example, three-strikes laws force judges to send to prison for life anyone convicted of a third felony (or, in some states, a third violent felony). Over the past two decades legislatures have passed dozens of mandatory sentencing laws, increasing the likelihood of prison and, in most cases, the length of sentences as well.

Another sentencing reform that has affected prison populations is presumptive sentencing, which was born of an effort to limit judicial discretion without removing it entirely. States with presumptive sentencing provide judges with a grid informing them which offenses should be punished with probation and which with prison time. (For an example of such a grid, see Chapter 5.) The grids also guide judges in deciding how much probation or prison time to give offenders according to their criminal histories. For instance, the grid might tell the judge that an offender with no criminal history convicted of second-degree assault should receive a sentence of 21 months on probation, whereas an offender with two prior minor convictions should receive a sentence of 30 months on probation for the same offense, and an offender with more serious prior convictions should receive a prison sentence of about three years.

The presumptive sentence is so named because it is the sentence that, presumably, the judge will impose. Presumptive sentencing gives judges some latitude to individualize sentences on the basis of prior record, but within narrow bounds. Thus sentences are more likely to be fair—about the same for everyone convicted of a specific offense and with a similar prior record. When judges depart from the presumptive sentence, they must explain in writing why they are doing so, a requirement that helps to eliminate the possibility of racial or some other form of bias in sentencing and makes it possible to review all departures from the presumptive sentence. By 1994, eight states had adopted presumptive sentencing laws.

Nearly all the recent changes in sentencing laws have lengthened the time a prisoner must serve before release. These changes thus are a key factor in the enormous increases in U.S. prison populations since the early 1970s.

Another factor driving up the prison population is the so-called war on drugs. In the late 1980s and 1990s widespread concern about drug sales and addiction encouraged lawmakers to enact laws providing especially harsh sentences for people convicted of possessing narcotics, especially crack cocaine. Mandatory sentencing and other types of strict laws aimed at drug-law violators put some sellers and users behind bars, but these laws have had many unanticipated, negative side effects.

The new drug laws have almost doubled the incarceration rate. They have not stopped the drug trade, which, because it is lucrative, merely passes into new hands when one seller goes to prison. The new drug laws have tended to net not the big-time dealers but small-time sellers and users. They have increased the proportion of blacks in the U.S. prison population, because crack cocaine, the target of the most draconian sentences, tends to be the drug of choice of black users, whereas white users prefer powdered cocaine and other types of drugs, such as marijuana. (Under federal law, possession of 5 grams of crack automatically leads to five years in prison, whereas possession of 5 grams of powdered cocaine, a nearly identical substance, is a misdemeanor that may result in no jail time at all.)

At the federal level, mandatory sentencing laws have repeatedly forced judges to send to prison, for very long terms and sometimes for life, minor offenders convicted of, for example, un-knowingly mailing a package containing crack for a friend. Some federal judges refuse to work in criminal courts because of these laws. New state-level drug laws added almost $10 billion in costs to state spending on corrections between 1993 and 1998. Com-menting on the extreme harshness of sentences for minor drug-law violations, Barry R. McCaffrey, head of the National Drug Control Policy Office, declared in 1999, "We have a failed social policy and it has to be reevaluated." Treatment of drug addiction, McCaffrey pointed out, would be far cheaper and more humane than sending minor drug offenders to prison for long terms.[6]

The huge growth in prison populations has led to a "private prisons" movement. During the 1980s and 1990s states found it difficult to keep up with the demand for more prison beds. Pri-vate, for-profit companies, many of them managed by former military or prison personnel, stepped up to offer an array of ser-vices to help states manage the overcrowding crisis. Some com-panies will run an entire prison, providing correctional officers, food and health services, and so on. Some companies will even build the prison that they then manage. Thus, the private prisons "movement" is not a social movement with broad social support but an entrepreneurial effort by private businesses to profit from the increases in prison populations. Whether states should con-tract with such businesses constitutes a major debate in U.S. cor-rections policy today.

Conclusion

The U.S. prison system has changed more over the past three decades than over the previous 100 years. Before 1970, a state might operate four to six prisons; by 1996 the state and federal prison systems were averaging twenty-nine correctional institu-tions, with some states operating about 100 prisons. Nationwide in 1996 the total number of correctional institutions was about 1,500; by 2001, it is expected to reach 1,800.[7] To keep up with the flood of new commitments, we need to add one 1,000-person-ca-pacity prison every week for the next decade.

The price tag for our current imprisonment binge is high. California, having created twenty-one new prisons in the past fif-teen years, currently (1999) spends $4 billion annually on its state prison system, which limits the amount it can spend in other areas such as education. Overall, states are now spending $30 billion annually on incarceration, double the rate of a decade ago.[8] Harder to estimate but no less important are the social costs of incarceration: broken homes, children raised with a parent missing, and prisoners' difficulty in finding jobs after release. Many experts feel that the primary effect of harsh drug laws has been to create an underclass of prisoners, former prisoners, and prisoners' families, a group with severe social problems and little or no stake in the broader society. This is the group most likely to be crime- and prison-prone in the future. If we want to reduce crime, criminologists argue, we should be reducing the size of the group, not encouraging its growth.

Many of those involved in the writing and implementation of the harsh drug penalties that have swelled our prison populations feel that these laws should be reevaluated or repealed so they no longer catch minor offenders in a net meant for drug kingpins. But the drug laws are so profitable for certain groups that repeal may be difficult or impossible. Correctional officers' unions have grown with the prison population, forming a strong lobby in favor of incarceration. The communities within which new prisons have been built, often in poor rural areas, form another group with an interest in keeping prisons open for business. Stockholders in the companies that build private prisons share this interest. Thus even with crime rates falling, Americans may be unable to stop the momentum toward yet further increases in prison populations.[9]

Notes

1. E. C. Wines and Theodore W. Dwight, *Report on the Prisons and Reformatories of the United States and Canada, Made to the Legislature of New York, January, 1867* (Albany, NY: Van Benthuysen & Sons' Steam Printing House, 1867), 62.

2. *The Transactions of the National Congress on Penitentiary and Reformatory Discipline Held at Cincinnati, Ohio, October 12–18, 1870,* edited by Enoch C. Wines (Albany, NY: Weed, Parsons and Company, 1871). The *Transactions* was reprinted in 1970 by the American Correctional Association to commemorate its Centennial Anniversary.

3. The Declaration of Principles, which can be found in its entirety in the Congress's *Transactions* (see note 2, above), is excerpted in Chapter 5 of this book.

4. James B. Jacobs, *Stateville: The Penitentiary in Mass Society* (Chicago: University of Chicago Press, 1977).

5. George Jackson, *Soledad Brother: The Prison Letters of George Jackson* (New York: Bantam Books, 1970).

6. McCaffrey, as quoted in the *New York Times*, 28 February 1999, 21.

7. These figures are from Camille Graham Camp and George M. Camp, *The Corrections Yearbook, 1996* (South Salem, NY: Criminal Justice Institute, 1996), 53.

8. *New York Times*, 7 March 1999, 16WK.

9. *New York Times*, 7 March 1999, 3WK.

Issues and Controversies

Prisons raise an almost infinite number of policy issues. This chapter focuses on eight issues or controversies that are particularly prominent in ongoing debates over prison policy:

- The purposes of incarceration
- Mandatory sentencing versus judicial discretion
- Prison expansion and overcrowding
- Prisoners' rights
- Equality for female prisoners
- Prison violence and its prevention
- Health care in prisons
- The private prisons movement

For each topic the chapter summarizes the nature of the controversy and key positions in the debate. It also provides some background information to explain the origins and development of the controversy, and in some cases it indicates likely outcomes in the future. The chapter's overall purpose is to introduce readers to the fundamental issues facing U.S. prisons today. Later chapters build on these discussions.

The Purposes of Incarceration

One major policy debate concerns the goals of the prison system. Neither prison managers nor the general public agree on the system's purposes. This disagreement stems from the fact that the goals of incarceration have changed considerably since the first state prison was founded over 200 years ago. When prisons failed to achieve one set of goals, another set would be adopted, only to fade in importance and in turn be replaced. The older goals were not forgotten, however, but persisted in the background, so that today a number of sometimes conflicting goals coexist. As a result Americans lack consensus on the aims of prisons. Moreover, because each goal implies a different set of prison policies, the lack of general consensus feeds into debates about sentencing and prison administration.

The goals that have been set over time for incarceration fall into four main categories: *punishment, deterrence, incapacitation,* and *rehabilitation.*

Punishment

The idea of punishing someone who commits a crime dates back at least to Old Testament days; in the Bible we find the phrase "an eye for an eye, a tooth for a tooth," meaning that the punishment should fit the crime. Punishment rests on the notion that crime upsets a balance in the social order. To restore that balance, we need to inflict on the offender an amount of pain equal to that he or she inflicted on the victim. Basic here is the concept of justice: to achieve justice, we must deliver a punishment proportionate to the crime.

Some people find the notion of punishment repellent. It is no more than simple revenge, they argue, and it serves no purpose other than the infliction of pain. It does no social good. To such objections, proponents of punishment reply that revenge achieves justice, and that is enough.

Since the emergence of nation-states and the writing of criminal codes, responsibility for punishing crimes has fallen on governments, acting on the victims' behalf. In the colonial period, criminal punishments tended to be physical, consisting of flogging, branding, public humiliation, hanging, and so on. Just after the Revolutionary War, however, Americans adopted incarceration as the primary means of punishing offenders. That the primary goal of incarceration is punishment was assumed without question until about 1870, when the goal of rehabilitation began to eclipse that of punishment. About 1970, when rehabilitation went out of fashion, the idea that punishment is one of the main aims of prisons returned, and it remains strong today.

Deterrence

Deterrence, another important rationale for prisons, involves the ideas of prevention and threat. If our goal is to prevent future crimes, we can pose a threat—punishment—to encourage people to abandon any plans they may have to break the law.

Criminologists distinguish between two types of deterrence, specific and general. *Specific deterrence* aims at discouraging a particular offender from committing another crime in the future. *General deterrence* aims at discouraging members of the general public from committing crimes. Thus, while both specific and general deterrence are concerned with preventing future crimes, specific deterrence targets people who have already committed offenses, and general deterrence targets people who have not yet committed a crime.

In the United States today, incarceration is the most common form of deterrent punishment. That is, many people support imprisonment as a form of criminal punishment because they feel it is the best way to deter people from committing serious offenses. However, few people recognize the all-important distinction between deterrence as a goal and as a reality. We may hope that the possibility of a prison sentence will deter crime (specifically or generally), but that does not mean that it actually does deter. Research suggests that some people and some offenses are more deterrable than others. Highly impulsive people seem less deterrable than more rational people. Moreover, it is easier to deter people from committing offenses like speeding in an automobile than homicide. Homicide is often committed when people are enraged and incapable of considering the consequences, whereas speeding occurs when people are more capable of forethought. Although the public believes that long sentences will deter violent crimes, the evidence indicates that stiff sentences have little deterrent effect on offenses of this type.

Deterrence as a goal of prisons became popular just after the Revolutionary War, when Cesare Beccaria first set forth deterrence theory. In his 1764 book *On Crimes and Punishments*, Beccaria, an Italian nobleman, argued that the only valid purpose of punishment is to deter, and he urged governments to adopt the punishment of incarceration. Periods of time in prison, Beccaria pointed out, can be made shorter or longer and thus proportional to the offense. If we write laws punishing each offense with an amount of pain that outweighs the benefits of the crime, and if we publicize these laws so that everyone is aware of the punishments, then crime rates will decrease. Behind Beccaria's advocacy of deterrence is a view of human beings as highly rational creatures who can weigh alternatives and choose the one that maximizes their own good. This view of human nature was shared by the early governors of the United States, who adopted imprisonment as the main form of punishing felons, and they agreed with Beccaria that deterrence should be one of prisons' main purposes. Even though prisons apparently have failed to achieve either general or specific deterrence, the idea of deterrence remains popular with prison policymakers and the general public.

Incapacitation

Incapacitation as a goal of imprisonment entails immobilizing offenders to protect society. Supporters of incapacitation argue that one of prisons' primary purposes is to get criminals off the streets. Today imprisonment is our major form of incapacitory punishment, and the notion of incapacitation is widely endorsed by lawmakers and the general public. Three-strikes legislation, mandatory prison sentences, and similar laws have been enacted in recent years in response to public demands that prisons be used to incapacitate offenders. Indeed, the concept of incapacitation has been a driving force behind the huge increases in our prison populations in recent years.

Rehabilitation

The notion of rehabilitating offenders or changing them for the better has been present as a secondary goal of incarceration since the prison system was formed. The Quakers who supported the first prisons believed that if criminals were locked up and left to reflect on their sins, repentance would follow. Indeed, the idea of penitence lies at the root of the word "penitentiary."

However, the concept of rehabilitation as a process distinct from religious conversion was not formulated until 1870, when delegates to the National Congress on Prison and Reformatory Discipline in Cincinnati developed their plan for encouraging prisoners to reform. (Excerpts of this plan appear in Chapter 5.) From 1870 to 1970, many Americans felt that one of prisons' most important functions was to rehabilitate. About 1970, however, the pendulum of public opinion swung in the other direction, and Americans generally rejected the rehabilitative ideal, adopting instead punishment, deterrence, and incapacitation as the chief goals of prisons.

There were many reasons for this rejection of the goal of rehabilitation. One was high recidivism rates, which suggested that rehabilitation programs had little effect. This view seemed to be confirmed by the 1974 publication of an article by the criminologist Robert Martinson in the journal *Public Interest* entitled, "What Works? Questions and Answers about Prison Reform." Martinson's article reported the results of an evaluation of all current rehabilitation programs, concluding, famously, that "Nothing works." Martinson later modified this view, but the public did not pay nearly as much attention to the modification as to the first report, which confirmed what people wanted to hear in the 1970s: that it is pointless to waste time and money "coddling criminals."

Another factor leading to rejection of the goal of rehabilitation was the opinion that prisoners do not deserve more programs than honest citizens. This view, sometimes referred to as the *principle of least eligibility,* holds that because criminals have broken the law, they should be last in line when it comes to eligibility for whatever benefits the society has to offer. Since 1970, the public has reacted angrily to news of prisoners earning law degrees, having exercise equipment, and otherwise enjoying advantages that are not available to many of the people who pay the taxes that support prisons.

History, then, has left us a legacy of four main justifications or goals for our prison system: punishment, deterrence, incapacitation, and rehabilitation. This mixed legacy can lead to arguments and confusion about the purpose of locking people up. Because each goal implies different policies for sentencing prisoners and administering prisons, the legacy of multiple goals has also fed into debates over prison management. However, there are advantages as well as disadvantages to this legacy. It has led to rich debates over the purposes of our prison system, to the involvement in prison management of people with a broad range of perspectives, and to the prospect of change in prison operations over time.

Mandatory Sentencing versus Judicial Discretion

A second significant debate concerns the degree of discretion sentencing judges should have to tailor the punishment to fit the individual offender. Should sentencing judges have a little discretion, a lot, or none at all? This issue is directly related to the rapid expansion of the prison system in recent decades.

Sentencing has been a hot topic since about 1970, when get-tough-on-criminals sentiment gave birth to a movement to deny judges discretion. Activists in this movement felt that judges were abusing their discretion by failing to impose prison sentences in some cases and by imposing overly brief prison sentences in others. The movement has led to a massive shift in governmental authority to determine sentences, from the judicial to the legislative branch of government.

Traditionally, all three branches of government participated in sentencing. Legislatures determined the framework within which judges had to act. For example, a legislature might decide that first-degree assault could be punished either with probation or two-to-six years in prison. Within the framework established by the legislatures, judges (constituting the judiciary branch) set the sentences for specific offenders, perhaps sending one person guilty of first-degree assault to prison for three to five years and sentencing a less serious offender guilty of the same crime to probation. The executive branch of government, which runs departments of correction, prisons, and parole boards, got into the act by determining exactly when a specific offender would be released from prison. Under indeterminate sentencing, someone sent to prison on a three-to-five year sentence might come before the parole board in, say, three and a half years, and if the parole board granted release, the prisoner would then be supervised in the community by a parole officer, who is also an employee of the executive branch.

Today more than at any other point in U.S. history, legislatures set sentences, with judges essentially presiding at sentencing ceremonies in which they have little or no authority to make the "in-out" decision (prison or probation) or to set sentence length. To a lesser but still significant degree, over the past three decades legislatures have also claimed for themselves some of the authority previously held by the executive branch to determine time served (the actual amount of time an inmate spends in prison). In recent years, then, many of the sentencing functions previously performed by the judicial and executive branches of government have been taken away by the legislative branch.

This shift was part of the reaction against indeterminate sentencing. Indeterminate sentences (terms with minimums and maximums—such as three-to-five year sentences) were introduced about 1870 as a way to rehabilitate prisoners, and for about a century, no one questioned their advisability. But about 1970, the public began taking a much harsher stance toward crime. Angry about crime, high recidivism rates, drugs, hippies, and what seemed to be deterioration of traditional values, conservatives complained that indeterminate sentences allowed criminals to be released before they had served their entire terms. Along with victim advocates, conservatives also demanded "truth in sentencing." They wanted prisoners with a three-to-five year sentence to serve something close to five years—and not to be released in less than three years as a result of good-time credits.

At the same time, liberals worried about whether judges and parole boards might be exercising their authority over sentence length in ways that reflected bias against blacks or other groups. As a result of all these concerns, some states abandoned indeterminate sentences, replacing them with flat or definite sentences of a set number of years (e.g., five years, or nine years) determined by the legislature. If the legislature decided that the punishment for first-degree assault was six years, the offender would now serve six years and not a moment less, except for good-time reductions.

Another aspect of the movement toward harsher sentencing involved the enactment of mandatory sentences. Mandatory sentencing laws remove judicial discretion by decreeing that anyone convicted of a particular offense has to go to prison; probation is not a possibility. Most mandatory sentencing laws also set a specific prison term for the offense in question. For example, a legislature might decide that anyone convicted of carrying an unregistered handgun should automatically be sentenced to one year of incarceration, or that anyone convicted of first-degree murder should automatically be sentenced to life in prison without parole. Since 1970, the state and federal governments have enacted a large number of mandatory sentences, limiting the influence of judges and representatives of the executive branch during the sentencing process.

Mandatory sentencing has been criticized from many angles. Judges resent the way it lessens their authority, and they point out that if sentences cannot be individualized, the results can often be unfair. Testifying before Congress in 1994, U.S. Supreme Court Justice Anthony M. Kennedy said, "I think I am in agreement with most judges in the Federal system that mandatory minimums are an imprudent, unwise and often unjust mechanism for sentencing."[1]

The sort of problem Justice Kennedy had in mind can be illustrated with the case of a woman who was recently sentenced. The mother of two small girls and a part-time secretary, this woman sometimes counted money for her drug-dealer boyfriend. She was convicted of conspiracy to distribute crack cocaine, and although she had no prior convictions she received the mandatory sentence: ten years in a federal prison.[2] Such tough mandatory sentences were enacted to punish major drug dealers. Unfortunately, they often seem to catch the "wrong" population, small-fry like the part-time secretary who had no information to trade for leniency, rather than drug dealers.

Another objection to mandatory sentences is that they do not really eliminate discretion but rather push it back to an earlier stage in the criminal justice process, to the point where the prosecutor decides what offense to charge. Prosecutors sometimes reduce charges, depending on circumstances. If a little old lady is caught carrying an unregistered handgun in a dangerous neighborhood because she is afraid of being mugged, a prosecutor might charge her with a lesser offense so that she will not receive the mandatory one-year in jail. Similarly, if a powerful organized crime figure offers a prosecutor information on the drug trade in return for leniency, the prosecutor may accept the deal in order to make further arrests. Thus, although mandatory sentences were enacted to remove judicial discretion, they often in fact increase prosecutors' discretion, which has less public visibility and thus is harder to control.

The most criticized aspect of mandatory sentencing is the way it has filled prisons with drug offenders. The United States stands alone among Western nations in addressing the drug problem by locking up drug users. Other countries concentrate on treatment, a less expensive and more effective approach that has the additional benefit of keeping families intact.

To avoid the drawbacks of mandatory sentencing, some jurisdictions have found ways to curtail judicial discretion without eliminating it entirely. One alternative is *presumptive sentencing.* In this approach the legislature approves a sentencing grid or chart that sets the "presumed" sentence for each offense. (For an example of this sort of chart, see Chapter 5.) The chart might indicate that anyone convicted of first-degree assault will presumably be sentenced to six years in prison. However, the chart would also give the judge some leeway to increase or reduce the term, depending on the particular offender's criminal history. (For example, the sentence could be somewhat reduced for an accomplice with no previous convictions.) Presumptive sentencing helps achieve fairness (everyone convicted of a certain offense receives about the same amount of punishment) without forcing judges to give sentences that cannot be modified according to the circumstances.

Another way of avoiding the rigidity of mandatory sentencing is to use *sentencing guidelines.* This approach is similar to that of presumptive sentencing except that the terms are set not by the legislature but by a sentencing board that includes citizens, prison administrators, judges, and others concerned with criminal justice. Of course the sentencing board's grid or chart must be approved by the legislature (or, at the federal level, by Congress) before it can become law, but such a board is more insulated from politics than legislators. When legislators themselves prepare a presumptive sentencing chart, they often act tough in order to ensure their reelection. This encourages very long sentences based on worst-case crime scenarios. But in reality most offenses are not of the worst-case sort, and the members of a sentencing board do not need to run for reelection; thus they tend to make more reasonable decisions in setting guidelines.

Most criminal justice officials see a need for some discretion if sentencing judges are to avoid injustices in unusual cases in which everyone agrees that the rules should not apply. The issue is: How much discretion is necessary? Too much discretion can lead to unfairness, just as too little can. Today, we are in the midst of this debate.

Prison Expansion and Overcrowding

During the past three decades the U.S. prison population has skyrocketed. We have been locking up an ever-greater proportion of our population and expanding the prison system with remarkable speed, adding the equivalent of one new 1,000-bed institution each week. Yet prisons are more overcrowded today than they were ten years ago. This raises a key policy question: How many more prisons should we build? According to statistical projections, the prison population will continue to soar if the mandatory and other harsh sentencing laws that are driving it upward are not modified. Shall we keep adding to what is already the largest prison system in the world, or should we stop at some point? And if the latter policy is best, where do we set that point?

Criminologists agree that 60 percent or more of the increase in the prison population is attributable to increases in drug cases, not violent or property offenders. In some jurisdictions today, three of every ten new prisoners are committed for drug offenses. The proportions are most dramatic in the federal system, which in the late 1980s enacted stiff mandatory sentencing for crack cocaine convictions. In 1988 about 20 percent of all federal inmates were serving time for drug-related crimes; today that figure is over 55 percent.[3]

And yet, the federal law is not working to put behind bars the drug kingpins at whom it was aimed. These big-time dealers have the means to evade capture; street-level dealers do not. Moreover, if caught, the big dealers can bargain their way out of stiff sentences in return for information. Street dealers and small-time users, in contrast, have little or no bargaining power. According to federal estimates, only 5 percent of those who have been jailed for selling crack were big-time dealers, whereas the majority of drug-offense prisoners are serving time for simple possession. In fact, more people are incarcerated for selling or possessing marijuana than for selling or possessing the drugs that inspired the tough drug laws—crack and powder cocaine.

What are the effects of the upward climb in the prison population? Some are positive. Crime rates have decreased, particularly rates of property crime, and some of this decrease may stem from the fact that so many offenders are behind bars. Moreover, thanks to the truth-in-sentencing movement, violent offenders are serving greater proportions of their sentences than they did ten or twenty years ago.

Drug use, however, seems to be unaffected, even though so many prisoners are now doing time for drug law violations. Rates of drug use began to decline before the new laws took effect, and they have stayed level since then, in terms of both the number of drug users and the types of drugs they use. To achieve a further decline in drug use, treatment is needed.

Other effects of the rise in prison populations are more negative. Overcrowding may have increased levels of prison violence. (Think of spending a year with a friend in the bathroom.

Then add two or three more people.) The price tag for incarcerating such large numbers is high both in dollars and in social costs. The proportion of prisoners who are black has increased because of stiffer penalties for possession or sale of crack cocaine (a form of cocaine preferred by blacks) than for powdered cocaine (a form preferred by whites). By 1996 over 8 percent of black men aged 25 to 29 years old were in prison, compared to less than 1 percent of white men in the same age bracket.

Another troublesome effect of the harsh sentencing laws has been to increase the proportion of older inmates, an effect that will intensify as we see the long-term results of three-strike and natural-life sentences. Because older people have low crime rates, incarcerating this population will do little to reduce crime, but it will increase the costs of prison medical care.

Ironically, another negative effect of mandatory sentencing and other tough sentencing laws has been to undermine the truth-in-sentencing movement that helped create these sentences in the first place. For example, when overcrowding becomes intolerable, courts declare a situation of cruel and unusual punishment and set caps on the number of prisoners an institution can hold. When prisons exceed their caps, they have to release inmates before their terms expire, thus undercutting truth-in-sentencing. Similarly, prisons have reduced the number of new inmates coming in the front door by starting boot camp programs. These give relatively young first offenders an opportunity to reduce their sentences by successfully completing a six- or nine-month military-type training program. Although boot camps help prisons cope with overcrowding, they release prisoners long before the expiration of the sentences they would otherwise serve.

The primary response of the state and federal governments to overcrowding is the construction of new prisons. A system that consisted of just over 1,000 institutions in 1987 now has over 1,500 and is expected to grow to nearly 1,800 by the year 2001. In 1995 alone, 70 new prisons were added, with about 70,000 beds; 62 more new prisons were under construction, and another 118 were being renovated, for a total of almost 100,000 beds added in 1996. Construction costs range from $31,000 per bed for minimum security facilities to $80,000 per bed for maximum security facilities, not including the cost of land. Moreover, it currently costs an average of $20,000 to hold a single prisoner for one year, a figure likely to rise quickly because of the growth and increasing clout of correctional-officer unions. In 1996 the total bill for prisons was $27.5 billion.[4]

How many more prisons do we want to build? If sentencing laws remain the same, we will have to keep building at the current rate for years to come. Eventually, of course, sentencing laws that are not working as planned will be modified or repealed as the public gets over its media-induced fear of crack cocaine and shifts away from its current punitive orientation. When that point comes, we may be left with numerous half-empty prisons, buildings that cannot easily be converted to other uses. We will also be left with a large underclass of former prisoners who are unemployed or minimally employed and whose families have disintegrated.

If the point of harsh drug sentences is to reduce drug use, we probably could achieve that result by providing drug treatment instead of prison sentences to all the drug offenders currently in prison and still save billions a year in prison costs. If the point is to reduce crime, we probably would do better by ceasing to lock up minor offenders and spending more on education, housing, and other programs associated with crime reduction. Thus the question becomes: When do we stop sending minor offenders to prison at such high rates and stop building new prisons? This is one of the weightiest and most intractable policy issues facing corrections today.

Prisoners' Rights

Should prisoners have rights? Should the U.S. Constitution apply in prisons? These questions have been debated since the start of the prison system and continue to form the basis for major controversies, with Supreme Court justices as well as ordinary citizens staking out strong positions.

For most of U.S. prison history, inmates had no rights whatsoever. If someone died under suspicious circumstances while in custody, there might be a newspaper scandal or executive-branch investigation; but the courts rarely intervened. Instead, from the start of the prison system until the early 1960s, courts followed the *hands-off doctrine,* a policy of refusing to become involved in matters of prison administration.

Courts were reluctant to intercede in prison matters partly because of the principle of separation of powers within our system of government. Judges kept their "hands off" because they thought that prison administration was none of their business. Prisons are run by the executive branch of government, judges reasoned, and thus courts have no authority to say how they should be run.

A second reason why judges traditionally upheld the hands-off doctrine lay in simple ignorance. They knew little of what went on behind prisons walls and so did not perceive that constitutional issues might be at stake. The third and most important reason for maintaining the hands-off doctrine was the opinion that prisoners, having been convicted of crimes, have no rights. Judges and the public alike believed that the U.S. Constitution simply did not apply inside prison walls.

Courts began to discard the hands-off doctrine in the early 1960s as the civil rights movement sensitized them—and the whole country—to the fact that millions of American citizens were not protected by the Constitution. At a time when prison populations were becoming predominantly black, white Americans woke up to the fact that blacks lacked the constitutional protections enjoyed by white men and, to a lesser degree, white women. Then, too, prison riots and other disturbances brought the media into penal institutions, where reporters discovered through interviews with inmates that conditions were much worse than outsiders had realized. Exposés of racism and guard brutality led civil rights lawyers and the public to wonder whether at some point the U.S. Constitution *should* apply in prisons.

These concerns led to the prisoners' rights movement, an effort by prisoners from about 1960 to 1980 to assert their entitlement to certain constitutional rights. During this period of the prisoner's rights movement, federal courts agreed with many (though certainly not all) of the prisoners' constitutional arguments. Since 1980 the prisoners' rights movement has slowed down, partly because inmates achieved their central goals and partly because the U.S. Supreme Court became more conservative and thus more reluctant to help prisoners.

Moreover, some judges are apparently returning to the hands-off doctrine or something close to it. One of these is Justice Clarence Thomas of the U.S. Supreme Court, who in his dissent to a recent prisoners' rights decision criticized "the pervasive view that the Federal Constitution must address all ills in our society. . . . The Eighth Amendment [prohibiting cruel and unusual punishment] is not, and should not be turned into, a National Code of Prison Regulation."[5] Similarly, some federal courts of appeals have recently overturned lower court decisions declaring that male and female prisoners should be treated equally. Prison conditions, in the judges' view, simply do not fall within the scope of the Constitution's equal protection clause. Some ordinary citizens, too, believe that anyone sent to prison for a crime does not deserve constitutional protections.

To illustrate the specific issues at stake in this controversy, the following sections review a few of the most important court decisions of the prisoners' rights era. (Excerpts from some of these decisions can be found in Chapter 5.)

Prisoners' Rights Case Law

Religious Freedom

The prisoners' rights movement was at first led by Black Muslims—well-organized, highly disciplined, intensely religious convicts who fought for the right to worship as Muslims, and especially for the right to keep copies of the Koran in their cells and to be fed a pork-free diet. Because of the Muslims' leadership, some of the earliest prisoners' rights cases concerned freedom of religion.

Prison administrators, the overwhelming majority of them white, fiercely resisted Muslim demands. They were made fearful by the sight of Muslims organizing and becoming a powerful force within the walls. The Muslims persisted, however, and eventually the courts granted them the right to worship, to have pork-free diets, and to keep copies of the Koran. This victory had a racial as well as religious dimension, demonstrating as it did that blacks, even prisoners, could stand as equals in court and win cases against whites.

Today, the rule of thumb in the area of prisoners' religious rights is that inmates can worship as they please, so long as their religious practices do not disrupt prison safety or routines.

Legal Rights

Another issue that became important early in the prisoners' rights movement was the question of whether inmates have legal rights such as the right of access to the courts. This was a particularly significant issue because if prisoners could gain access to the courts, they could then argue other issues as well.

In the first of the big legal rights cases, *Johnson v. Avery* (1969), the U.S. Supreme Court gave prisoners the right to act as "jailhouse lawyers." Previously, officials had tried to prevent inmates from learning about the law and helping one another with their cases; they did not want protests against poor prison conditions to reach the courts. But in *Johnson v. Avery,* the Supreme Court declared that inmates have the right to practice as jailhouse lawyers, helping themselves and one another with legal matters, because they have no other form of legal assistance. The alternative was for prisons to provide free legal counsel to inmates—which, of course, they could not afford to do.

The second key decision in this area came eight years later, when the U.S. Supreme Court decided in *Bounds v. Smith* (1977) that prisons are obligated to provide inmates with an adequate law library. This was a logical extension of the jailhouse lawyer decision, since obviously a jailhouse lawyer cannot be effective without law books. Hence today, prisons have small law libraries.

Medical Care

Traditionally courts refused to hear cases based on allegations of denial of medical treatment. The situation changed in 1976 with the U.S. Supreme Court decision in *Estelle v. Gamble.* Here the court defined the level of care that prisons must provide, declaring that "deliberate indifference to the serious medical needs of prisoners constitutes the unnecessary and wanton infliction of pain . . . proscribed by the Eighth Amendment." Locked up and unable to reach physicians on their own, prisoners are essentially helpless; the state is not free to leave them to sicken and die. Prisoners are sentenced to loss of liberty, not loss of health or preventable death from illness.

In *Estelle v. Gamble* the Court said that prison officials violate the Eighth Amendment only when they demonstrate "deliberate indifference" to serious medical needs—that is, when they intentionally ignore the medical needs of a prisoner who is very sick. (Indifference through ignorance is not a violation.) This fairly low standard does not obligate prison officials to provide much in the way of health care. However, with the help of guidelines developed by organizations such as the American Medical Association and the American Public Health Association, prison officials generally adhere to a higher standard, and today professional medical groups are deeply involved in prison health care delivery.

Due Process in Punishments

Historically courts were uninterested in how prison officials reached decisions on prison discipline. More recently, they have issued decision-making guidelines for cases in which discipline involves some kind of loss of liberty, such as loss of good-time credits or removal from the general population to solitary confinement. The key case in this area is *Wolff v. McDonnell*, decided by the U.S. Supreme Court in 1974. McDonnell, a prisoner, had been denied good-time credits without any kind of a hearing to determine whether the denial was fair. He argued that he should have had a chance to explain his side of the situation, and the Supreme Court agreed. When the prisoner stands to lose a degree of liberty, the Court held, he or she is entitled to some due process, including:

- A 24-hour written notice of the charges
- A hearing before a discipline committee
- Permission to present some evidence and to call witnesses, so long as institutional control is not jeopardized
- A written statement from the disciplinary committee, announcing its decision and explaining its reasoning

On the other hand, in *Wolff* the Court also said that in these situations prisoners do not have a right to cross-examine witnesses or to have a lawyer present, although in some cases an inmate may have the assistance of a lawyer-substitute such as another prisoner or a staff member. In sum, in *Wolff* the Court held that in disciplinary proceedings in which the prisoner faces some loss of liberty, the prisoner is entitled to some due process of law but not the full amount that defendants have at trial.

General Conditions of Confinement

In addition to deciding cases based on prisoner claims to specific rights, courts have also decided cases on the basis of general conditions of confinement, declaring that the totality of conditions in a penal institution may be so bad as to constitute cruel and unusual punishment. The first case of this type decided by a federal court was *Holt v. Sarver* (1970). In it, a federal district court found that inmates at the Arkansas penitentiary were lashed with a leather strap until bruised and bloody; given electric shocks on their genitals; worked in the fields 60 hours per week with only hand tools; forced in winter to work outdoors in freezing temperatures with inadequate clothing and no shoes; and fed food containing maggots. These and other specific circumstances led the court to decide that the general conditions of confinement at the penitentiary amounted to cruel and unusual punishment. Declaring that the entire Arkansas prison system operated in an unconstitutional manner, the court ordered reforms.

In other conditions-of-confinement cases, courts have examined the constitutionality of overcrowding and, in the Texas case *Ruiz v. Estelle* (1980), of a disciplinary system, the "building tender system," in which inmates supervised and punished other inmates on behalf of the administration.

The Realities of Prisoners' Rights and Recent Cases

It is important to recognize that when prisoners challenge officials, they sometimes suffer retaliation, and that even when they win, they do not necessarily get what they sought. The *Ruiz v. Estelle* case, which dragged on for years, documented extensive retaliation against the prisoner-plaintiffs by staff of the Texas Department of Corrections and by the building tenders, including maimings and murders. Similarly, although *Wolff* gave prisoners some due process rights under some circumstances, the hearings specified by *Wolff* do not necessarily occur, or they may be run by an official who is not impartial.

The 1979 U.S. Supreme Court decision in *Bell v. Wolfish* is said to mark the waning of the prisoners' rights movement. In this case pretrial detainees in a New York City jail complained that they were being double-bunked and thus denied the recommended minimum amount of space. The Court said, essentially, "Too bad." It pointed out that double-bunking was not intended as a punishment and that, in any case, the government had no alternative.

Nevertheless, in 1992, long after the prisoners' rights movement had passed its prime, the U.S. Supreme Court gave prisoners another important victory in *Hudson v. McMillian.* This case involved Keith Hudson, a prisoner at the Louisiana State Penitentiary at Angola, who had been beaten brutally and maliciously by prison guards (one of them named McMillian) while he was chained and handcuffed. One guard held Hudson from behind, while McMillian and a fellow guard, both of them over six feet tall and weighing over 200 pounds, kicked and punched him, causing bruises, facial swelling, and the cracking of Hudson's dental plate. The Court declared that the key issue here was not whether there was any obvious injury but whether that degree of force was necessary to maintain prison discipline. It found that the guards had used excessive force, in violation of Hudson's Eighth Amendment rights.

Thus prisoners' rights remain a matter of concern to the courts. How long they will remain so is, however, an open question. *Hudson v. McMillian* was the case in which Justice Thomas argued in his dissent that "primary responsibility for preventing and punishing such conduct [the beating suffered by Keith Hudson] rests not with the Federal Constitution but with the laws and regulations of the various States."[6] If Thomas's view prevails in the long run, prisoners would no longer fall under the protections of the U.S. Constitution.

Equality for Women Prisoners

Related to prisoners' rights is the issue of whether women prisoners have a right to be treated as well as men prisoners. This issue goes beyond legal rights, however, in that it also involves controversies over what "equal treatment" might mean. Some advocates of equal treatment argue that female prisoners should be treated just as male prisoners are. Others, however, argue that identical treatment would be inherently unfair, because the standard would be set by male prisoners, who have different needs and concerns. True fairness, this second group argues, lies in treatment that meets the unique needs and concerns of women prisoners.

Actually providing equal treatment has proved very difficult, for several reasons.

The "Numbers" Problem

One obstacle to equal treatment is the fact that there are so many fewer female than male prisoners, an imbalance that has existed since the prison system began. In nineteenth-century penitentiaries, it was easy for officials to overlook the few women prisoners, especially when they had special problems (such as pregnancy) that the male officers did not know how to deal with. Later, when women were removed to separate reformatories, it was still easy for state officials to pay less attention to them than to the much more numerous (and demanding) population of male prisoners. Departments of correction have tended to wait to fund their one women's institution until funds have been allocated to all their men's institutions. Thus women's prisons have had trouble providing the same level of treatment as can be found in men's prisons.

Also relevant is the matter of economies of scale: Per capita costs are lower when the population is large. A prison with 1,000 inmates can feed and clothe each inmate more cheaply than can a prison with 100 inmates. Women's penal institutions tend to be much smaller than men's, but each still needs a superintendent, a physician, an engineer to fix the furnace, and so on. These prisons simply cannot be run as economically as men's institutions. As a result, corners are sometimes cut.

The "Nature" Problem

A second complication in the provision of equal treatment is beliefs about women's "nature." Many people believe that women are so different from men that they need entirely different types of programs. In nineteenth- and early-twentieth-century reformatories, women prisoners were taught to clean, cook, and wait on tables so that on release they would make good domestic servants. Into the 1970s and 1980s the primary program in many women's institutions was "cosmetology"—hairdressing and makeup. Such training did not prepare women to compete for jobs on release; indeed, cosmetology programs sent the message that women's main job is to appear attractive.

Treatment based on the traditional belief that women are more childish in nature than men has historically led to harsher sentences. In the late nineteenth century, as a result of the reformatory movement, women could be sent to state prisons for out-of-wedlock sexual activity and minor public-order violations that were overlooked in the case of men. Moreover, the reformatory prisons could hold these women for relatively long periods. Additionally, women convicted of regular crimes such as burglary could be sentenced for longer terms than men convicted of the same offenses. The rationale was that because women were weaker, they needed more "help." Thus female-specific care led to unequal and harsher treatment.

The "Same" or "Different" Debate

In the 1970s and 1980s feminist lawyers worked with women prisoners to argue for equal treatment. They forced courts to strike down some of the older laws that made women liable to harsher sentences. They also forced departments of correction to institute more job-training programs in women's prisons and to ensure that these programs trained women for competitive jobs.

However, this push for equal treatment soon hit a barrier: recognition that the treatment needs of incarcerated women simply are not the same as those of male counterparts. As summarized in a recent report: "Women in prison have some needs that are quite different from men's, resulting in part from women's disproportionate victimization from sexual or physical abuse and in part from their responsibility for children. Women offenders are also more likely than men to have become addicted to drugs, to have mental illnesses, and to have been unemployed before incarceration."[7]

The realization that women have different treatment needs has led to a *parity movement*—an effort to provide incarcerated women with programs that are as numerous and adequate as those available to incarcerated men but designed with women's particular needs in mind. Whereas the push for "equality" tends to be translated into "same" or "identical" programs, the push for "parity" leaves room for differences in program content.[8]

Over the coming ten to twenty years the parity movement may bring considerable change to the way female prisoners are treated. One area in which change may occur is that of prisoner classification. Currently most states use the same questionnaires and tests to classify incoming female and male prisoners by security level, program needs, and so on. However, because these instruments were developed for use with male populations, their application to women prisoners sometimes leads to misclassification.

Advocates of parity point out that a key difference between male and female prisoners has to do with children. More than two-thirds of all women in prison have children younger than eighteen years of age, and most of these women were the chief provider of child care before they were incarcerated. Male prisoners, in contrast, are much more likely to have been living apart from their children at the time they entered prison and to have taken little or no responsibility for their care. When asked, women emphasize that the worst aspect of incarceration is separation from their children and anxiety about their children's welfare. On release, most of them will once again be responsible for these children. Meanwhile, the separation can be damaging for the children as well. Children sometimes think that they have done something to cause their mother's incarceration. Others think their mother has deserted them.

Thus one of the main thrusts of programming for women prisoners has related to children and child care. Some programs bring children to the prison for regular visits. The women's prison at Bedford Hills, New York, enables mothers to keep infants with them in prison for the first year or so. Still other programs provide courses in child care.

Another area being addressed by the parity movement is that of physical and sexual abuse. Over 43 percent of women in prison report having been physically or sexually abused before incarceration. (For men in prison, the corresponding figure is 12 percent.)[9] Some institutions have developed programs to help women cope with a history of abuse and to teach them how to escape abusive situations in the future. Related are programs that teach women prisoners how to cope when they are tempted to use violence with children or a partner.

Legal Issues

Despite these efforts, women's prisons continue to provide fewer and less adequate programs than men's prisons. This failure has led to lawsuits based on the Fourteenth Amendment's Equal Protection Clause. Although no prisoner has a right to certain programs, if one group of prisoners (in this case, males) is systematically given more programs than another group (females), the equal protection clause may be violated.

Equal-protection litigation has not proved an effective remedy, however. Typically the suits take many years to reach a conclusion. When women win their cases, the decisions are sometimes reversed by a higher court. When the decisions stand, it is very difficult to force states to implement them. Even the best-intentioned department of correction has trouble overcoming the challenges posed by the much smaller number of female prisoners, sexist traditions, and the differences in the needs of male and female inmates.

An emerging legal issue concerns the sexual abuse of women prisoners by male officials. That such abuse occurs has been known at least since the mid–nineteenth century, when discovery of a prostitution ring at the Indiana penitentiary led to the establishment of the first separate prison for women. Recently, interest in the problem has been revived by a 1996 publication by Human Rights Watch entitled *All Too Familiar: Sexual Abuse of Women in U.S. State Prisons.*[10] Today, women held in separate women's prisons are likely to be guarded by men. The study reports sexual misconduct including vaginal, anal, and oral rape and other forms of sexual assault. "In addition to engaging in sexual relations with prisoners," the report states, male officers have used mandatory pat-frisks or room searches to grope women's breasts, buttocks, and vaginal areas and to view them inappropriately while in a state of undress in the housing or bathroom areas. Male correctional officers and staff have also engaged in regular verbal degradation and harassment of female prisoners, thus contributing to a custodial environment in the state prisons for women that is often highly sexualized and excessively hostile.[11]

Sexual abuse raises Eighth Amendment issues about cruel and unusual punishment. Because incarcerated men are less vulnerable to sexual abuse than incarcerated women, the problem also raises Fourteenth Amendment issues of equal treatment.

As this example of sexual abuse demonstrates, the issue of providing adequate care to female prisoners is likely to remain a serious controversy in the years ahead. No aspect of this issue has yet been successfully resolved, despite thirty years of effort. The courts have still not decided whether women prisoners have a right to treatment equal to that of men prisoners. Nor have advocates of equality settled the issue of whether "equal" treatment should mean identical care or different care based on women prisoners' different needs. And as yet, no one has discovered ways to overcome the obstacles to equal treatment posed by the "numbers" and the "nature" problems.

Prison Violence and Its Prevention

Violence has always been a part of prison life. The prison itself, with its metal bars, locked doors, and body-cavity searches, is a symbol of violence. Throughout prison history, administrators have relied on intimidation and force to control inmates. Moreover, many inmates engage in violent and unmanageable behavior as a result of problems such as mental illness, emotional distress, alcoholism, and drug addiction.

Given these underlying conditions, what can or should be done to prevent prison violence? How much should be spent to ensure the safety of inmates and staff? These questions have plagued American prisons for two centuries and still constitute one of the major debates in prison management.

Debates over how to handle prison violence involve different considerations depending on whether one is discussing men's or women's prisons. Rates of interpersonal violence are much higher in men's prisons. Although male prisoners tend to inflict violence against one another, female prisoners are more apt to be victims of violence inflicted by staff or by themselves in acts of self-mutilation.

In order to take an informed position on issues of prison violence, one must know something about the types and causes of violence in penal institutions and about current strategies for violence reduction.

Causes and Types of Violence

There is little agreement on the causes of prison violence. Factors that seem to cause violence in one institution do not do so in another, and a factor that evidently plays a key role in one historical period may have negligible effect in another. Confusion over the causes of prison violence can be reduced by distinguishing between background factors and immediate or triggering causes. Although the immediate causes tend to be highly specific and therefore resistant to generalization, it is easier and more productive to identify background factors that contribute to prison violence.

One important background factor in recent disturbances has been overcrowding. Overcrowding can lead to elevated rates of depression, anxiety, stress, boredom, and mental breakdown, causing disciplinary infractions, assaults, and riots. Although prison construction has proceeded rapidly over the past few decades, it has not kept up with the growth of the population. Consequently, overcrowding continues to be a problem in most prison systems. Cells built to hold one inmate now house two, three, and even four inmates. Few states are able to provide program and treatment opportunities to even half their prison populations. Idleness and boredom lead to frustration and violence.

Another background factor is the breakdown of faith in government that began in the 1960s. Political turmoil and civil unrest stemming from issues like the Vietnam War and the civil rights and Black Power movements led to a violent period in American society. Youth no longer shared the moral standards of their elders. Violent crime and gang delinquency escalated; violence exploded in the streets, on college campuses, and inside prison walls. As crime rates rose and prison populations grew, staff and inmates alike turned to violence to achieve control.

Inspired by the civil rights movement and social upheaval, prisoners began to fight for their own constitutional rights. They complained about poor prison conditions, staff mistreatment, racism, and inadequate services. Prison guards also responded to the stress of their environment and to their own mistreatment by administrators. Staff rebelled against centralized power, restrictive work conditions, and dangerous prison environments. As they became less willing to conform to the strict rules and regulations of their leaders, key elements of social control and prison security deteriorated. Taking advantage of weakened security, inmates engaged in protests and violence to send messages to prison administrators and the public. When authoritarian prison administrators ignored their complaints or punished those who did the complaining, prisoners became further frustrated and angry.

Another significant background factor in recent prison violence has been a breakdown of earlier agreement over the goals of incarceration and the best methods of prison administration. Around 1970, the American public rejected rehabilitation in favor of retribution, deterrence, and incapacitation as the goals of prisons. Supporters of prisoners' rights, racial equality, and determinate sentencing policies questioned the legitimacy of prisons and prison officials' authority. This crumbling of agreement over the goals of imprisonment and the principles that govern their operation resulted in a loss of control by old-fashioned hard-line officers. By the early 1970s larger state prisons were faced with protests and accelerating violence.[12]

To analyze prison violence, it is useful to distinguish among three levels or types: individual violence, gang-related or group violence, and the large-scale collective violence of riots. Individual violence takes many forms, including assault, murder, rape and other forms of sexual coercion, and self-mutilation. Prisoners incite violence against each other and staff, but staff, too, may inflict violence.

Gang-related violence emerged as a problem in the 1950s; today nearly every prison system has to deal with it. Many male prisoners affiliate with a gang for protection, social status, and access to illicit goods and services. Most male prison gangs are racially exclusive. Gang rivalries are so fierce in some prisons that gang members ask to be segregated from the general population just to be safe from their rivals. Prisoners without a gang affiliation are vulnerable to gang intimidation, threats, and abuse.

Collective violence has played a major part in prison history. Often influenced by external social and political pressures, riots generally erupt when security and administrative controls become lax. If prisons operate below constitutional standards or fail to meet court-ordered reforms, inmates may respond with collective violence. Destruction of property, interpersonal violence, and demands to the administration are characteristic of prison riots.

The Attica, New York, riot in 1971 and the Santa Fe, New Mexico, riot in 1980 were the deadliest in U.S. prison history. Both involved the taking of hostages and numerous deaths, and in both cases, officials' failure to pay attention to inmate grievances was an important background factor. Otherwise, however, the two riots were quite different.

At Attica, although the uprising began as a spontaneous violent outburst, Black Panthers and Muslim leaders quickly organized inmates, bringing solidarity and control to a chaotic situation and initiating negotiations with the administration. Inmates treated the guard-hostages with some respect and killed few other prisoners. Nearly all of the deaths—a total of forty-three—occurred when state troopers, on the orders of Governor Nelson Rockefeller, shot into the yard, killing hostages and inmates. When the news media went in to cover the Attica takeover, the public witnessed for the first time the reality of what was happening inside prison walls. The facility's physical deterioration, the abhorrent living conditions, racism, overcrowding, and mistreatment of prisoners and staff became vivid to anyone following the riot on television.

During the New Mexico riot, in contrast, inmates were disorganized, with no leadership or solidarity. Instead of collaborating, they brutalized, terrorized, and murdered one another. They had little ground for negotiating with authorities, as they could agree on little among themselves.[13] Whereas television coverage of Attica tended to arouse public sympathy with the inmates as well as the hostages, scenes of carnage and mutilation at Santa Fe alienated the public from the inmates' cause.

An interesting turn of events occurred during a 1986 riot at the West Virginia Penitentiary. Inmates could have escaped by walking out the front door if they chose to, but no one did. When state police finally came in and took control of the facility, inmates were having parties in the basement with drugs and local prostitutes. The place was filthy, but very little violence had actually occurred. Inmates were simply protesting against the wretched conditions in the prison. Their intent was not to escape or to brutalize anyone; they simply sought better conditions and treatment.

Strategies for Violence Reduction

Strategies for reducing violence may involve improving prison conditions, establishing grievance procedures, improving security and classification systems, and developing a highly trained staff and a riot control plan.

Improving the conditions of a run-down facility and reducing overcrowding may help to prevent incidents of violence. When the overcrowding problem is resolved, other problems may evaporate. More jobs and program opportunities decrease prisoner idleness. If health and sanitation problems are solved, the institution may need less rigid security measures, and inmates may develop fewer psychological and emotional problems. Responding to prisoner grievances may prevent the growth of larger problems associated with violence. A simple and direct grievance process reduces prisoner discontent and tension. Moreover, ombudsmen can form a useful link between prisoners and administrators, monitoring conditions associated with victimization and abuse.

New strategies for increasing security include redesigning facilities to increase surveillance and control, creating barriers between housing units so that riots cannot spread, and upgrading hardware such as locks and cell doors. Policies that outline security and safety procedures and policies for disciplining staff who use excessive force also increase the level of social control and order.

An important method for controlling prison violence is an accurate and efficient classification system for determining the level of security for inmates. The distribution of power among prisoners is a major determining factor in the level of violence. Today many prisons use a gang identification system to separate gang leaders and members and to reduce gang rivalries. They also reward members for severing ties to their gang while in prison. Ultimately, such systems decrease the power of gangs in prison.

A recent development in prison security is the building of "supermax" facilities or "control units" for prisoners who, because of violent and disruptive behavior, threaten the safety and security of a prison. At supermax institutions, prisoners are kept in solitary confinement in tiny six- by eight-foot cells for twenty-two to twenty-three hours a day, and there is no opportunity for congregate dining, exercise, or religious services. Using methods for handcuffing prisoners from the opposite side of a door and for opening and closing doors by remote control, correctional officers can avoid contact with prisoners in these facilities. Today there are more than twenty supermax units and separate facilities in the United States, and five more are projected to open in 1999.[14]

Increasing the size and quality of staff, improving the level of training, and requiring annual recertification procedures can reduce a penal institution's vulnerability to inmate violence. Training should include conflict management and resolution skills as well as strategies for preventing, controlling, and containing a violent outburst. Policies outlining consistent responses to disciplinary infractions and ensuring that appropriate sanctions are enforced can thwart inmate manipulativeness and increase staff control. Riot control plans are required in most prison systems today.

However, although these strategies may reduce the problem of prison violence, they do not solve it. Many people feel that incarcerating people in supermax institutions merely increases their propensity to violence. Few prisons try to train inmates in anger management and other techniques for controlling their own aggression. Rape and other forms of assault remain common in most prisons; sometimes guards will actually encourage such attacks on the theory that if inmates are fighting with one another, they will not fight with the administration. Although people agree that we must reduce prison violence, it is clear that we are far from solving the problem.

Health Care in Prisons

The prison health care debate involves one major issue and a host of minor ones. The major controversy is over how much health care prisoners should receive. Until the 1970s, prisons were obliged only to deliver emergency and life-sustaining treatment. By the late 1970s, two developments had improved the quality of prison health care. The first involved a U.S. Supreme Court decision, *Estelle v. Gamble* (1976), defining how much health care prisons must provide. The Supreme Court ruled that institutions could not be "deliberately indifferent" to prisoners' serious medical needs.

The second development was the start of an ongoing collaboration between health-care professionals and prison administrators. Today, many prisons hire professional health-care agencies to provide medical care for inmates. Various types of collaboration exist for training staff, developing education and prevention programs, writing health-care policies, administering medical tests, and following up on treatment plans after inmates return to the community.[15]

More specific health-care controversies emerge as new diseases appear, as the medical needs of the prison population change, as new ways are found to prevent diseases, and as laws mandate new types of care. Recent examples include the concentration of HIV and AIDS cases in penal institutions, the resurgence of tuberculosis, increases in the number of inmates with a history of mental illness or substance abuse, and legal challenges to cigarette smoking.

HIV and AIDS

Infection with the human immunodeficiency virus (HIV) and the development of the acquired immunodeficiency syndrome (AIDS) pose the most serious set of management issues facing prison health-care administrators today. Treating inmates afflicted with AIDS is costly, and there is considerable debate over how much treatment should be provided to prisoners who knowingly exposed themselves to infection. In addition, AIDS raises the difficult issue of whether to grant compassionate early release to prisoners near death. HIV and AIDS also force prison administrators to deal with prejudice on the part of inmates and staff members who object to contact with infected inmates. Most controversial of all are proposals to halt the spread of HIV and AIDS in prisons by recognizing illicit sexual activity and drug use through the distribution of preventatives such as condoms and bleach to clean intravenous injection needles.

A 1994 National Institute of Justice survey revealed that AIDS is nearly six times more prevalent among prisoners than in the general U.S. population.[16] By 1995, the number of state and federal prisoners testing positive for the HIV virus passed the 28,000 mark.[17] The two principal ways the virus is communicated are through sexual contact and through use of contaminated intravenous needles. Although homosexual and drug-injecting behaviors are prohibited, both are common in prison.

Prisons have introduced various programs to control and prevent the spread of HIV. One of the most controversial is testing programs aimed at identifying infected inmates. Should such testing be voluntary or coerced? Who should have access to the test results? Can confidentiality be guaranteed in the small world of a prison? Should the tests be given when inmates enter a facility, on release, or both? And what kinds of action should follow after the identification of an HIV-positive inmate? All of these questions are being debated by prisoners, prison administrators, health-care agencies that provide medical care to inmates, and the general public.

Another controversial policy involves the segregation of HIV-positive inmates from the general prison population. When HIV-positive prisoners and those with AIDS first began to appear in prison populations, the reaction of prison administrators was to isolate them. This led to fierce reactions from the infected inmates, who complained that isolation was based on ignorance and prejudice and that it cut them off from the programs that were available to other inmates, thus in effect punishing them for being ill. Prisons now limit their segregation policies to living quarters, allowing HIV-positive prisoners access to most prison programs. Some institutions provide hospice care in an isolated section of the prison where dying prisoners can self-administer pain-relieving drugs.

Other controversial proposals involve the distribution of condoms and bleach and the creation of clean needle exchange programs. Prison administrators have been reluctant to approve any plan that seems to condone prohibited behavior. As a result, only five jurisdictions give prisoners access to condoms. The distribution of bleach and clean needles, although approved by prison systems in Europe, Australia, and New Zealand, has received little support in the United States. Nearly all U.S. prisons provide "safer sex" education programs, but critics complain that these are ineffective.

Tuberculosis

Tuberculosis (TB), a highly infectious disease spread by coughing, sneezing, spitting, and even unnoticed expectoration during conversation, at one time accounted for up to one-quarter of all deaths per year in the United States. It was brought under control in the early twentieth century, only to reappear in the 1980s. In this resurgence, TB spread particularly quickly in prisons and jails, where people must live and work in close proximity and air circulation is often poor. In 1994, state and federal prisons reported that as many as 69,000 prisoners tested positive for TB.[18] A 1991 TB outbreak in New York State led to the deaths of thirty-six prisoners and one correctional officer.

Although TB is now curable, treatment is difficult, requiring prolonged medication and isolation of the infected person. Isolation is important not only to prevent carriers from infecting others but also to prevent reinfection of carriers themselves while in the process of recovery. Prevention is a matter of special concern for administrators who deal with short-sentence prisoners, who can contract TB and carry it into the community before there has been time for full treatment. However, the extent to which governments can force prisoners and ex-prisoners with TB to live in confined and isolated circumstances and take medicines constitutes a major debate.

In recent years multiple-drug-resistant TB (MDR-TB) has developed as a result of patients failing to complete long-term antibiotic treatment, which encourages the growth of stronger types of TB. To treat MDR-TB, the patient must take a combination of drugs for ten or twelve months. However, it is difficult for prisoners and ex-prisoners who may also be coping with mental illnesses and AIDS to follow such rigorous treatment plans.

Again, the key issue is how far such prisoners can be coerced into confinement designed to cure them and prevent the spread of TB. A secondary issue concerns who should supervise and administer the treatment. Isolation and mandatory treatment policies have led to prisoner complaints of cruel and unusual punishment. To date, the courts have ruled in support of the security and safety of the prison, approving isolation and mandatory treatment and TB testing. But the question of enforced treatment beyond the prison term remains unanswered.

Mental Health Issues

Mental illness has always been a major problem in prisons, where rates of mental illness are higher than in the general population. In the nineteenth century special prisons were created to house criminally insane inmates. At the same time, many states established institutions to hold people in the general population who suffered from mental illness, senility, and mental retardation.

A decision of great consequence for prisons occurred in the 1970s, when governments "deinstitutionalized" their mental hospitals and homes for the mentally retarded. As a result of deinstitutionalization, many former civilian mental hospital inmates were pushed into the community. Some ended up as homeless derelicts; others ended up in prisons. Thus the proportion of mentally disabled prisoners has increased considerably in recent decades.

Although many inmates enter prison with mental disabilities, others develop mental illnesses in prison. For example, elderly prisoners serving life sentences sometimes develop

Alzheimer's disease. Other prisoners break down emotionally from the stress of prison conditions. Prisoners suffering from mental health problems take longer to adjust to prison life, and some never do. Those with severe mental disabilities often have trouble following rules, and others exhibit violent or unpredictable behavior.

How to care for such prisoners without bankrupting the prison system has been one of the major intractable issues of prison management since the prison system began. Nineteenth-century physicians bitterly debated whether mentally disabled prisoners should be treated as "mad" or "bad"—as mental patients or criminals. To some extent this debate continues today as mentally disabled persons are shunted from hospitals to prisons. Drugs now give us the ability to sedate disruptive prisoners, but the degree to which such drugs should be administered is hotly debated.

In the past decade the debates have been complicated by the Americans With Disabilities Act (ADA), passed in 1990. This law defines a mental disability as any "mental or psychological disorder," including organic brain syndrome, severe emotional or mental illness, specific learning disabilities, and retardation.[19] It requires jails and prisons to make their programs and activities accessible to eligible mentally disabled inmates. Institutions need not provide such access to prisoners whose behavior threatens others, but the ADA forces them to justify exclusions.

Thus one effect of the ADA is to push prisons toward much more careful intake screening for inmates with mental disabilities. Recent court decisions declaring that prisons cannot show deliberate indifference to an inmate's mental disabilities are pushing prisons in the same direction. This means that in the future penal institutions will have to spend more on psychological screening. It also means that they will identify a large number of mentally disabled prisoners with treatment needs that are difficult to provide, particularly in confined and punitive settings. How to handle such prisoners will remain a thorny issue well into the twenty-first century.

Substance Abuse

Many prisoners enter prison with serious drug and alcohol addiction problems. Although the numbers vary across jurisdictions, one recent study found that four out of five prisoners are addicted to some form of drug. Nearly the same proportion were under the influence of drugs or alcohol at the time of their crime, and most have a long history of drug and alcohol abuse.[20] A surprising number of prisoners test positive for drugs while incarcerated, and some who did not use drugs before start in prison.

The central controversy in this area is whether to provide in-prison drug rehabilitation treatment that will help inmates stay off drugs in the long run. About one in six inmates receives treatment for addiction, but in most cases the "treatment" consists of "just say 'No'" instructions that have little impact. Some treatment programs have proved effective, but they add to the cost of incarceration. Only 2 percent of offenders receive this kind of treatment.[21]

In the programs that actually reduce prisoners' dependency on drugs, enrolled inmates live in a separate section of the prison in a "therapeutic community" where they work on their problems in a highly structured program for periods of 12 to 18 months. (The shorter the program, the weaker its effect.) These programs cost an additional $10 to $15 per day per inmate, but they dramatically reduce recidivism rates. That is, inmates who successfully complete the programs are much less likely to be rearrested after release.[22]

Critics of such programs point to their costliness and argue that the prison system has more pressing needs, such as relief of overcrowding. Many critics are opposed to rehabilitation on general principles, arguing that deterrence and incapacitation are more important goals.

Proponents of drug treatment counter that we would save money in the long run by treating addicts. A California study indicates that for every $1 spent on a drug program of proven effectiveness, the state saves $7 in the costs of future crime and incarceration. Proponents also note that prisons, where addict populations are concentrated, are ideal places for treatment, and that in prison addicts have a particularly strong motivation for kicking their habit, not least because treatment programs offer alternatives to boredom.[23]

Cigarette Smoking

As much as 80 percent of the prison population is addicted to cigarettes. Although most offenders began smoking before entering prison, some start smoking in prison as a way to reduce stress or simply pass the time.

In the 1990s, prison administrators had to respond to general health concerns about smoking and to lawsuits claiming that second-hand smoke is a health hazard. In 1993, the U.S. Supreme

Court ruled that prisoners have a right not to be subjected to the hazards of second-hand smoke.[24] A year later the Federal Bureau of Prisons established a no-smoking policy, designating all facilities and vehicles as no-smoking areas unless specified otherwise. Today most state prisons also have policies that forbid smoking. Some prohibit smoking in the entire institution, whereas others provide nonsmoking living areas.

Several issues are associated with the creation of a smoke-free prison environment. Some prisoners' lawsuits claim that exposure to smoke creates an unnecessarily cruel and harmful environment, in violation of the Eighth Amendment. Others claim that it is cruel and painful to be forbidden to smoke. Critics of the ban on smoking claim that it increases stress and prison violence. (One administrator who was concerned about increased stress handed out carrot and celery sticks, potato chips, and popcorn to calm jittery nerves.)[25] To eliminate some of the stress associated with smoking cessation, programs have been developed to help prisoners gradually wean themselves from cigarettes. Recent health care standards call for treating cigarette withdrawal in the same way as other types of addiction.

A related issue has to do with the way no-smoking rules turn cigarettes into valuable contraband. Cigarettes have long served as a type of currency in prison, where they are used like money to gamble and barter for goods and services. Smoking bans drive up cigarettes' value. In response to this problem, prison officials have reduced the seriousness of smoking infractions and in some cases loosened restrictions to allow smoking in outdoor areas.

Despite these controversies, the trend is in the direction of further restrictions and the eventual banning of all tobacco products from state and federal prisons.

The Private Prisons Movement

Several factors have contributed to the recent development of private, for-profit prisons. These include overcrowding, soaring prison budgets, court-ordered "caps" on the number of prisoners an institution can hold, and a sociopolitical climate that calls for less government control and overall downsizing. The private sector can build new prisons faster and more cheaply than government bureaucracies can. Thus privatization has become a quick solution for state correction systems bulging with convicted offenders and no place to house them.

Prison facilities financed and operated by private enterprises aim at making a profit. When the private prisons movement began, people expected that the corporations would limit themselves to small, low-security facilities—and initially they did. The first private adult prisons housed inmates who spent most of the day on work-release programs and needed little in the way of programs and security. Today, however, private corporations own and operate prisons at all security levels, with populations of up to 2,000 inmates. Moreover, privatization has come to involve all types of adult facilities, including detention centers, reformatories, penitentiaries, and supermax prisons.

Privatization has raised weighty issues about governance. In the opinion of many, it conflicts fundamentally with the traditional view that state and federal governments should be responsible for the punishment and control of serious offenders. Critics argue that privatization enables the private sector to deprive individuals of their liberty, a power traditionally reserved for government agencies.

Critics of privatization also raise issues of accountability, quality, and security. They argue that many private prisons are dangerous, unsanitary, and poorly staffed. Recent escapes and violence have led to further concerns that private prisons do not have the same standards as public institutions for hiring qualified officers, training, and maintaining security.[26] Critics further point out that for-profit businesses tend to cut corners in areas such as security, employee benefits, and programs. In their opinion, the interests of corporations often are antithetical to those of the nation as a whole.

Advocates of privatization counter that the private sector can provide higher-quality services at lower costs and can provide better job opportunities for prisoners. They also argue that privatization reduces the role of big government and that the private sector is more flexible in its responses to change. Another important argument on behalf of private prisons is that they merely extend the practice of contracting with private enterprises that prisons have engaged in since the early nineteenth century.

Since the first privately run adult prisons opened in 1984, more than 160 such institutions have come into being. Today more than 25 states and the federal prison system include privately run institutions. Some appear to be well run, but others have had problems. The most alarming problems have cropped up in the so-called speculative prisons, which corporations establish by contracting not with a prison system that has too many prisoners, but with a town that needs jobs. For instance, the Northeastern Ohio Correction Center, founded in the impoverished former steel town of Youngstown, was plagued by stabbings and escapes in the late 1990s. Investigators found that although it was a medium-security institution, it was taking maximum-security prisoners from out of state. State and local officials had not been informed of this change, nor could they do anything about it, for the contract with the corporation gave them no authority for oversight.[27]

Because of such problems, it is likely that in the future local jurisdictions will insist on reserving for themselves the authority to regulate and inspect privately run prisons. The private prisons movement will probably survive recent scandals, but it may become less profitable as its institutions are forced to conform to state and federal standards. In the long run, its institutions may end up being very similar to traditional prisons in both operations and costs.

Notes

1. *New York Times*, 10 March 1994, A22.

2. *New York Times*, 28 February 1999, NE20.

3. *New York Times*, 28 February 1999, NE21.

4. Camille Graham Camp and George M. Camp, *The Corrections Yearbook, 1996* (South Salem, NY: Criminal Justice Institute, 1996), 53, 60, 63, 65.

5. Justice Clarence Thomas, dissent to *Hudson v. McMillian*, 503 U.S. 1, at 28.

6. Ibid.

7. Merry Morash, Timothy S. Bynum, and Barbara A. Koons, *Women Offenders: Programming Needs and Promising Approaches* (U.S. Department of Justice, Office of Justice Programs, August 1998), 1.

8. Nicole Hahn Rafter, *Partial Justice: Women, Prisons, and Social Control*, 2d ed. (New Brunswick, NJ: Transaction Publishers, 1990), 185–189.

9. Morash, Bynum, and Koons, 1.

10. This report has been published internationally by Human Rights Watch. For information on ordering, contact Human Rights Watch, 485 Fifth Avenue, New York, NY 10017-6104; tel. 212-972-8400; e-mail hrwnyc@hrw.org. The website address is http://www.hrw.org.

11. Human Rights Watch, 1996, 1–2.

12. Bert Useem and Peter Kimball, *States of Siege: U.S. Prison Riots, 1971–1986* (New York: Oxford University Press, 1991).

13. Roger Morris. *The Devil's Butcher Shop: The New Mexico Prison Uprising* (Albuquerque: University of New Mexico Press, 1983).

14. LIS, Inc., *Supermax Housing: A Survey of Current Practice* (Longmont, CO: National Institute of Corrections Information Center, March 1997).

15. Theodore Hammett, *Public Health/Corrections Collaborations: Prevention and Treatment of HIV/AIDS, STDs, and TB* (Research brief) (Washington, DC: National Institute of Justice and Centers for Disease Control and Prevention, 1998).

16. Laura Maruschak, *HIV in Prisons and Jails, 1995* (Washington, DC: Bureau of Justice Statistics, August 1997), 4.

17. Kathleen Maguire and Ann Pastore, eds., *Sourcebook of Criminal Justice Statistics, 1997* (Washington, DC: U.S. Department of Justice, Bureau of Justice Statistics; Government Printing Office, 1998), 523.

18. Karen Wilcok, Theodore Hammett, Rebecca Widom, and Joel Epstein, *Tuberculosis in Correctional Facilities, 1994–1995* (Research brief) (Washington, DC: National Institute of Justice, 1996).

19. Paula N. Rubin and Susan W. McCampbell, *The Americans With Disabilities Act and Criminal Justice: Mental Disabilities and Corrections* (Washington, DC: National Institute of Justice, July 1995).

20. National Center on Addiction and Substance Abuse, *Behind Bars: Substance Abuse and America's Prison Population* (New York: National Center on Addiction and Substance Abuse at Columbia University, January 1998).

21. Joseph B. Treaster, "Drug Therapy: Powerful Tool Reaching Few Inside Prisons," *New York Times*, 3 July 1995, 26.

22. Ibid., 1, 26.

23. Ibid., 26.

24. *Helling v. McKinney*, 509 U.S. 25 (1993).

25. *New York Times*, 5 February 1995, A37.

26. Charles Logan, "Proprietary Prisons," in *The American Prison: Issues in Research and Policy*, ed. Lynne Goodstein and Doris McKenzie (New York: Plenum Press, 1989), 45–62; Pam Belluck, "As More Prisons Go Private, States Seek Tighter Controls," *New York Times*, 15 April 1999, 1, 20.

27. Belluck, 1, 20.

Chronology 3

This chapter presents a chronological overview of major events in U.S. prison history. It focuses on the evolution of the eight issues and controversies outlined in Chapter 2.

1764   Cesare Beccaria publishes *On Crimes and Punishments,* a book urging that imprisonment be used as the main form of punishing offenders. Influential throughout Europe and among the American colonial leaders, Beccaria's treatise sets forth the theory of deterrence as the basis for punishment and argues against the harsh physical punishments of the past.

1773   Connecticut establishes the Newgate Prison at Simsbury, in an old copper mine, and holds Tory prisoners there. In a sequence typical of post–Revolutionary War efforts to incarcerate felons, Connecticut turns Newgate into a state prison in 1790, but sickness, violence, and escapes prove its inadequacy. Eventually Connecticut abandons this makeshift prison and builds the Connecticut State Prison at Wethersfield, opening it in 1827.

1776   Pennsylvania Quakers establish the Philadelphia Society for Alleviating Distressed Prisoners (later renamed the Philadelphia Society for Alleviating the Miseries of Public Prisons). This step demonstrates their commitment to prison reform and prepares them to take the lead in devising the new punishment of incarceration.

1797   New York State opens its first prison, in the Greenwich Village section of New York City.

1817   Auburn State Penitentiary opens in Auburn, New York. Inmates are housed in cell blocks but marched to workshops for silent labor during the day.

The first good-time law is enacted by New York, permitting prison officials to reward good behavior with sentence reduction. This law covers only first-term inmates with sentences of less than five years; it enables them to earn a maximum of a one-fourth reduction in sentence length.

1825   Sing Sing State Prison opens in Ossining, New York, operating on the plan previously instituted at New York's Auburn State Penitentiary.

1829   Eastern State Penitentiary opens in the Cherry Hill section of Philadelphia, Pennsylvania. Its operations, designed to ensure solitary and silent confinement, become known as the Pennsylvania system. Critics charge that the Pennsylvania system drives prisoners mad with solitude; nonetheless, this system impresses European visitors, who adopt it when they return home. (After 142 years of use, Eastern State Penitentiary was abandoned in 1971. Today it offers historic tours.)

1839   Mount Pleasant Prison for women opens in Ossining, New York, near the Sing Sing Prison for men. The first separate penal unit for females, Mount Pleasant replaces the attic room at Auburn State Penitentiary where women were held in squalid conditions for many years. Mount Pleasant is also innovative in appointing a woman to superintend the female prisoners. The first warden is Eliza Farnham, an advocate of rehabilitation who is far in advance of her time—and of the managers of Sing Sing—in attempting to reform prisoners. Farnham is forced out after a few years, however, by male officials at Sing Sing who do not approve of her progressive techniques.

1841   John Augustus, a shoemaker in Boston, Massachusetts, initiates the practice of probation. Augustus asks a municipal court judge to give him several weeks to reform an offender, instead of sending the man to jail. The offender reforms, and Augustus goes on to work on a volunteer basis with many other such cases, thus beginning the practice of sentencing lesser offenders to community supervision instead of prison. Today probation is the most common form of punishment for crimes; without it, our prisons would have to hold many more offenders than they do.

1859   New York State Lunatic Asylum for Insane Convicts opens in conjunction with the state prison at Auburn, New York. It is the first separate unit for mentally impaired prisoners, indicating awareness that prisoners need to be classified into separate units, depending on their needs.

1865   In the aftermath of the Civil War, Southern states begin to enact "black codes" and "pig laws" to ensure massive incarceration of recently freed slaves. These states also greatly expand the lease system, renting prisoners out to plantation owners, who work them under miserable conditions.

1867   Enoch Wines and Theodore Dwight present their detailed *Report on the Prisons and Reformatories of the United States and Canada* to the New York Prison Association. Outlining the results of their survey, the report concludes that no state is trying to reform prisoners, many of whom leave penitentiaries worse than when they entered. Their report lays the foundation for the prison reform movement that starts three years later in Cincinnati, Ohio.

1868   Zebulon R. Brockway, superintendent of the Detroit House of Correction, establishes an adjacent but separate unit for women, the House of Shelter, where prostitutes

1868   can be held on indeterminate sentences. This unit is sig-
cont.   nificant for several reasons. It anticipates the women's
        reformatory movement by separating women from the
        men prisoners and appointing female staff members to
        supervise them. It anticipates the rehabilitation move-
        ment that starts in 1870 by introducing indeterminate
        sentences and prisoner education. And it enables Brock-
        way, soon to become the most influential penologist in
        the United States, to test out his innovative ideas about
        prisoner management and reform.

1870   National Congress on Penitentiary and Reformatory Dis-
        cipline meets in Cincinnati, attracting reformers from all
        over the country. The delegates endorse a Declaration of
        Principles that becomes the basis of the rehabilitative ap-
        proach that dominates U.S. prison philosophy for the
        next 100 years. This conference is now recognized as the
        first meeting of the group later known as the National
        Prison Association and today as the American Correc-
        tional Association. Presiding at the Cincinnati meeting is
        Rutherford B. Hayes, later president of the United States.

1874   Indiana establishes the first entirely independent refor-
        matory for adult women in the United States.

1876   New York State opens its Elmira State Reformatory, the
        first reformatory prison for men in the United States. The
        superintendent, Zebulon Brockway, runs the facility for
        over twenty-five years, advertising it as a model institu-
        tion that puts into practice the rehabilitative principles en-
        dorsed by the Cincinnati conference in 1870. Reformers
        from around the world flock to Elmira to observe the in-
        novative institution in operation. Brockway emphasizes
        prisoner classification, education and vocational training,
        indeterminate sentencing, and parole. But in fact his sys-
        tem is less effective than he proclaims. Behind the scenes,
        he whips prisoners, starves some, feeds others contami-
        nated food, and transfers those who break down under his
        harsh rule to prisons for the insane. Scandals bring in state
        investigators, who eventually force Brockway to retire.

1895   Construction begins on the first federal prison at Fort
        Leavenworth, Kansas.

1901   New York opens its Reformatory for Women at Bedford Hills under Dr. Katharine Bement Davis. Davis becomes the most innovative prison administrator of the early twentieth century and a firm believer in the theory of eugenics. With the help of grants from wealthy philanthropists, she implements the medical model and arranges to have "feeble-minded" inmates held on indefinite, eugenic sentences. She also builds the Psychopathic Hospital for the treatment of particularly difficult inmates.

1920   New York State enacts the nation's first eugenic sentencing law, making it possible for the state to commit women to the Division for Mentally Defective Delinquent Women at Bedford Hills on totally indefinite sentences.

1921   New York State enacts a eugenic sentencing bill for men, establishing the Napanoch Prison as the state Institution for (Male) Defective Delinquents and enabling it to hold prisoners for up-to-life on indefinite sentences.

1925   Stateville Prison opens in Illinois with several buildings constructed on the model of Jeremy Bentham's panopticon or circular design.

1927   Alderson Federal Prison for women opens in Alderson, West Virginia, superintended by Dr. Mary Belle Harris.

1930   The Federal Bureau of Prisons is established by the U.S. Congress to administer the federal prison system.

1934   The U.S. Penitentiary at Alcatraz ("the Rock") opens on an island off the coast of San Francisco, California, to hold the most violent and dangerous federal prisoners. Its inmates come to include Robert Stroud, famous as "the Birdman of Alcatraz," and the gangster Al Capone. (Closed in 1963 because of the high cost of building maintenance, today Alcatraz is a tourist attraction.)

1960s   The prisoners' rights movement emerges out of the civil rights movement, marking the end of the courts' traditional hands-off policy.

1968   Former U.S. Attorney General Ramsay Clark and other prison reformers argue for the abolition of parole. This is one of the first signs that indeterminate sentencing and the rehabilitative goal are about to come under attack from the political left.

1969   U.S. Supreme Court issues its decision in *Johnson v. Avery*, giving prisoners the right to serve as jailhouse lawyers. This decision improves prisoners' access to the courts, where they argue for other constitutional rights.

1970   Beginning of the rapid increase in prison populations and the upward climb in incarceration rates that persist today.

        George Jackson, a California prisoner and black revolutionary, publishes his incendiary collection of letters, *Soledad Brother*. These become a key document in the prisoners' rights and Black Power movements.

        In *Holt v. Sarver,* a federal district court rules that conditions of confinement in the Arkansas prison system, taken as a whole, constitute cruel and unusual punishment in violation of the Eighth Amendment.

1971   Publication of *Struggle for Justice*, a report sponsored by a Quaker group, the American Friends Service Committee, that mounts a radical attack on the rehabilitative ideal and indeterminate sentencing. With this report, Quakers again take a lead in U.S. prison reform, much as they had in the late eighteenth century.

        Prisoners take over a section of New York's Attica State Prison, marking the beginning of a decade of disturbances at prisons throughout the United States. Forty-three hostages and prisoners are killed at Attica, most of them by troopers who at the command of Governor Nelson Rockefeller storm the prison to regain control. Rockefeller is later denied the Republican nomination for president of the United States, mainly because of what many viewed as his unwillingness to compromise at Attica.

1972   A moratorium on capital punishment begins. In *Furman v. Georgia*, the U.S. Supreme Court rules that Georgia's death penalty is administered in an arbitrary, discriminatory, and hence unconstitutional manner. As a result of this ruling, no executions are conducted in the United States until 1976.

        David Ruiz, a Texas prisoner, files a handwritten petition in federal court questioning the constitutionality of conditions in the Texas prison system. This initiates the case that became *Ruiz v. Estelle.*

1973   Under Governor Nelson Rockefeller, New York State passes its "Rockefeller" drug laws. Harsh and controversial, this legislation swells the state's prison population and gives the country a foretaste of the overcrowding that will later result from the enactment elsewhere of severe drug laws.

1974   Robert Martinson publishes "What Works? Questions and Answers About Prison Reform" in the journal *Public Interest.* Reporting results of prison rehabilitation programs, the article concludes that "Nothing works." This helps shift the goal of the U.S. prison system away from rehabilitation and toward punishment, deterrence, and incapacitation, the main aims of the system today. Although Martinson later softens his conclusions, his modified view attracts less attention than his initial attack on rehabilitation.

        U.S. Supreme Court decides *Wolff v. McDonnell*, the leading case on due process in prison discipline. The Court declares that when prisoners stand to lose a degree of liberty in disciplinary proceedings, they must have some due-process protections, but not as many as defendants in a court of law.

1975–   Judge William Wayne Justice of the Fifth Circuit Court is-
1977   sues orders protecting prisoners who are suffering retaliation from staff as a consequence of involvement in the *Ruiz v. Estelle* class action suit against the Texas prison system.

1976   Maine enacts a definite sentencing law, becoming the first state to reject indeterminate sentencing.

U.S. Supreme Court decides *Estelle v. Gamble,* holding that prisons cannot exhibit "deliberate indifference" to inmates' serious medical needs. This Eighth Amendment case sets a relatively low standard for prison health care, but today many jurisdictions exceed its requirements.

With *Gregg v. Georgia,* the U.S. Supreme Court lifts the moratorium on capital punishment, and death row units begin to fill. By 1 January 1996 there are 3,099 state and federal prisoners awaiting execution.

1977   U.S. Supreme Court issues its decision in *Bounds v. Smith,* ruling that prisons are obligated to provide inmates with an adequate law library.

1978–   Judge Justice of the Fifth Circuit Court presides over the
1979   lengthy trial in the Texas prisoners' rights case *Ruiz v. Estelle.*

1979   The U.S. Supreme Court issues a decision in *Bell v. Wolfish,* a case that many take as a sign of the waning of the prisoners' rights movement. This decision, although it does not affect previous prisoners' rights decisions, denies new inmate claims to certain constitutional rights.

1980   On 2 February, convicts take over the New Mexico State Penitentiary at Santa Fe and during the next thirty-six hours rape, pillage, mutilate, and kill, leaving 33 prisoners dead and the prison in ruins. Although more lives were lost during the Attica rebellion of 1971, the Santa Fe riot is the deadliest prison riot in U.S. history in terms of the number of inmates killed by other prisoners. Investigators identify overcrowding, rotten food, lax security, and corrupt officials as causes of the riot.

In the Texas prisoners' rights case *Ruiz v. Estelle,* Judge Justice finds the totality of conditions in the Texas prison system to be unconstitutional and orders massive changes.

1983   First boot camp opens in Georgia. Boot camps, also
        known as shock incarceration, combine military training
        with the traditional rehabilitation philosophy. This type
        of program is designed for young, first-time, nonviolent
        offenders.

1984   U.S. Congress establishes the United States Sentencing
        Commission to write sentencing guidelines.

1986   The Marion Adjustment Center in Kentucky becomes the
        first privately owned and operated prison in the United
        States. A minimum-security institution, Marion is run by
        the Corrections Corporation of America.

1987   U.S. Sentencing Commission submits federal sentencing
        guidelines to U.S. Congress. They are approved quickly
        and go into effect in November 1987. The guidelines de-
        fine punishment, deterrence, and incapacitation as the
        primary goals of the prison system. They set mandatory
        minimum sentences for federal drug law violations, sen-
        tences later copied by many states.

1992   In a victory for prisoners' rights advocates, the U.S.
        Supreme Court declares in *Hudson v. McMillian* that
        guards may not use excessive force to maintain prison
        discipline. The key issue, the Court holds, is not the de-
        gree of injury but whether the guards used more force
        than necessary.

1994   U.S. Congress passes the Violent Crime Control and Law
        Enforcement Act. It establishes a truth-in-sentencing pol-
        icy that metes out longer terms for serious violent
        crimes. It also expands the number of federal crimes
        punishable by death. To increase the amount of prison
        time served by violent offenders at the state level, the
        legislation includes $4 billion in funds for prison con-
        struction in states that adopt truth-in-sentencing laws
        guaranteeing that violent offenders will serve at least 85
        percent of their sentences. It further provides over $1 bil-
        lion for states to establish separate drug courts and pro-
        vide drug treatment, graduated sanctions, and intensive
        supervision for nonviolent offenders with substance
        abuse problems.

1994   No-smoking policy is implemented by the Federal Bu-
cont.   reau of Prisons.

"Three-strikes" sentencing legislation is passed in California, mandating sentences of twenty-five years to life
for third-time felons.

The U.S. prison population passes the 1 million mark.

1995   Chain gangs are reintroduced in Alabama, Arizona, and
Florida.

1996   State and federal governments spend $27.5 billion on in-
carceration.

1997   Federal regulations are changed to allow juveniles convicted of violent crimes to be housed in adult prisons.

1998   Private corporations are managing 159 adult prisons
holding more than 116,000 prisoners.

By mid-year, federal and state prisons hold an estimated
total of 1.2 million inmates, an increase of nearly 60 percent since 1990.

On 6 June, after a 26-year court battle against New York
State, Frank "Big Black" Smith, a leader of the 1971 Attica
prison riot, now sixty-four years old, is awarded $4 mil-
lion by a federal jury. Smith's suit claimed that he was
beaten and tortured by prison guards and state police
after the riot was terminated.

Biographical Sketches

This chapter presents biographical sketches of twenty-three people who have contributed importantly to the development of American prisons, including administrators, jurists, philosophers, prisoners, reformers, and researchers. Since the birth of the American prison in the late eighteenth century, a large number of people have affected the institution's evolution and growth, some working within the system, others trying to reform it from the outside. These sketches thus cover only a small fraction of the hundreds of men and women who changed the course of U.S. prison history. The individuals represented here were selected either because they had a particularly strong influence on prison development or because they played a crucial role in the controversies summarized in Chapter 2. They illustrate the range of actors on the stage of prison history.

Cesare Beccaria (1738–1794)

In his treatise *On Crimes and Punishments* (1764), Italian author and philosopher Beccaria argued passionately for using prisons as a method of punishing crimes on the ground that proportional prison sentences would deter future crimes. It had a major impact on the founding of the American prison system, appearing as it did at a time when colonial leaders were thinking about how the new country should be governed.

Beccaria, who had been born into an aristocratic family in Milan, Italy, was the first to argue from philosophical premises for imprisonment as a form of punishment. In Europe and to some degree in the United States as well, punishments for crimes in the late 1700s tended to be physical and brutal, taking such forms as flogging, mutilation, and free use of the death penalty. Beccaria sought a more humane form of punishment. He was concerned, moreover, that wealthy people were more likely to escape punishment than the poor and that torture, which he said was still widely used in Italy to extract confessions, led to the conviction of innocents. But his major interest was in identifying a form of punishment that would actually prevent future crimes.

In the United States just after the Revolutionary War, leaders were devising new strategies of government that would, they hoped, promote liberty. Thus Beccaria's argument for replacing older forms of punishment with imprisonment had great appeal. Sentences to imprisonment, Beccaria reasoned, can be adjusted in length, so that the punishment can fit the crime. This principle of proportional punishment remains one of the key ideas in American jurisprudence today. Beccaria argued further that just punishments, if well publicized, would deter people from committing future crimes. This concept of deterrence, too, continues to play a major role in U.S. sentencing philosophies.

Beccaria's ideas were influential partly because they coincided with and reinforced beliefs also held by leaders of the newly freed colonies. Beccaria conceived of humans as rational beings, capable of choosing whether or not to commit crimes; and he conceived of government as a social contract between citizens and their representatives, with citizens giving up a degree of liberty in return for a safe and well-managed society. From these premises, for Beccaria and the U.S. founding fathers, it followed that imprisonment would be the best manner of punishing felons.

Jeremy Bentham (1748–1832)

Bentham was an English social philosopher, reformer, and prison architect. Born in London, England, and deeply influenced by Beccaria's writing, Bentham helped create the philosophical foundation on which the early penitentiaries were built. Developing further Beccaria's theme of deterrence, Bentham formulated his "greatest happiness principle," according to which rewards and punishments can be used to encourage people to make sure that their own greatest happiness coincides with the greatest happiness of their group. That is, if threatened with punishments, people will refrain from committing punishable acts and thus behave in ways that maximize not only their own good but also the good of the group, which includes a crime-free society. Closely associated with Bentham, this type of reasoning is often called *utilitarianism,* meaning that we calculate the "utility" or usefulness of our actions. Bentham believed that people break the law because they make inaccurate calculations about the consequences of their actions. Hence the punishments for crime should be made very clear to everyone, and they should be inevitable.

Bentham designed a type of prison known as the *panopticon* (literally the "see everywhere"), which would enable a single guard to see every prisoner at once and keep them all under constant surveillance. In this plan, the prison is shaped like a half sphere, with tiers of cells circling a central area. A guard in a tower in the structure's center would be able to watch the prisoners, but because the guard would be concealed, the prisoners would never know when they were being observed. Bentham urged England to build a panopticon in Australia, to replace its prison colonies. England declined, but several prisons in the United States adopted the panopticon plan (notably Stateville, in Illinois). Traces of the panopticon idea also appear in the spokes-and-hub architecture used at Pennsylvania's Eastern State Penitentiary in Philadelphia.

George Beto (1916–1991)

Beto, a penologist and prison commissioner, was associated with authoritarian methods and Texas's "building tender" system. An ordained Lutheran minister with a doctorate in education, Beto began his career in corrections by serving on the Illinois Board of Parole during the 1950s. There he met and was strongly influenced by the hard-nosed superintendent of the Stateville and Joliet prisons, Joseph Ragen. Beto moved to Texas, becoming president of Concordia College and serving on the Texas Board of Corrections. He was then appointed Commissioner of the Texas Department of Corrections, a position he held from 1962 to 1972.

Adopting the tough disciplinary style of Joseph Ragen, Beto ruled the Texas Department of Corrections with an iron hand, emphasizing discipline and control. Although Texas prisons under Beto were known as safe and efficient, an inmate class action suit, *Ruiz v. Estelle* (1980) later declared the entire system unconstitutional, condemning in particular the building tender system, which empowered the most brutal convicts to run the cell blocks. Beto nonetheless had many supporters who admired his emphasis on inmate obedience, hard labor, and literacy training.

Zebulon R. Brockway (1827–1920)

A prison administrator, reformer, penologist, and one of the most celebrated figures in American prison history, Brockway began his extensive career in penology as a twenty-one-year-old clerk at Connecticut's Wethersfield Prison. From there he moved to prison administration positions in Albany and Rochester, New York, and in 1861 he became superintendent of the Detroit House of Correction. In Detroit Brockway began developing his ideas for rehabilitating prisoners through education, trade training, and incentive programs that rewarded prisoners for good behavior.

In 1868 Brockway established a House of Shelter for women as an adjunct to the Detroit House of Correction. There he introduced a form of indeterminate sentencing that rewarded good behavior with early release. This was the first step toward the system later known as parole. By 1870, with national sentiment gathering for an entirely new, reformational approach to prisoners, Brockway and his innovations at the Detroit House of Correction were on the cutting edge of prison management.

At the 1870 meeting of the National Congress on Penitentiary and Reformatory Discipline, Brockway was poised to become a national leader in prison reform. He delivered the Congress's most influential paper, advocating methods of prisoner reformation, and he helped write the Congress's famous Declaration of Principles, the document that became the foundation of the rehabilitative approach to incarceration and determined the course of "corrections" for the next 100 years.

At this point, Brockway was recognized as the most innovative prison administrator in the United States. Hence when New York State established a new reformatory for young men at Elmira and decided that it should be operated along the lines Brockway had outlined at the 1870 prison congress, it was natural for the state to invite Brockway to superintend this experimental prison. He accepted and ran the famous Elmira Reformatory for the next twenty-five years, implementing indeterminate sentencing and claiming very high rates of success in rehabilitating inmates. At Elmira he also introduced the first formal parole system and a method of rewarding prisoners with promotion to better "grades" with more privileges. Adopting medical terminology, he did much to persuade the general public and other penologists that criminals are less bad than sick. Thus he was influential in promoting the "medical model" of criminology.

Under the surface, however, Elmira's system operated far less well than Brockway claimed. Investigated twice by the New York State Board of Charities on charges of using cruel and excessive punishments, Brockway was finally ousted for his brutal floggings of prisoners, for feeding them inferior foods and allowing diseases to flourish, and for mental cruelty. This ouster did little to harm his reputation, however, and even today prison administrators regard him as one of the great humanitarians in American prison reform. In 1912 he published an autobiography entitled *Fifty Years of Prison Service.*

Rhoda M. Coffin (1826–1909)

Born in Xenia, Ohio, and raised as a Quaker, prison reformer Rhoda Johnson married Charles Coffin of Richmond, Indiana, in 1847. Following the example of Pennsylvania Quakers, the Coffins became involved in prison reform and attended the 1870 National Congress on Penitentiary and Reformatory Discipline. Coffin may have helped persuade the congress to adopt its Principle XIX, which advocated separate prisons for women. In any case, she became instrumental in the founding of the first all-female prison, the Indiana Reformatory Institution for Women and Girls, in Indianapolis in 1873. She and her husband had been horrified, during earlier investigations of the Indiana State Prison at Jeffersonville, to discover that the women prisoners had sexual contact with male prisoners and were sometimes whipped into sexual submission by male guards. Thus she worked to have the female prisoners removed to a separate institution.

The Indiana Reformatory Institution was the first completely independent women's prison. It was also the first to be run by an entirely female staff. Although most prison histories tout the men's reformatory at Elmira, New York, as the first adult reformatory in the United States, in fact that distinction belongs to the Indiana women's reformatory, which Rhoda Coffin helped open several years before Elmira received its first inmates.

Sir Walter Crofton (1815–1897)

Crofton, a director of the Irish Convict Prisons, created the "progressive stage" system of enabling convicts to earn "marks" or points for good behavior, which strongly influenced American prison administrators in the move to adopt the philosophy of rehabilitation. Crofton, a retired army officer, was appointed director of Irish Convict Prisons in 1854 and devised his progressive stage system over the next eight years. Influenced by the British penologist Sir Alexander Maconochie, who had worked out similar ideas as head of a penal colony in Australia, Crofton was laying the groundwork for what became indeterminate sentencing and parole.

Crofton's system involved an early form of classification and several stages for offenders to work through toward rehabilitation and early release. In the first stage convicts started with three months in solitary confinement, followed by six months with short periods of labor and increased rations. In the second stage convicts were shipped to Spike Island, off the coast of Ireland, for vocational training or, if they had work skills, sent to another town to help build a new prison. This stage involved educational and vocational training designed to develop work skills. In the third stage inmates were sent to dormitories where they were assigned to jobs and continued their vocational training. Convicts gradually earned increased privileges that allowed them some mobility in the local community. The final stage was a work-release program allowing the offender to work in the community without supervision.

Crofton improved the "ticket of leave" system developed by Maconochie in Australia by granting convicts their ticket of leave, or parole, once they were reestablished in the community. If the convict did not meet the terms of this conditional pardon, the "ticket" would be revoked. The ticket of leave remained in effect until the date of completion of the original sentence.

Crofton's mark system, sometimes called the Irish system, became part and parcel of the American reformatory plan in the 1870s. Zebulon Brockway, who had experimented with a similar system at the Detroit House of Correction, folded Crofton's mark system into indeterminate sentencing, thus producing an overall plan of rewards and punishment that enabled prisoners to work their way upward through "grades" or classifications to parole.

Crofton's Irish mark system was eventually adopted by other countries as well.

Katharine Bement Davis (1860–1935)

A social worker and penologist, Davis superintended the New York State Reformatory for Women at Bedford Hills from 1901 through 1913, a period during which it was the most innovative and influential penal institution in the country. Born in Buffalo, New York, Davis began her career as a teacher. In 1893, after earning a bachelor's degree from Vassar College, she became head of a settlement house in Philadelphia, where she worked until 1897. Davis then enrolled at the University of Chicago, earning a Ph.D. in political economy in 1900, a time when it was still unusual for women to graduate with a doctoral degree.

Josephine Shaw Lowell, an activist on behalf of women's prisons, invited Davis to become superintendent of the new women's reformatory at Bedford Hills. Like many reformers of the time, Davis endorsed eugenic principles, according to which crime and other social problems can be eradicated by preventing "inferior" people from reproducing. Armed with this philosophy, Davis persuaded several influential foundations to fund research at Bedford. The research seemed to prove that many of the prisoners were "feeble-minded" and thus (so the reasoning then ran) inferior through heredity. Though eugenics doctrine has since been disproved, the research that Davis initiated at Bedford remains important as an early effort to conduct scientific studies of the causes of crime. Moreover, because Davis usually hired female researchers, she opened doors for some of the country's first women social scientists.

On the basis of her research, Davis concluded that "feeble-minded" prisoners should be segregated for life to prevent them from "breeding." With financial assistance from John D. Rockefeller Jr., one of the richest men in the United States and a fellow eugenicist, Davis arranged for "feeble-minded" inmates to be removed to separate quarters and held on completely open-ended or indefinite sentences. Later she helped arrange an agreement between Rockefeller and New York State whereby he actually owned part of the women's reformatory and paid for studies done there on female mental defects and psychopathy.

After leaving Bedford, Davis served as New York City's commissioner of corrections (the first female appointed to that position) and, later still, as chairperson of the city's parole board.

Louis Dwight (Reverend) (1793–1854)

Dwight was a prison reformer, head of the Boston Prison Discipline Society, and chief advocate of the congregate method of prison management. At the time the first penitentiaries were constructed, a fierce battle raged between advocates of the Pennsylvania or segregate system and of the New York or congregate system of prison discipline. As a leading supporter of the New York system, which eventually won the struggle, Dwight helped determine the architecture and management methods of prisons as we know them today. Although it is now difficult to comprehend how tempers could have flared so high over the choice between alternative methods of administering prisons, this debate dominated the literature on prisons in the early nineteenth century. Dwight headed the Boston Prison Discipline Society, which championed the New York system, from the time he organized the group in 1825 until his death in 1854; during that time the Philadelphia Prison Society, leader of the forces in favor of the Pennsylvania system, constituted his chief opponent.

Dwight originally hoped to enter the ministry but gave up that plan when an accident damaged his lungs. Touring the countryside to distribute Bibles to prisoners, he became familiar with the appalling conditions in penal institutions and became determined to change them. The Pennsylvania system, most notably implemented in the Eastern State Prison at Philadelphia, held convicts in separate cells and allowed no group activities from the moment of commitment until release. Dwight, claiming that this system led to high rates of insanity, preferred the system first realized at New York's Auburn Prison, where convicts were separately celled but allowed to congregate during the day in factory-like workshops, under conditions of total silence. The New York system eventually triumphed in the United States because it cost less per capita. Cells could be stacked in tiers, a cheaper method of construction than was possible with the segregate system; the cells could be smaller, because prisoners did not inhabit them twenty-four hours a day; and money could be made from the sale of goods produced by inmate labor. At the time, the triumph of the New York system seemed to owe a great deal to the combative Dwight, who, whenever he heard that a state was drawing up plans for a new prison, would rush into battle, armed with charts and statistics, to push for what he was certain was the superior plan. Dwight was so committed to the concept of silent labor that he advocated that it be implemented in schools as well as prisons. In part because of the vigor with which he argued for the merits of silence, many U.S. prisons maintained a silence rule well into the twentieth century.

Eliza Farnham (1815–1864)

As the first women to head a state prison unit and a pioneer in prisoner rehabilitation, Farnham served as chief matron at New York's Mount Pleasant Prison for women, the first separate women's penal unit in the country, from 1844 to 1847. At the time of her appointment, Farnham was only twenty-eight years old, but through a combination of kindness and firmness, she was able to bring order to the chaotic new prison, built adjacent to the more famous Sing Sing men's prison. Born in Rensselaerville, New York, into a Quaker family, Farnham had been impressed by what she had heard about Elizabeth Fry, the English advocate of female prison reform. Like many of her contemporaries, Farnham endorsed phrenology, the theory that behavior is governed by various separate "faculties" within the brain. Criminal behavior, phrenologists taught, results from underdevelopment or atrophy of one or more of the faculties. From this, it followed that the way to cure criminal behavior was through treatment that would restore undeveloped faculties to normality. Thus Farnham's phrenological treatments of women prisoners at Mount Pleasant constituted very early forms of prisoner rehabilitation and presaged what later came to be known as the "medical model" of criminology, according to which offenders are sick and in need of cure.

Farnham tried to educate her inmates and allowed them to read in their cells. She also broke from the Sing Sing practice of perpetual silence among inmates by allowing thirty minutes of quiet conversation per day. In other innovations, Farnham classified prisoners to target their treatment needs and established incentives for good behavior. Moreover, she established the first prison nursery in the country. However, her radical approaches roused the ire of more traditional prison administrators, especially the chaplain of Sing Sing, who considered novel-reading irreligious. Attacked by her critics, Farnham was eventually forced to resign.

Jean Struven Harris (1924–)

In 1981 Harris, who later became a prison reformer and advocate of incarcerated mothers, was convicted of second-degree murder and sentenced to a term of fifteen years to life for the murder of her lover, the "Scarsdale Diet" author Herman Tarnower. The case was all the more electrifying because Harris had led a life of considerable privilege and at the time of the crime headed an elite girls' prep school. Raised in the wealthy Shaker Heights neighborhood of Cleveland, Ohio, Harris attended Smith College before she began a career in administration at private secondary schools, where she was known as a strong and somewhat preachy disciplinarian.

Harris had no prior history of criminal behavior, and indeed, throughout her trial and years of incarceration, she maintained her innocence, claiming that the gun she intended to use to kill herself went off by accident when Tarnower tried to take it from her. But the relationship with Tarnower was known to have been nearing an end, and the prosecution built a persuasive case that Harris had meant to kill him to keep him from leaving her. Incarcerated at the Bedford Hills, New York, women's prison, Harris spent most of her time helping other inmates. In particular, she became known for her work in the prison nursery. She taught parenting classes to young mothers and was a major force behind the establishment of the Children's Center, a program that brings children to the prison for visits with their mothers. As a result of Harris's work, Bedford Hills today is a national model for prisoner parenting programs. Harris has authored several books, including *Stranger in Two Worlds* (1986), an autobiography focused on her experience of incarceration. In 1993, Harris was released from prison and placed on parole for the remaining four years of her sentence.

George Jackson (1941–1971)

A militant political activist, California prisoner, and author, Jackson participated in a 1969 incident of racial violence at Soledad Prison and was shot and killed two years later during a violent disturbance at San Quentin. Because of the success of his book *Soledad Brother: The Prison Letters of George Jackson*, his death received international attention and he became a martyr of the militant black prisoners' movement.

Jackson's first encounter with the law occurred in Chicago, when he was fourteen years old. When his family moved to Los

Angeles, his criminal behavior escalated from petty theft to robbery and burglary. Jackson spent most of his adolescent years in and out of juvenile detention facilities. In 1961, at nineteen years of age, Jackson pleaded guilty to armed robbery and received a lengthy indeterminate sentence. In prison Jackson became a revolutionary, a change reflected in his letters, which are intense, dramatic calls to battle against racial injustice. A powerful leader of black prisoners, Jackson was also revered by radical youths of the 1970s.

Transferred to Soledad Prison, Jackson participated in political study groups and declared himself a Marxist. In early 1969, with racial tensions running high, violence at Soledad resulted in the shooting deaths of three black prisoners by a white officer. Several days later, a white guard was beaten to death. Jackson and two other inmates were charged with this murder; they became known as the "Soledad brothers" and received widespread attention in the media. Transferred to San Quentin and held in solitary confinement to await trial, Jackson was now facing the death penalty.

The Soledad brothers became national celebrities and heroes of the black revolution, gaining even more status with the 1970 publication of *Soledad Brother*. When the trial finally began in late 1971, Jackson had already been killed during a mysterious encounter with prison officers about which little is known. In August 1971 Jackson had come into possession of a gun; there followed an outbreak of violence that left a number of guards and convicts dead, including Jackson. The remaining two Soledad brothers were acquitted.

Josephine Shaw Lowell (1843–1905)

As a women's prison reformer and state charities commissioner, Lowell was a major figure in the establishment of separate prisons for women and the most prominent and effective woman involved in "charity" (state welfare) work in the late nineteenth century. Born in West Roxbury, Massachusetts, into an antislavery family, she was the sister of the famous Civil War Commander Robert Gould Shaw, who led a black regiment into battle in the South and died there. Her husband of one year, Charles Russell Lowell, also died in action during the war, leaving her with a daughter. Instead of retreating into grief, Lowell helped direct the Women's Central Association of Relief for the Army and Navy.

In 1876, Lowell was appointed the first female commissioner of the New York State Board of Charities, where she became a strong advocate for "scientific philanthropy," or state aid based on sociological studies as opposed to haphazard alms-giving. Coming face-to-face with the conditions of women held in predominantly male jails and prisons, Lowell campaigned vigorously for the establishment of separate prisons for women that would be run by other women.

In the 1870s Lowell read Richard Dugdale's electrifying study of the infamous "Juke" family, from which she concluded that poverty, criminality, and other social ills are hereditary traits, passed through the generations of the poor. From this study she, like other welfare experts of her day, concluded that one of the most significant causes of social problems is "feeble-mindedness" (what we today call mental retardation) and that feeble-mindedness and other social problems are spread mainly by promiscuous, feeble-minded women. Thus Lowell became one of the first U.S. advocates of the doctrine later known as *eugenics*, a plan for eliminating social problems by encouraging law-abiding citizens to produce more children and preventing the poor, criminal, and feeble-minded from reproducing. She was the most instrumental figure in the founding of the first U.S. eugenic institution, the Newark (New York) Custodial Asylum for Feeble-Minded Women of Child-Bearing Age. Lowell also founded several reformatories for criminal women, including the reformatory prison at Bedford Hills, New York.

Elam Lynds (1784–1855)

In 1816 Lynds, a former army captain and strict disciplinarian, was appointed principal keeper (chief warden) of the new state prison at Auburn, New York, one of the earliest U.S. state penal institutions. Discipline was harsh in all early penal institutions, but Lynds's name became a synonym for militaristic routines and brutality.

Lynds believed that inmates should be known only by their number and that everyone should be treated exactly the same. Inmates wore black-and-white striped clothing, partly to eradicate their individuality and partly for security reasons. Lynds often resorted to the form of punishment used in the military: flogging. He did not believe that good behavior should be rewarded, and in fact he doubted that convicts could reform. Under his rule, convicts were not allowed to communicate with the outside world; there were no visitors, nor was letter-writing permitted. The only reading material allowed in the prison was the Bible. Local citizens could pay to come into the prison to look at the inmates, much as they might view animals at a zoo.

When Auburn prison became full in 1825, Lynds was commissioned to build a new prison using convict labor at Ossining, New York. Within three years the new institution, Sing Sing, was ready for occupancy, and Lynds became its first principal keeper. Lynds remained at Sing Sing until 1830, resigning shortly after an investigation of his management methods.

Edna Mahan (1900–1968)

One of the most respected, innovative, and effective prison administrators in U.S. history, Mahan spent more than forty years as superintendent of the Reformatory for Women in Clinton, New Jersey. Long after the rehabilitative thrust of the women's reformatory movement had weakened in other states, Mahan continued to advocate methods of encouraging prisoners to become independent and to take responsibility for their own lives.

Born in 1900 in Yreka, California, Mahan was raised by her mother and graduated from the University of California at Berkeley in 1922 with a bachelor's degree in education. She completed postgraduate work at the California Bureau of Juvenile Research, where she established a close friendship with the Superintendent of the Los Angeles County Juvenile Hall, Dr. Miriam Van Waters, who later became superintendent of the Framingham, Massachusetts, women's reformatory. In 1923, Van Waters brought Mahan into the Los Angeles County Probation Department, and in 1924 she hired her to work at Juvenile Hall.

Mahan's first appointment as a superintendent in the field of corrections was at El Retiro, a school for female juveniles in Los Angeles. In 1927, when her mentor, Dr. Van Waters, moved to Boston to work on a research project at Harvard Law School, Mahan accompanied her. In Boston Mahan met leaders in the field of corrections. In 1928, she became the superintendent of Clinton Farms, New Jersey's reformatory for women, where she fought long and hard for humane treatment of prisoners. Under her supervision, Clinton Farms became known as one of the most progressive institutions in the country.

Mahan supported the philosophy of an open institution: She maintained low levels of security, removed iron bars from the windows, and created more housing units of the "cottage" design.

Under her administration, Clinton Farms resembled a campus more than a prison. Mahan instituted an inmate self-government system in which inmates elected representatives to help manage the institution. Student government was a system of self-discipline, inmate supervision, and mentoring; it promoted positive behavior and rehabilitation. In addition, all inmates were encouraged to be leaders and to assume responsibility for the behavior of everyone living in their cottage.

Mahan also devoted a great deal of her career to developing programs for inmate mothers and their children. She maintained a nursery cottage for infants born at Clinton Farms until 1949, when overcrowding forced relocation of the nursery to the hospital. In 1967, Mahan opened the doors to the first halfway house for women in New Jersey, Carpenter House, which could accommodate up to eight inmates at a time. Mahan was an active member of the American Prison Association and the Osborne Association. A role model for women in corrections, she strongly advocated equal compensation and opportunities for women in prison administration. In remembrance of Mahan, Clinton Farms has been renamed the Edna Mahan Correctional Facility for Women.

Robert Martinson (1927–1979)

Martinson conducted one of the most influential studies of correctional treatment of the 1970s, a survey of the effectiveness of programs designed to rehabilitate offenders. Martinson's research pointed toward the conclusion that "Nothing works."

Martinson received a bachelor's degree in economics and a master's degree and Ph.D. in sociology from the University of California at Berkeley. As a doctoral student in 1961 Martinson joined the Freedom Riders protesting the segregation of institutions in the South. Arrested in Jackson, Mississippi, he was convicted of breach of peace and sentenced to four months in jail and a $200 fine. Martinson served forty days at Parchman State Prison in Mississippi before being released on appeal. His prison experience had such a strong impact that he devoted his career to the study of corrections, teaching first in California and later at the City College of New York, where he was head of the department of sociology and director of the Center for Knowledge in Criminal Justice Planning.

In 1974, in the journal *Public Interest*, Martinson published one of the most controversial research reports in the history of American corrections: "What Works? Questions and Answers about Prison Reform." Having surveyed the results of 231 correctional treatment evaluations conducted between 1945 and 1967, Martinson concluded that none had been effective in rehabilitating inmates. At a time when the pendulum of public opinion was fast swinging from liberal to conservative in the criminal justice arena, Martinson's report was used to support the abolition of rehabilitation programs and the return to "flat" or definite sentencing. Ironically, liberals, too, pounced on Martinson's conclusions to support their contention that treatment programs and indeterminate sentencing often resulted in unfairness, including longer terms for black prisoners than for white prisoners. Thus politicians of all stripes cited Martinson's article, which was widely quoted and reprinted.

Other researchers came to similar conclusions, but within a few years yet another group of scholars began to insist that some rehabilitation programs work some of the time with some inmates. By 1979 Martinson himself had moderated his original conclusions, but he remained famous for the original report that seemed to say, "Nothing works." Martinson died before he could complete his follow-up research and speak definitively about the success of rehabilitation programs.

Thomas O. Murton (1929–1990)

Murton's efforts to reform the Tucker Farm at the Cummins Farm Unit of the Arkansas State Penitentiary drew attention to scandalous conditions at the state's prisons. Although Murton was fired, actor Robert Redford publicized his work as a reform warden in the movie *Brubaker* (1980).

Formerly a criminal justice professor and head of a U.S. Army stockade in Alaska, Murton was appointed in 1966 to run the Tucker Prison Farm, a 300-bed unit of the state penitentiary. At Tucker Farm Murton ended the use of corporal punishment and overhauled prison nutrition and housing conditions. In 1967 he became warden at the Cummins Farm Unit, a 1,300-bed unit. When Murton arrived at Cummins, he found brutality, buried bodies of prisoners whose deaths had not been recorded, and other deplorable conditions.

Murton was a strong advocate for the abolition of life sentences and the death penalty. These opinions, as well as Murton's liberal approach to prisoner and prison reform, embarrassed the state's correctional establishment, one of the most backward in the nation. Murton was forced to resign two years into his term, but his reform efforts eventually led to a federal court decision declaring that conditions at Cummins Farm violated the Eighth Amendment prohibition against cruel and unusual punishment. Despite years of repeated efforts, Murton was unable to find another job in corrections, which led him to conclude that he had been blacklisted. In 1970 he published *Accomplices to the Crime: The Arkansas Prison Scandal*, describing his experience as an administrator in the Arkansas prison system. After a number of years as a criminal justice professor at the University of Minnesota, he retired to raise poultry in Oklahoma and wrote two more books, *The Dilemma of Prison Reform* (1982) and *Crime and Punishment in Arkansas* (1985).

Helen Prejean (Sister) (1939–)

A nun, Prejean became famous for her humanitarian work as spiritual adviser to death row inmates in the state of Louisiana. Born and raised in Baton Rouge, Louisiana, she joined the Sisters of St. Joseph of Medaille in 1957. She received a bachelor's degree in English and education from St. Mary's Dominican College, New Orleans, and a master's degree in religious education from St. Paul's University in Ottawa, Canada. Prejean is the author of *Dead Man Walking: An Eyewitness Account of the Death Penalty in the United States* (1994). This book became the basis for a major motion picture, *Dead Man Walking* (1996), in which she is portrayed by the actor Susan Sarandon. The book and the movie describe how Prejean became the pen pal of a death row inmate at the Louisiana State Penitentiary at Angola. After they had exchanged numerous letters, inmate Patrick Sonnier asked her to visit him in prison; this was the start of her prison ministry.

Prejean's work has forced her to confront both sides of the death penalty issue. Working with the condemned, Prejean aims at helping death row prisoners find some serenity and accept responsibility for their crimes before they die. In addition, she founded Survive, an advocacy group for families of murder victims.

Joseph E. Ragen (1896–1971)

Warden of the Stateville and Joliet penitentiaries in Illinois for twenty-six years, Ragen was one of the last of the old-style, tough-guy wardens who ruled their institutions like little kingdoms and enjoyed almost unchecked power.

After eight years in a sheriff's department, Ragen began his career as a prison administrator in 1935 at the Menard prison in Southern Illinois. He became known for the paramilitary strictness with which he maintained discipline not only among the inmates but also among the correctional officers. More concerned with security than with rehabilitation, Ragen was a no-nonsense, authoritarian manager. State legislators and the public alike respected his ability to prevent riots and escapes and to minimize prison violence. Working in a period before the civil rights revolution, Ragen was able to impose his will on prisoners and staff without interference from the courts and to keep critical reporters out of his institutions. After his retirement in 1961, however, the Illinois prison system opened up to the outside world. Inmates began taking their grievances to the courts, and discipline broke down.

After his resignation as warden, Ragen served for four years as Illinois' director of public safety and taught at Southern Illinois University. He also served as a consultant to prisons throughout the country and authored a book on Joliet, *Inside the World's Toughest Prison* (1962).

Wilbert Rideau (1943–)

Wilbert Rideau (pronounced REE-doh), who has become an author, editor, and filmmaker, is the most famous prisoner in America and the focus of a nationwide campaign for commutation of his life sentence. For the past thirty-eight years he has been held on a life sentence at the Louisiana State Penitentiary at Angola.

In 1961, Rideau committed bank robbery and murder. He was tried three times. The first conviction was reversed because of excessive pretrial publicity and the second because of improper jury selection, but the third resulted in a death sentence. Rideau spent over a decade on death row, but in 1972, when the U.S. Supreme Court temporarily invalidated the death penalty, his sentence was changed to one of natural life. He has confessed to his crime and takes full responsibility for it while also pointing out that nearly every other Louisiana prisoner in similar circumstances has had a commutation of sentence.

Rideau feels—as do many of his supporters—that he may be a victim of his own success. If he had a lower profile, the governor could quietly pardon him, but given his fame, a pardon could make the governor look soft on crime. The state's pardon board has repeatedly recommended release, but the governors who must make the final decision on clemency have repeatedly refused to follow the board's recommendation.

Rideau's case seems to contradict the belief that prison cannot rehabilitate. Pulling himself up by his own bootstraps, in 1975 Rideau became editor in chief of *The Angolite,* the institution's journal. Excerpts from *The Angolite* were published in 1992 as *Life Sentences: Rage and Survival Behind Bars,* a book that subsequently became required reading in many criminal justice courses. Since then Rideau has worked in broadcasting and filmmaking. His most recent movie, *The Farm,* about life at Angola, shared the Grand Prize Award at the Sundance Film Festival and was a 1999 Oscar nominee for best documentary.

Robert Stroud ("The Birdman of Alcatraz") (1890–1963)

Stroud, an ornithologist who was portrayed by Burt Lancaster in the famous 1962 film *Birdman of Alcatraz,* became a federal prisoner in 1909 at the age of nineteen and remained behind bars for the rest of his life. Convicted of a murder committed in Alaska, he was sentenced to the McNeil Island Federal Penitentiary in Washington, but after stabbing an inmate he was transferred to Leavenworth Penitentiary in Kansas. There he continued to behave violently. Stroud stabbed and killed a guard in 1916, and after three trials, his final conviction of first-degree murder was upheld by the U.S. Supreme Court. In 1920 President Woodrow Wilson commuted his death sentence to life imprisonment. To prevent further violence, Stroud was classified at the highest custody level and in 1942 transferred to the U.S. Penitentiary at Alcatraz, off the coast of San Francisco.

It was while serving more than thirty years in solitary confinement at Leavenworth that Stroud raised and studied canaries, research that led to his being nicknamed the "Birdman of Alcatraz." Stroud's research on birds was published in two books: *Stroud's Digest on the Diseases of Birds* (1943, 1964) and *Diseases of Canaries* (1933). At Alcatraz, where he was no longer allowed to work with birds, Stroud spent his time writing about the history of the prison system. In 1959 he was transferred to the Medical Center for Federal prisoners in Springfield, Missouri, where he died in 1963.

Miriam Van Waters (1887–1974)

Van Waters was superintendent of the Massachusetts State Reformatory for Women from 1932 through 1957. Born in Greensburg, Pennsylvania, she grew up in Oregon and after obtaining a Ph.D. in psychology returned to Oregon to supervise a Portland youth detention home. From there Van Waters moved to Los Angeles, where she briefly served as superintendent of the Los Angeles County Juvenile Hall and later as a judge in the California juvenile court system.

While working in California's juvenile justice system, Van Waters befriended Edna Mahan, later superintendent of the New Jersey Reformatory for Women; the two remained allies in prison reform for decades. In 1925, Van Waters published her first book, *Youth in Conflict*, which deals with the treatment of juvenile delinquents. Taking Mahan with her, Van Waters moved to Boston in 1929 to work on a juvenile delinquency project at Harvard Law School. President Herbert Hoover appointed her to the Wickersham Commission to report on the treatment of juvenile delinquents in the federal system.

Like most criminal justice reformers of her day, Van Waters strongly supported the philosophy of rehabilitation. In her view, no woman was incapable of reformation. She put this philosophy into practice when she became superintendent of the Massachusetts State Reformatory for Women. However, her liberalism attracted critics, and in 1947, after an inmate committed suicide and stories began circulating about inmate homosexuality, her administration was investigated. In hearings and in the press, Van Waters was accused of mismanagement, but a March 1949 decision cleared her name and enabled her to return to the prison, where she remained for another thirteen years.

Earl Warren (1891–1974)

Not long after becoming governor of California in 1942, Warren ordered an investigation of the state's prison system. This led to a reorganization of the system intended to implement inmate rehabilitation. At the heart of this reorganization lay an indeterminate sentencing law that enabled the state to hold inmates on open-ended sentences and release them only when they appeared to be rehabilitated. When Warren was later appointed to the U.S. Supreme Court, he continued to work on criminal justice reform. The liberal "Warren Court" led the 1960s legal revolution that expanded the rights of racial minorities, the poor, minors, criminal defendants, and prisoners. Although the most famous of the Warren Court's decisions dealt with arrest and police investigations, the principles it endorsed, especially its emphasis on due

process and fundamental rights, eventually affected the treatment of prisoners as well. At the request of President Lyndon
Johnson, Warren headed the investigation of the assassination of
President John F. Kennedy. The "Warren Commission" report
found that Lee Harvey Oswald acted alone.

Documents and Statistics

5

For most of U.S. prison history, penal institutions operated with little oversight. Wardens reported annually on their operations to boards of overseers, legislatures, and prison commissions, but usually these groups accepted the wardens' reports without asking tough questions. Prominent and effective wardens—Elam Lynds in the early penitentiaries of New York State, Zebulon Brockway at New York's Elmira Reformatory in the late nineteenth century, Joseph Ragen at Illinois' Stateville prison in the early twentieth century, George Beto in Texas in the mid–twentieth century—ruled with almost unchecked authority, using force as they saw fit to maintain institutional order.

Standards for acceptable physical force have changed, however; today we are less tolerant of violence—in the home as well as in prisons—than in the past. Moreover, prison history and social science experiments have demonstrated that the key to a humane prison system is monitoring and inspection by outsiders who are free to criticize the administration. Without oversight, prison authorities can become authoritarian, oppressive, and even cruel, valuing smoothness in operations above respect for inmates as human beings. As demonstrated by Philip Zimbardo's famous experiment with a mock prison managed by college students, exercising total control over others seems to bring out the worst in people.[1]

Today various groups exercise formal and informal control over prison operations, monitoring institutions to ensure that officials do not exceed their authority, charting new paths for reform, or simply publishing data on prisons' operations. Perhaps the most important source of oversight is the federal court system, which decides how the U.S. Constitution should be applied in prison settings. Prison reformers constitute another significant source of oversight; over time, critics unaffiliated with government have turned prison management in new directions and introduced major changes in sentencing laws. A third source is the agencies and organizations that produce data on prisons, enabling the press and ordinary citizens to discover how many prisons there are in this country, how many inmates they hold, how states differ in their incarceration rates, how many institutions are run for profit by private companies, and so on. Without such information, true oversight is difficult.

This chapter presents two types of data: documents basic to understanding prison oversight and information on the operation of prisons today. The documents excerpted here include the U.S. Constitution, prisoners' rights cases, and the 1870 Declaration of Principles produced by the National Congress on Penitentiary and Reformatory Discipline. Although these are just a few of the many documents that have regulated the operation of prisons over time, they are arguably the most consequential documents of this type. The information on prison operations includes current data on sentencing, prison system growth and costs, prisoner characteristics, and private prisons. The tables and graphs illustrate the type and quality of data available on prisons and prisoners in this country.

U.S. Constitution

Until the 1960s, the Constitution did not apply within prison walls. Adhering to a hands-off doctrine, courts refused to intervene in the internal operations of prisons and dismissed prisoners' lawsuits regarding the conditions of confinement. In the 1960s, however, a prisoners' rights movement emerged out of the civil rights movement. Today, courts recognize that prisoners have constitutional rights based on the First, Fourth, Eighth, and Fourteenth Amendments.

First Amendment (1791)

Congress shall make no law respecting an establishment of religion, or prohibiting the free exercise thereof;
or abridging the freedom of speech, or the press; or the
right of the people peaceably to assemble, and to peti-
tion the government for a redress of grievances.

According to court decisions, the First Amendment gives
prisoners freedom of speech, access to reading materials, and
freedom in religious practices. These rights are available as long
as their provision does not jeopardize security at the prison.

Fourth Amendment (1791)

The right of the people to be secure in their persons,
houses, papers, and effects, against unreasonable
searches and seizures, shall not be violated, and no
Warrants shall issue, but upon probable cause, supported by Oath or affirmation, and particularly describing the place to be searched, and the persons or
things to be seized.

The Fourth Amendment, designed to protect people from
unreasonable searches and seizure of personal property by government officials, applies to prisoners in limited ways. Courts
have given prison officials authority to conduct cell and body-
cavity searches and to seize property for security purposes. On
the other hand, courts have restricted the seizure of prisoners'
legal and religious materials.

Eighth Amendment (1791)

Excessive bail shall not be required, nor excessive
fines imposed, nor cruel and unusual punishments
inflicted.

Today, the Eighth Amendment's prohibition against cruel
and unusual punishment is interpreted to include excessive punishment, unnecessary use of force or coercion, sexual abuse,

inhumane living conditions, and inadequate food and health services. Although prisons may send inmates to solitary confinement without violating the Constitution, they must provide materials for basic hygiene, and the length of time in solitary confinement must be proportionate to the offense. The Eighth Amendment also helps to prevent medical experimentation on prisoners, involuntary treatment with drugs or chemicals, and particularly painful methods of execution.

Fourteenth Amendment (1868)

> Section 1. All persons born or naturalized in the United States and subject to the jurisdiction thereof, are citizens of the United States and of the State wherein they reside. No State shall make or enforce any law which shall abridge the privileges or immunities of citizens of the United States; nor shall any state deprive any person of life, liberty, or property, without due process of law; nor deny to any person within its jurisdiction the equal protection of the laws.

The Fourteenth Amendment protects prisoners against discrimination on the basis of sex, age, race, religion, and other individual characteristics. According to current case law, the Fourteenth Amendment also entitles prisoners to some due process when they are charged with violations that could lead to a loss of statutory good time, solitary confinement, or (in some cases) punitive transfer to another prison. When prisoners face such consequences, officials must give them notice of upcoming disciplinary proceedings and some opportunity to defend themselves during a hearing. However, the hearing committee may consist of correctional officers, and prisoners do not have the full range of due process rights available to defendants in a court of law.

Prisoners' Rights Cases

This section excerpts seven important court cases pertaining to the constitutional rights of prisoners, some decided by the U.S. Supreme Court, others by lower federal courts.[2] These cases were selected to illustrate how in recent decades courts have applied the First, Fourth, Eighth, and Fourteenth Amendments of the

U.S. Constitution to prisoners' issues. Although it is impossible to cover the entire spectrum of prisoners' rights cases in this section, we have chosen the excerpts to indicate some of the most significant rights that inmates have been granted since the advent of the prisoners' rights movement in the 1960s.

Johnson v. Avery (1969)[3]

David Johnson, an inmate serving a life sentence at the Tennessee State Penitentiary, was disciplined for violating a regulation that prohibited prisoners from serving as "jailhouse lawyers" or assistants to other prisoners preparing legal materials. The regulation stated: "No prisoner will advise, assist or otherwise contract to aid another, either with or without a fee, to prepare Writs or other legal matters. . . . Inmates are forbidden to set themselves up as practitioners for the purpose of promoting a business of writing Writs."[4] Johnson complained of being disciplined, arguing that he should be able to help other prisoners prepare petitions to the courts. In *Johnson v. Avery*, the U.S. Supreme Court decided as follows:

> This Court has constantly emphasized the fundamental importance of the writ of habeas corpus in our constitutional scheme. . . . Since the basic purpose of the writ is to enable those unlawfully incarcerated to obtain their freedom, it is fundamental that access of prisoners to the courts for the purpose of presenting their complaints may not be denied or obstructed. . . . Tennessee does not provide an available alternative to the assistance provided by other inmates. . . . [There is no] regular system of assistance by public defenders. . . . [U]nless and until the State provides some reasonable alternative to assist inmates in the preparation of petitions for postconviction relief, it may not validly enforce a regulation such as that here in issue, barring inmates from furnishing such assistance to other prisoners.[5]

One of the earliest decisions in the prisoners' rights movement, *Johnson v. Avery* was significant in enabling prisoners to bring other issues before the courts. Having achieved the right of assistance in preparing court petitions, prisoners could then proceed to argue in court for other rights.

Holt v. Sarver (1969)[6]

Holt and other prisoners at the Cummins Farm Unit of the Arkansas Penitentiary asked the court to examine the constitutionality of the conditions under which they were confined. The federal court responded as follows:

> The principal complaints of petitioners are that confinement in cells in the isolation unit of the Farm amounts to cruel and unusual punishment prohibited by the Eighth Amendment . . . ; that they are denied adequate medical attention . . . ; and that the Penitentiary authorities [including Robert Sarver, Commissioner of Corrections] have failed to take adequate steps to protect inmates from assaults by other inmates. . . .
>
> [T]he State owes to those whom it has deprived of their liberty . . . [a] fundamental constitutional duty to use ordinary care to protect their lives and safety. . . .
>
> The Court does find . . . that the State has failed and is failing to discharge its constitutional duty with respect to the safety of certain convicts, and that the conditions existing in the isolation cells, including overcrowding, render confinement in those cells under those conditions unconstitutional.[7]

The court went on to observe that conditions had improved under reform warden Thomas O. Murton. However, it also found that:

> Convicts still work long hours in the fields and in institutional facilities; they are paid nothing . . . for their labor. . . . They are still guarded principally by armed trusties. . . . Trusties smuggle in contraband, including liquor and knives. . . . A serious question can be raised . . . as to the constitutionality of the system at Cummins where inadequately supervised trusties, many of whom are hardened criminals, . . . are permitted to guard and exercise authority over other inmates some of whom are less evil and dangerous than the trusties themselves.[8]

Inmates were unable to sleep in their barracks, the court went on, for fear of being knifed; four convicts had recently died of knife wounds. As for the isolation cells, the court found that

> the prolonged confinement of numbers of men in
> the same cell under the conditions that have been
> described is mentally and emotionally traumatic. . . .
> It is hazardous to health. It is degrading and debas-
> ing; it offends modern sensibilities, and, in the
> Court's estimation, amounts to cruel and unusual
> punishment.[9]

The court declared the entire Arkansas prison system unconstitutional under the Eighth Amendment and the Fourteenth
Amendment's guarantee of procedural due process. In reaching
this conclusion, it used the concept of "totality of conditions."
The "totality" of all conditions covered by the suit violated the
Constitution, even though each condition taken alone might not
constitute a constitutional violation. The court directed the
prison system to improve its standards of confinement or close
the institutions. The legal dispute continued for over thirteen
years until, in 1982, Arkansas persuaded the courts that its prisons met minimum constitutional standards.

Estelle v. Gamble (1976)[10]

J. W. Gamble, a prisoner, filed a suit against Wayne J. Estelle, the
director of the Texas Department of Corrections, complaining
that the quality of medical treatment he received after an injury
subjected him to cruel and unusual punishment. Quoting from
earlier cases, the Supreme Court affirmed that the Eighth
Amendment

> proscribes more than physically barbarous punish-
> ments. The Amendment embodies "broad and idealis-
> tic concepts of dignity, civilized standards, humanity,
> and decency . . ." against which we must evaluate
> penal measures. . . . These elementary principles es-
> tablish the government's obligation to provide med-
> ical care for those whom it is punishing by
> incarceration. An inmate must rely on prison authori-
> ties to treat his medical needs; if the authorities fail to
> do so, those needs will not be met.[11]

Although the Court found that Gamble had in fact received adequate medical treatment, it outlined a standard against which
prison medical care must be measured:

> We therefore conclude that deliberate indifference to serious medical needs of prisoners constitutes the "unnecessary and wanton infliction of pain" proscribed by the Eighth Amendment. This is true whether the indifference is manifested by prison doctors in their response to the prisoner's needs or by prison guards in intentionally denying or delaying access to medical care or intentionally interfering with the treatment once prescribed.[12]

This "no deliberate indifference" standard remains in force today for determining the constitutional adequacy of prison health care.

Bell v. Wolfish (1979)[13]

In this class action suit, pretrial detainees at a federal jail challenged the constitutionality of the conditions under which they were confined, including double-bunking, body-cavity searches, and restrictions on the packages and books they could receive. Part of the prisoners' argument rested on the fact that they had not yet been convicted of the crimes with which they were charged. The court rejected the claim that their First, Fourth, and Eighth Amendment rights had been violated, explaining that the key question was whether the conditions of confinement "amount to punishment of the detainee."[14]

> Not every disability imposed during pretrial detention amounts to "punishment" in the constitutional sense. . . . [I]n addition to ensuring the detainees' presence at trial, the effective management of the detention facility once the individual is confined is a valid objective that may justify imposition of conditions and restrictions of pretrial detention and dispel any inference that such restrictions are intended as punishment.[15]

In words that people interpreted as a death knell for the prisoners' rights movement, the Court also declared:

> There was a time not too long ago when the federal judiciary took a completely "hands-off" approach to the problem of prison administration. In recent years,

however, these courts . . . have waded into this complex arena. . . . [M]any of these same courts have, in the name of the Constitution, become increasingly enmeshed in the minutiae of prison operations. . . . [Henceforth] the inquiry of federal courts into prison management must be limited to the issue of whether a particular system violates any prohibition of the Constitution.

Bell v. Wolfish did not mark the end of prisoners' rights litigation, and the extent to which it applies to other types of institutions is unclear. However, the decision did establish that the security and safety needs of a prison can validly serve to restrict inmates' constitutional rights, so long as they are not designed to punish.

Ruiz v. Estelle (1980)[16]

Prisoner David Ruiz and other inmates filed a federal class action suit against Wayne J. Estelle, director of the Texas Department of Corrections, and other department officials. This case became one of the longest proceedings in the history of American corrections, starting in 1972, when Ruiz originally filed suit, running through the trial decision excerpted here, and continuing into appeals. The trial itself involved nine months of testimony from 349 witnesses and over 1,600 evidentiary exhibits. Judge William Wayne Justice of the U.S. District Court for the Southern District of Texas blamed the lengthiness of the litigation on the fact that "prison officials . . . vigorously contested the allegations of the inmate class on every issue."[17] He found that:

Crowded two or three to a cell or in closely packed dormitories, inmates sleep with the knowledge that they may be molested or assaulted by their fellows at any time. Their incremental exposure to disease and infection from other prisoners in such narrow confinement cannot be avoided. They must urinate and defecate, unscreened, in the presence of others. Inmates in cells must live and sleep inches away from toilets; many in dormitories face the same situation. There is little respite from these conditions, for the salient fact of existence in Texas prisons is that prisoners have wholly inadequate opportunities to escape the overcrowding in their living quarters.[18]

Judge Justice's detailed opinion, covering overcrowding, security and supervision, health care, discipline, access to the courts, and other general conditions of confinement, is grisly in its details, including evidence of violent physical retaliation by Texas Department of Corrections officials against the prisoners who brought the suit and a whisper campaign to discredit Judge Justice. The judge concluded:

> [I]t is impossible for a written opinion to convey the pernicious conditions and the pain and degradation which ordinary inmates suffer within [Texas Department of Corrections] prison walls—the gruesome experiences of youthful first offenders forcibly raped; the cruel and justifiable fears of inmates, wondering when they will be called upon to defend [sic] the next violent assault; the sheer misery, the discomfort, the wholesale loss of privacy for prisoners housed with one, two, or three others in a forty-five [square] foot cell or suffocatingly packed together in a crowded dormitory; the physical suffering and wretched psychological stress which must be endured by those sick and injured who cannot obtain adequate medical care; the sense of abject helplessness felt by inmates arbitrarily sent to solitary confinement or administrative segregation without proper opportunity to defend themselves or to argue their causes; the bitter frustration of inmates prevented from petitioning the courts and other governmental authorities for relief from perceived injustices.

The judge found that in their totality, these conditions "contravene the constitution."[19] "Plaintiffs' most fundamental constitutional rights have been violated in numerous ways."[20] Because Texas Department of Corrections officials had so often broken state laws and ignored Judge Justice's own injunctions to stop "harassing, abusing, or discriminating against inmate writ writers,"[21] the judge also appointed a supervisor to monitor their compliance with his decision.

Hudson v. McMillian (1992)[22]

"This case," Justice Sandra Day O'Connor writes at the start of the opinion, "requires us to decide whether the use of excessive physical force against a prisoner may constitute cruel and unusual punishment when the inmate does not suffer serious injury."[23] Keith Hudson, an inmate at the Louisiana State Penitentiary at Angola, sued three correctional officers (one named McMillian) who, while Hudson was handcuffed and shackled, punched him in the mouth, eyes, chest, and stomach. During the incident a second officer held him and punched and kicked him from behind. The third officer, a supervisor, watched while advising the other two "not to have too much fun." Hudson suffered bruises, swelling, loosened teeth, and a cracked dental plate. He argued that the beating violated the Eighth Amendment protection from cruel and unusual punishment. The Supreme Court agreed:

> [W]e hold that whenever prison officials stand accused of using excessive physical force in violation of the Cruel and Unusual Punishments Clause, the core judicial inquiry is . . . whether force was applied in a good-faith effort to maintain or restore discipline, or maliciously and sadistically to cause harm. . . . When prison officials maliciously and sadistically use force to cause harm, contemporary standards of decency always are violated. This is true whether or not significant injury is evident. Otherwise the Eighth Amendment would permit any physical punishment, no matter how diabolic or inhuman, inflicting less than some arbitrary quantity of injury.[24]

Hudson v. McMillian set a national standard for determining when prison physical punishments violate the Eighth Amendment.

Jordan v. Gardner (1993)[25]

Prisoners at the Corrections Center for Women in Gig Harbor, Washington, claimed that their constitutional rights were violated when they were forced to submit to random, nonemergency, clothed body pat-searches by male prison guards. The policy was instituted in 1989 as a result of two factors. First, the previous policy of conducting nonrandom pat-searches using only female guards placed a burden on the institution's female guards, who occasionally had to interrupt their lunch breaks when such searches were required. Second, the new superintendent, Eldon Vail, believed he could better control contraband with a policy of random searches. The text of the Ninth Circuit Court decision explains as follows:

> Before mid-1989, routine, suspicionless searches of inmates were performed only at fixed checkpoints by female guards. Male guards were permitted to search inmates only in emergency situations. Vail decided to change the policy . . . [d]espite warnings from psychologists on his staff that the cross-gender clothed body searches could cause severe emotional distress in some inmates. . . . According to the prison training material, a . . . guard must "[p]ush inward and upward when searching the crotch and upper thighs of the inmates." All seams in the leg and the crotch area are to be "squeez[ed] and knead[ed]." Using the back of the hand, the guard also is to search the breast area in a sweeping motion, so that the breasts will be "flattened." At a minimum, each response and movement [sic] officer was expected to perform ten random searches per shift during the two daytime shifts.
>
> Several inmates were searched by male guards on the first (and only) day of implementation. One, who had a long history of sexual abuse by men, . . . suffered severe distress: she had to have her fingers pried loose from bars she had grabbed during the search, and she vomited after returning to her cell block.[26]

Without deciding the inmates' claim that the search policy violated their Fourth Amendment right to be free of unreasonable searches, the court decided the case only on Eighth Amendment grounds:

> We conclude that the Eighth Amendment prohibition against the unnecessary and wanton infliction of pain forbids these searches under the circumstances of this case.[27]

In reaching this decision, the court noted that women with a history of sexual or physical abuse may react differently than men to cross-gender pat-searches. It also noted that the prison's "security is not dependent upon cross-gender clothed body searches" and that "Superintendent Vail urges, in effect, that it is proper to inflict serious psychological pain on the inmates because otherwise it may be necessary to interrupt the lunch periods of female guards."[28] This case recognizes significant differences between male and female inmates in both their personal histories and treatment needs.

The Declaration of Principles (1870)

The most effective prison reform movement in U.S. history was launched in 1870 in Cincinnati, Ohio, by the National Congress on Penitentiary and Reformatory Discipline. Delegates to the conference produced a Declaration of Principles that guided U.S. penology for the next 100 years. The conference illustrates how powerfully a private reform organization can influence prison management.

Principle II of the Declaration emphasizes rehabilitation rather than the more traditional goals of punishment, deterrence, and incapacitation:

> II. The treatment of criminals by society is for the protection of society. But since such treatment is directed to the criminal rather than to the crime, its great object should be his moral regeneration. Hence the supreme aim of prison discipline is the reformation of criminals, not the infliction of vindictive suffering.

In Principles IV and XV, the Declaration proposes specific methods to achieve the goal of rehabilitation:

> IV. Since hope is a more potent agent than fear, it should be made an ever-present force in the minds of prisoners, by a well-devised and skillfully applied system of rewards for good conduct, industry and attention to learning. Rewards, more than punishments, are essential to every good prison system.
>
> XV. In prison administration, moral forces should be relied upon, with as little admixture of physical force as possible, and organized persuasion be made to take the place of coercive restraint, the object being to make upright and industrious freemen, rather than orderly and obedient prisoners. Brute force may make good prisoners; moral training alone will make good citizens.

The rehabilitative goal requires indeterminate sentences, according to Principle VIII.

> VIII. Peremptory [definite or determinate] sentences ought to be replaced by those of indeterminate length. Sentences limited only by satisfactory proof of reformation should be substituted for those measured by mere lapse of time.

Rehabilitation programs must emphasize religion, education, and labor:

> IX. Of all reformatory agencies, religion is first in importance, because it's most potent in its action upon the human heart and life.
>
> X. Education is a vital force in the reformation of fallen men and women. . . .
>
> XVI. . . . Steady, active, honorable labor is the basis of all reformatory discipline. It not only aids reformation, but is essential to it. . . .

In the delegates' view, classification of prisoners and prisons is also crucial if the goal of rehabilitation is to be achieved:

> XIX. Prisons, as well as prisoners, should be classified or graded so that there shall be prisons for the untried, for the incorrigible and for the degrees of depraved characters, as well as separate establishments for women, and for criminals of the younger class.

Although today many Americans have rejected the goal of rehabilitation, specific reforms endorsed by the Declaration of Principles remain in effect, and private prison-reform organizations continue to have strong input into American prison policy.

Prison Data

This section illustrates the kinds of information available on incarceration and provides specific data on sentencing, the growth and costs of the prison population over time, prisoner characteristics, prisoner health and mortality, and private prisons.

Sentencing

Utah's Criminal History Assessment form (see Figure 5.1, p. 108) illustrates the results of sentencing reforms over the past twenty-five years. Before the 1970s, in Utah and elsewhere, each offense had its own penalty; today, Utah and other jurisdictions classify offenses into crime categories, in this case ranging from Category A (first-degree murder) through Category I (minor offenses, third degree). (The specific offenses in each category other than Category A are listed elsewhere.)

The differing grades of shading on the form indicate the type of punishment that should typically be given to people convicted of crimes in the various categories. The actual length of sentence, however, also depends on the offender's *criminal history score* (left side of the grid), which is calculated by adding up numbers from the top of the page. Someone with one prior felony conviction, for example, would get 2 points on the criminal history score; if the same person had two to four prior misdemeanor convictions, another 2 points would be added to the score; if the same offender had more than four prior juvenile adjudications, 3 more points would be added; and so on.

At the end, a *total placement score* is calculated, and that total is used to determine which criminal history row of the grid the judge should look at when sentencing the particular offender. Moreover, as indicated under the grid, sentences can be "enhanced" for other factors. Thus this sentencing guidelines grid, like the presumptive sentencing grids used in other jurisdictions, controls judicial discretion while also enabling judges to make some adjustments to a sentence according to the individual's criminal history.

Figure 5.2 (p. 109) shows the type of sentences being served by all adults under correctional supervision in 1997. The most common form of punishment for crimes in 1997 was probation, with over 57 percent of all adults under correctional supervision serving probationary sentences. Prison, the next most common form of criminal punishment, was being used with almost 21 percent of the total population of adults under correctional supervision. Parole was less common than prison, with 12 percent of adults under correctional supervision, and jail was least common of all, with a little less than 10 percent of adults under correctional supervision being in jail on the census date.

Table 5.1 (p. 106) lists average sentence lengths by offense type for state and federal prisoners in 1994. People convicted of murder and manslaughter received the longest prison sentences, with an average of 267 months, which is more than 22 years. Rape convictions resulted in the next longest prison sentences, with an average of 157 months or 13 years, and nonviolent offenses in the "other" offenses category received the shortest prison sentences (41 months or about three and a half years). Other data (not shown here but available from the federal government) indicate that most offenders do not serve the entire length of their imposed sentences but rather are released early on parole, through earning good-time credits, or both.

Prison System Expansion

The next two figures illustrate the growth of the prison population over time and incarceration costs. Figure 5.3 (p. 110) charts the number of state and federal prisoners from 1925 to mid-year 1998. In 1925 there were about 100,000 inmates in state and federal prisons. The numbers dipped slightly during World War II (1939–1945) and then again during the war in Vietnam (late 1960s), when the prison-prone population entered the armed forces. Starting in 1970, the U.S. prison population soared, crossing the 1 million mark in 1994 and standing at about 1.2 million by mid-year 1998.

Figure 5.4 (p. 111) charts expenditures of state and federal prisons from 1980 through 1993. In 1980, state and federal prisons spent over $4 billion. By 1993 the total had risen to almost $24 billion, a sixfold increase in less than fifteen years. As Figure 5.4 also shows, most of these expenditures were made by state governments.

Prisoner Characteristics

Figure 5.5 (p. 112) shows the numbers of female state and federal prisoners from 1925 to 1997. In 1925 there were fewer than 5,000 female prisoners nationwide (the actual figure was 3,438). As the overall prison population began its steep increase about 1970, so did the female prisoner population. By the end of 1997, it was nearing 80,000 nationwide.

Figure 5.6 (p. 113) shows the numbers of male state and federal prisoners from 1925 to 1997. In 1925 there were fewer than 100,000 male prisoners nationwide (the actual figure was 88,231). Following the overall steep increase that began about 1970 (and, indeed, accounting for most of it), by the end of 1997 the male prisoner population was nearing 1.2 million (with an actual figure of 1,197,590). Thus the increases follow the same patterns in both female and male prisoner populations, although the male population is far larger in terms of raw numbers.

Figure 5.7 (p. 114) illustrates the racial distribution of state and federal prisoners in 1995. Blacks comprised nearly one-half of the total prisoner population in 1995; whites comprised the next largest category; and other racial groups comprised much smaller percentages. As we know from other sources, blacks comprise only about 15 percent of the total U.S. population; whites comprise about 72 percent of the total, yet only about 40 percent of the prison population is white. Scholars have tried to explain these troubling racial imbalances, but the imbalances remain the source of a great deal of concern and debate.

Figure 5.8 (p. 115) shows the proportion of state and federal prisoners who in 1995 were of Hispanic origin (any race). Hispanics constituted nearly 18 percent of the total state and federal prisoner population in 1995. Yet, as we know from other sources, people of Hispanic origin constituted only about 10 percent of the U.S. population in 1995. Thus here, too, there is an imbalance, with Hispanics being overrepresented in prison populations, though not to the extent of blacks.

Prisoner Health and Mortality

Figure 5.9 (p. 116) provides information on the numbers of prisoners who, in 1996, tested positive for HIV or were diagnosed with AIDS. HIV-positive cases greatly outnumber confirmed AIDS cases in both state and federal prisons. In 1996, state prisons had 5,521 confirmed AIDS cases, and federal prisons had 353. Despite their relatively small numbers, however, the confirmed AIDS cases constitute a large expense, because of the high costs of treatment.

Figure 5.10 (p. 117) summarizes the numbers and causes of deaths in state and federal prisons in 1995. More than 3,000 people died in state and federal penal institutions during 1995. The major cause of death was "natural" causes, including non-AIDS illnesses. Next in significance was AIDS, with a death toll of almost 1,000. Fifty-six prisoners were executed nationwide in 1995. Because of variations in states' methods of reporting, it was impossible to specify the causes of death in 426 cases.

Private Prisons

Table 5.2 (p. 107) provides data on the numbers and capacities of private adult prison facilities in use in 1998. There were 159 private institutions for adult prisoners in 1998, with a total capacity exceeding 116,000 inmates. Texas led the other states both in the raw number of institutions (43) and in their capacity (29,577). California came in second, with 24 private prisons with a total capacity in excess of 11,000 inmates. Eighteen states have not enacted legislation permitting private, for-profit companies to operate prisons.

TABLE 5.1

Average Sentence Length by Offense Type, U.S. State and Federal Prisoners, 1994

Offense Type	Average Prison Sentence Imposed (in months)
Murder/manslaughter	267
Rape	157
Robbery	115
Aggravated assault	79
Other violent offenses[a]	70
Burglary	69
Larceny	45
Motor vehicle theft	50
Other theft	44
Fraud	50
Forgery	50
Drug possession	50
Drug trafficking	70
Weapons offenses	54
Other offenses[b]	41

[a]Includes negligent manslaughter, sexual assault, and kidnapping.
[b]Includes nonviolent offenses such as receiving stolen property and immigration offenses.
Source: Sourcebook of Criminal Justice Statistics, 1997, p. 430.

TABLE 5.2
Private Adult Prison Facilities: Number and Capacity, 1998

State[a]	Number of Facilities	1998 Year-end Capacities
Arizona	6	6,860
Arkansas	2	1,200
California	24	11,294
Colorado	9	4,644
District of Columbia	1	866
Florida	10	6,255
Georgia	5	6,418
Idaho	1	1,250
Illinois	1	220
Indiana	1	670
Kansas	2	529
Kentucky	4	2,631
Louisiana	2	2,948
Michigan	1	480
Minnesota	1	1,338
Mississippi	6	4,630
Missouri	2	660
Montana	1	512
Nevada	1	500
New Jersey	1	300
New Mexico	7	4,696
New York	1	200
North Carolina	2	2,112
Ohio	2	2,256
Oklahoma	8	9,702
Pennsylvania	1	1,200
Puerto Rico	4	3,000
Rhode Island	1	302
Tennessee	6	7,326
Texas	43	29,577
Utah	1	400
Virginia	1	1,500
Washington	1	150
Totals	159	116, 626

[a]Eighteen states have not passed legislation to permit the operation of private prisons in their jurisdictions.
Source: Private Corrections Project, University of Florida, Gainesville, Florida, 1999.

108

Figure 5.1 Utah Criminal History Assessment Form

FORM 1
CRIMINAL HISTORY ASSESSMENT

These are guidelines only. They do not create any right or expectation on behalf of the offender.

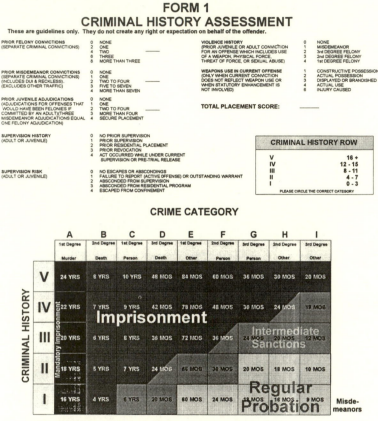

PRIOR FELONY CONVICTIONS
(SEPARATE CRIMINAL CONVICTIONS)
- 0 NONE
- 2 ONE
- 4 TWO
- 6 THREE
- 8 MORE THAN THREE

PRIOR MISDEMEANOR CONVICTIONS
(SEPARATE CRIMINAL CONVICTIONS)
(INCLUDES DUI & RECKLESS)
(EXCLUDES OTHER TRAFFIC)
- 0 NONE
- 1 ONE
- 2 TWO TO FOUR
- 3 FIVE TO SEVEN
- 4 MORE THAN SEVEN

PRIOR JUVENILE ADJUDICATIONS
(ADJUDICATIONS FOR OFFENSES THAT
WOULD HAVE BEEN FELONIES IF
COMMITTED BY AN ADULT)(THREE
MISDEMEANOR ADJUDICATION EQUAL
ONE FELONY ADJUDICATION)
- 0 NONE
- 1 ONE
- 2 TWO TO FOUR
- 3 MORE THAN FOUR
- 4 SECURE PLACEMENT

SUPERVISION HISTORY
(ADULT OR JUVENILE)
- 0 NO PRIOR SUPERVISION
- 1 PRIOR SUPERVISION
- 2 PRIOR RESIDENTIAL PLACEMENT
- 3 PRIOR REVOCATION
- 4 ACT OCCURRED WHILE UNDER CURRENT SUPERVISION OR PRE-TRIAL RELEASE

SUPERVISION RISK
(ADULT OR JUVENILE)
- 0 NO ESCAPES OR ABSCONDINGS
- 1 FAILURE TO REPORT (ACTIVE OFFENSE) OR OUTSTANDING WARRANT
- 2 ABSCONDED FROM SUPERVISION
- 3 ABSCONDED FROM RESIDENTIAL PROGRAM
- 4 ESCAPED FROM CONFINEMENT

VIOLENCE HISTORY
(PRIOR JUVENILE OR ADULT CONVICTION
FOR AN OFFENSE WHICH INCLUDES USE
OF A WEAPON, PHYSICAL FORCE,
THREAT OF FORCE, OR SEXUAL ABUSE)
- 0 NONE
- 1 MISDEMEANOR
- 2 3rd DEGREE FELONY
- 3 2nd DEGREE FELONY
- 4 1st DEGREE FELONY

WEAPONS USE IN CURRENT OFFENSE
(ONLY WHEN CURRENT CONVICTION
DOES NOT REFLECT WEAPON USE OR
WHEN STATUTORY ENHANCEMENT IS
NOT INVOLVED)
- 1 CONSTRUCTIVE POSSESSION
- 2 ACTUAL POSSESSION
- 3 DISPLAYED OR BRANDISHED
- 4 ACTUAL USE
- 6 INJURY CAUSED

TOTAL PLACEMENT SCORE: _____

CRIMINAL HISTORY ROW	
V	16 +
IV	12 - 15
III	8 - 11
II	4 - 7
I	0 - 3
PLEASE CIRCLE THE CORRECT CATEGORY	

CRIME CATEGORY

CRIMINAL HISTORY	A 1st Degree Murder	B 2nd Degree Death	C 1st Degree Person	D 3rd Degree Death	E 1st Degree Other	F 2nd Degree Person	G 3rd Degree Person	H 2nd Degree Other	I 3rd Degree Other
V	24 YRS	6 YRS	10 YRS	48 MOS	84 MOS	60 MOS	36 MOS	30 MOS	20 MOS
IV	22 YRS	7 YRS	9 YRS	42 MOS	78 MOS	48 MOS	30 MOS	24 MOS	18 MOS
III	20 YRS	6 YRS	8 YRS	36 MOS	72 MOS	36 MOS	24 MOS	20 MOS	12 MOS
II	18 YRS	5 YRS	7 YRS	24 MOS	66 MOS	30 MOS	20 MOS	18 MOS	10 MOS
I	16 YRS	4 YRS	6 YRS	20 MOS	60 MOS	24 MOS	18 MOS	16 MOS	9 MOS

Mandatory Imprisonment

Imprisonment / Intermediate Sanctions / Regular Probation

Misde-meanors

CONSECUTIVE ENHANCEMENTS: 40% of the shorter sentence is to be added to the full length of the longer sentence.

CONCURRENT ENHANCEMENTS: 10% of the shorter sentence is to be added to the full length of the longer sentence.

Matrix timeframes refer to imprisonment only. Refer to the categorization of offenses.
Capital offenses are not considered within the context of the sentencing guidelines.

	ACTIVE CONVICTIONS	CRIME CATEGORY	TIME
MOST SERIOUS			
NEXT MOST SERIOUS			
OTHER			
OTHER			
		TOTAL	_____

OFFENDER NAME: _____   DATE SCORED: _____   SCORER'S NAME: _____

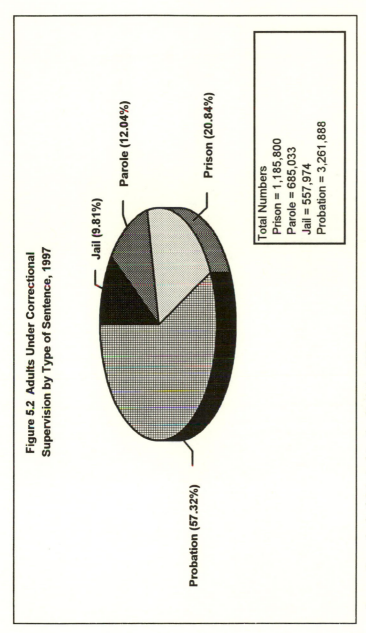

Figure 5.2 Adults Under Correctional Supervision by Type of Sentence, 1997

Jail (9.81%)

Parole (12.04%)

Prison (20.84%)

Probation (57.32%)

Total Numbers
Prison = 1,185,800
Parole = 685,033
Jail = 557,974
Probation = 3,261,888

Source: Sourcebook of Criminal Justice Statistics, 1997, p. 464.

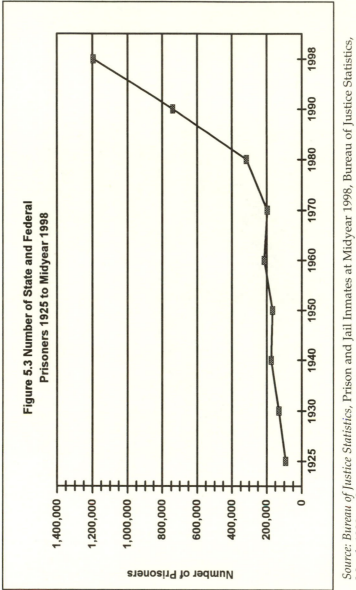

Figure 5.3 Number of State and Federal Prisoners 1925 to Midyear 1998

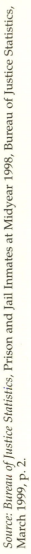

Source: Bureau of Justice Statistics, Prison and Jail Inmates at Midyear 1998, Bureau of Justice Statistics, March 1999, p. 2.

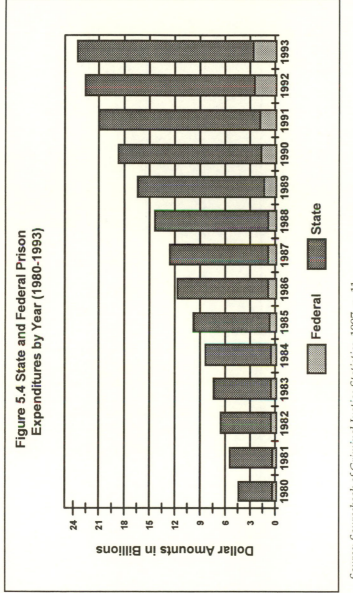

Figure 5.4 State and Federal Prison
Expenditures by Year (1980-1993)

Source: Sourcebook of Criminal Justice Statistics, 1997, p. 11.

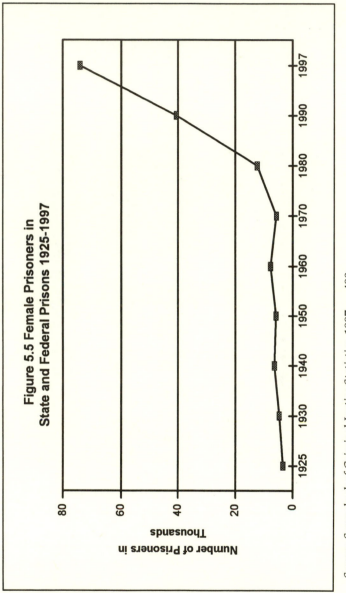

Figure 5.5 Female Prisoners in
State and Federal Prisons 1925-1997

Number of Prisoners in
Thousands

Source: Sourcebook of Criminal Justice Statistics, 1997, p. 490.

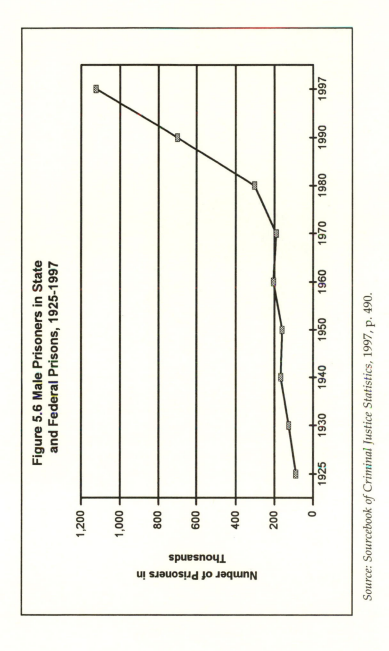

Figure 5.6 Male Prisoners in State and Federal Prisons, 1925-1997

Source: Sourcebook of Criminal Justice Statistics, 1997, p. 490.

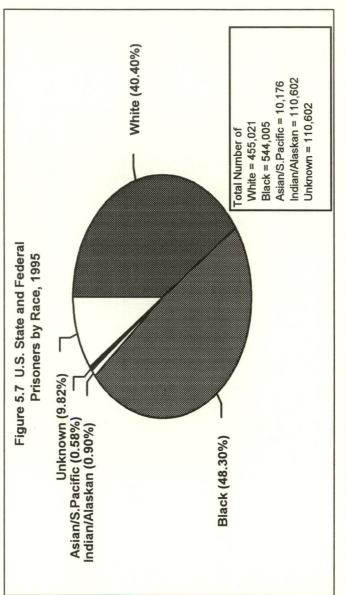

Figure 5.7 U.S. State and Federal Prisoners by Race, 1995

White (40.40%)

Black (48.30%)

Unknown (9.82%)
Asian/S.Pacific (0.58%)
Indian/Alaskan (0.90%)

Total Number of
White = 455,021
Black = 544,005
Asian/S.Pacific = 10,176
Indian/Alaskan = 110,602
Unknown = 110,602

Source: Sourcebook of Criminal Justice Statistics, 1997, p. 499.

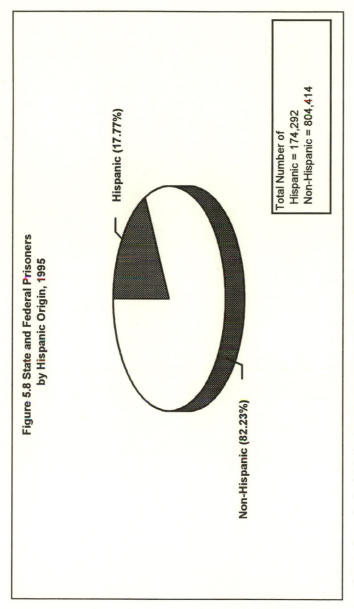

Figure 5.8 State and Federal Prisoners by Hispanic Origin, 1995

Hispanic (17.77%)

Non-Hispanic (82.23%)

Total Number of
Hispanic = 174,292
Non-Hispanic = 804,414

Source: Sourcebook of Criminal Justice Statistics, 1997, p. 499.

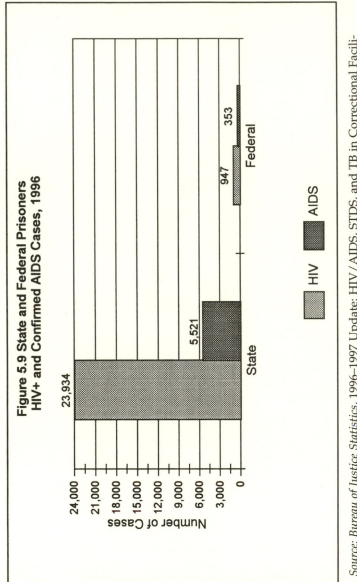

Figure 5.9 State and Federal Prisoners
HIV+ and Confirmed AIDS Cases, 1996

Source: Bureau of Justice Statistics, 1996–1997 Update: HIV / AIDS, STDS, and TB in Correctional Facilities, March 1999, pp. 7–8.

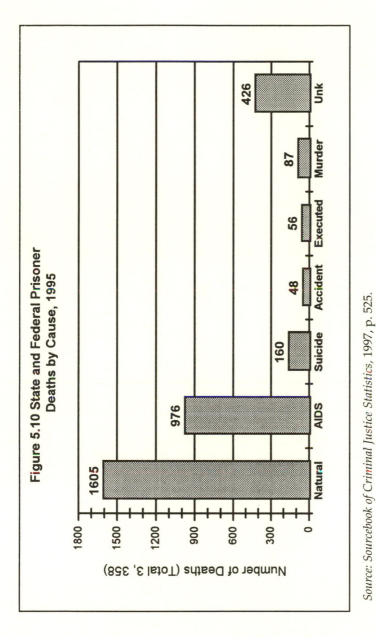

Figure 5.10 State and Federal Prisoner
Deaths by Cause, 1995

Source: Sourcebook of Criminal Justice Statistics, 1997, p. 525.

Notes

1. A video based on this experiment is cited in Chapter 8.
2. Our quotations omit the decisions' footnotes.
3. *Johnson v. Avery,* 393 U.S. 483.
4. Ibid., 484.
5. Ibid., 484–490.
6. *Holt v. Sarver,* 300 F. Supp. 825.
7. Ibid., 826–828.
8. Ibid., 829–830.
9. Ibid., 833.
10. *Estelle v. Gamble,* 419 U.S. 97.
11. Ibid., 102–103.
12. Ibid., 104–105.
13. *Bell v. Wolfish,* 441 U.S. 520.
14. Ibid., 535.
15. Ibid., 540.
16. *Ruiz v. Estelle,* 503 F. Supp. 1265.
17. Ibid., 1391.
18. Ibid., 1277.
19. Ibid., 1384.
20. Ibid., 1388.
21. Ibid., 1389.
22. *Hudson v. McMillian,* 503 U.S. 1.
23. Ibid., 4.
24. Ibid., 6–7, 9.
25. *Jordan v. Gardner,* 986 F.2d 1521.
26. Ibid, 1523.
27. Ibid, 1524.
28. Ibid, 1530.

Agencies and Organizations

Because the United States has a decentralized criminal justice system in which responsibilities are spread over city, county, state, and national jurisdictions, the nation's penal institutions are administered by a wide range of organizations. Some of these organizations are local, bearing responsibility for the management of city and county jails. These local lockups traditionally have held only misdemeanants (minor offenders) and people awaiting trial on more serious charges. State-level organizations operate penitentiaries and prisons, which are institutions for felons (offenders convicted of serious crimes for which the possible punishment is one year or more of incarceration). At the federal level are the federal prisons, run by the Federal Bureau of Prisons, in which felons convicted of federal crimes such as racketeering, tax evasion, or treason are incarcerated. In addition to these governmental organizations, the United States has a large number of private agencies concerned with such issues as the rights and welfare of prisoners, maintaining contacts between prisoners and their families, and sentencing reform.

In reality, there is often some overlap among the various types of agencies and organizations. For example, in recent decades

119

huge increases in the number of state and federal prisoners have sometimes led to the incarceration of serious felons in local jails. Or when a new, privately funded organization introduces a successful program, a government agency may begin contributing to the organization's costs. Thus the reality is a network of hundreds of collaborating, intersecting, and sometimes competing agencies.

This chapter provides information on the major federal organizations, some state-level organizations, and a cross-section of private agencies concerned with the operation of U.S. prisons. Some of these are well-established organizations that work at the national level, whereas others are less stable local organizations concerned with issues important to the immediate community. Some have existed since the nineteenth century; others are of recent vintage, and some are maintained by one or two dedicated individuals and liable to close when the personnel can no longer keep them going. More state-level information can be obtained at the Federal Bureau of Prisons' website on the Inmate Information page (www.bop.gov/inmate.html); this website lists the phone numbers of the departments of corrections in every state and the District of Columbia.

American Civil Liberties Union
125 Broad Street, 18th floor
New York, NY 10004-2400
(212) 344-3005
Internet: http://www.aclu.org

Founded in 1920, the American Civil Liberties Union (ACLU) is a private organization that provides legal counsel and support to defend constitutional rights. Its involvement in inmates' legal issues has had a major impact on prison reform in such areas as prisoners' rights, privacy, security, and safety; overcrowding and other prison conditions; and the management of prisons and jails. Supported by annual dues, contributions, and grants but not by government funds, the ACLU litigates cases involving prisoners' rights and also devotes resources to educating the public through its National Prison Project (see below). It has over 275,000 members and more than 2,000 lawyers who offer legal services at no fee in each of the 50 states.

American Correctional Association
Main Office:
4380 Forbes Boulevard
Lanham, MD 20706-4322

(800) 222-5646
E-mail: aca@corrections.com
Internet: http://www.corrections.com/aca
Publications Office:
8025 Laurel Lakes Court
Laurel, MD 20707
(301) 206-5100

Founded in 1870, the American Correctional Association (ACA) is the oldest U.S. organization for correctional practitioners. Its primary purpose is to promote professional development and influence policy and practice. With more than seventy chapters and affiliated organizations, the ACA has over 20,000 members, including policymakers, researchers, academics, and agency personnel. It publishes agency and program directories, videos, and teaching materials. It also offers national workshops and on-site technical support, and it develops correctional standards for the accreditation of penal institutions. Before 1954, the ACA was known as the National Prison Association.

American Correctional Health Services Association
Box 2307
Dayton, OH 45401-2307
(937) 586-3708
Fax: (937) 586-3699
E-mail: achsa@corrections.com
Internet: http://www.corrections.com/achsa

The American Correctional Health Services Association (ACHSA), an organization for people involved in delivering health-care services in prisons and jails, assists with programming and provides guidelines and educational programs. As an affiliate of both the American Correctional Association and the American Jail Association, it reviews standards for health care in correctional facilities. The ACHSA publishes research reports, program plans, education manuals, and bulletins on health-care issues in prisons and jails, and it sponsors an annual conference.

American Friends Service Committee
1501 Cherry Street
Philadelphia, PA 19102
(215) 241-7000
Fax: (215) 241-7275

E-mail: afscinfo@afsc.org
Internet: http://www.afsc.org

The American Friends Service Committee (AFSC) is a Quaker organization that includes people of various faiths committed to
working for social justice and peace. Its work is based on the Religious Society of Friends (Quaker) belief that each person has
worth and that the power of love can overcome violence and injustice. Founded in 1917, today the AFSC runs programs that
focus on issues related to criminal and social justice, among other
causes. The organization has offices throughout the world and in
many areas of the United States.

Association for the Treatment of Sexual Abusers
10700 SW Beaverton-Hillsdale Highway, Suite 26
Beaverton, OR 97005-3035
(503) 643-1023
Fax: (503) 643-5084
E-mail: atsa@atsa.com
Internet: http://www.atsa.com

Incorporated in 1984, the Association for the Treatment of Sexual
Abusers (ATSA) is an example of a type of organization that does
not deal directly with prisons but nonetheless intersects in its interests with a population of concern to specialists in sentencing,
corrections, and penology. A nonprofit, interdisciplinary organization, ATSA was founded to foster research, facilitate information exchange, and promote professional development for those
involved in sex offender evaluation and treatment. It is an international organization focused on the prevention of sexual abuse
through effective management of sex offenders. ATSA publishes
a journal, *Sexual Abuse: A Journal of Research and Treatment*, sponsors graduate research awards, issues public policy statements,
and organizes an annual conference.

Association of State Correctional Administrators
Spring Hill West
South Salem, NY 10590
(914) 533-2562
Internet: http://www.asca.net

The Association of State Correctional Administrators (ASCA), established in 1970, was incorporated as a New York State nonprofit organization in 1985. Its primary goal is to enhance
correctional services and practices. To achieve this goal, the

ASCA promotes the exchange of ideas and philosophies at the top administrative level of correctional planning and policymaking. Areas of focus include: (1) advancing correctional techniques, particularly in the areas of program development, design of physical and correctional management facilities, and staff training; (2) encouraging public support for corrections and the reintegration of offenders; (3) research; (4) developing and applying correctional standards; (5) fostering legislative and other measures that further the organization's objectives; and (6) exchanging information with correctional agencies and organizations in other countries. Membership is limited to those responsible for the administration of correctional institutions.

Association on Programs for Female Offenders
Mary V. Leftridge Byrd, President and Superintendent
State Correctional Institution
500 East 4th Street
Chester, PA 19013
(610) 490-5412
Fax: (610) 447-3042

The Association on Programs for Female Offenders (APFO), an affiliate of the American Correctional Association, was founded in 1974. It is an outgrowth of earlier women's committees within the ACA. Its goal is to stimulate awareness and encourage cooperation in identifying the unique needs of female offenders. APFO communicates with individuals, agencies, and organizations dedicated to the improvement of services to female offenders. It publishes a quarterly newsletter that goes out to more than 500 individuals and agencies.

Bureau of Justice Statistics
Office of Justice Programs
U.S. Department of Justice
810 7th Street, NW
Washington, DC 20531
(202) 307-0765
E-mail: askbjs@ojp.usdoj.gov
Internet: http://www.ojp.usdoj.gov/bjs

The Bureau of Justice Statistics (BJS) is responsible for researching and reporting on a wide range of criminal justice phenomena. It administers, analyzes, and disseminates information from the National Victimization Crime Survey; conducts sample surveys of individuals under the custody of criminal justice jurisdictions; collects and analyzes crime data from national, state, and local criminal justice agencies; publishes research reports, statistical bulletins, and program manuals; and conducts an annual conference on justice statistics, research, and policy analysis. The BJS distributes information on the number and type of crimes, convictions, and prisoners and on related areas; it also collects data on the characteristics of inmates under correctional supervision. It further disseminates information on federal offenders and case processing, felony convictions, and the operation of criminal justice systems at all levels of government. The BJS website provides a list of publications by topic. Many publications are available on-line, including more than two dozen major data series. The site also provides on-line access to the database of state activities and research.

California Coalition for Women Prisoners
100 McAllister Street
San Francisco, CA 94102
(415) 255-7036, ext. 4
Fax: (415) 552-3150
E-mail: ccwp@igc.org
Internet: http://www.prisonactivist.org/ccwp

The California Coalition for Women Prisoners (CCWP) was founded in 1995 in response to concerns about the human and civil rights of female prisoners in California. The membership includes community members, female prisoners, former prisoners, and prisoners' families. Initially the main focus of the CCWP was to build support for a lawsuit filed by prisoners at the Central California Women's Facility and the California Institution for Women to achieve access to better medical care. Today CCWP also works to raise public consciousness about conditions for women in prison and to press for reforms. It has advocated the release of inmates dying of AIDS and other terminal illnesses; the protection of female prisoners from sexual assault and abuse by correctional staff and by other prisoners; the improvement of health care services; and justice for battered women. CCWP community members devote time to maintaining contacts with coalition members in prison. The organizations' newsletter, *The Fire Inside*, is published five times per year.

Center on Crime, Communities, and Culture
Open Society Institute

400 West 59th Street
New York, NY 10019
(212) 548-0668 or (212) 548-0600
Fax: (212) 548-4679
Internet: http://www.soros.org/crime/index.html

The Center on Crime, Communities, and Culture funds programs that work with families and communities to reduce the harmful effects of incarceration, to train correctional officers and judges to respond better to the needs of prisoners and their families, and to help former prisoners and parolees establish healthy lives through education, parenting classes, and reconnecting with the community. The Center's website provides detailed information on its activities, publications, training and educational resources, upcoming workshops and conferences, funding and grant opportunities and guidelines, fellowship opportunities for students of criminal justice, employment opportunities, and daily news stories.

CHIPS—Children of Incarcerated Parents Program
Center for Community Alternatives
115 East Jefferson Street, Suite 300
Syracuse, NY 13202
(315) 422-5638
Fax: (315) 471-4924
E-mail: ccacny@dreamscape.com

The Center for Community Alternatives (CCA), a private, non-profit agency established in 1981, aims at providing direct services to clients in the criminal justice and human service systems, together with training and technical assistance to professionals in those fields. CCA developed and administers the CHIPS program, a support group for children of incarcerated parents, especially students prone to disciplinary problems and violence. CHIPS helps children and parents preserve family bonds and rebuild broken ties. Its goals include increasing school attendance, decreasing school suspensions, decreasing disciplinary infractions, developing educational materials for caregivers and community agencies, and increasing community awareness of the effects that incarcerating parents may have on children. CHIPS support groups meet once a week in groups of five to ten children. Support group sessions cover issues of isolation, self-esteem and shame, making positive choices, goal-setting, self-reliance, developing support systems, substance abuse, visitations in correctional institutions, family contacts, parole and release, and legal matters. CHIPS students may participate in other CCA programs and activities such as community service, job training and employment, peer education, and mentoring. CCA offers training and publishes a manual for professionals working with children of incarcerated parents. It also provides an on-line list of resources for use with young children, teens, and people who work with youth.

Chicago Legal Aid to Incarcerated Mothers
205 Randolph, Suite 830
Chicago, IL 60606
(312) 332-5537
Fax: (312) 332-2570
E-mail: info@c-l-a-i-m.org

Chicago Legal Aid to Incarcerated Mothers (CLAIM) was founded in 1985 to address the gap in legal aid and advocacy for women prisoners and their families. It has grown from a one-woman office to a staff of four (including two former prisoners), an active board, and two volunteer lawyer programs. CLAIM's goal is to provide legal services and educational programs that will help women prisoners and their families remain intact. The organization also works with government agencies to help imprisoned mothers, their children, and other family members.

Citizens United for Rehabilitation of Errants
PO Box 2310
National Capital Station
Washington, DC 20013-2310
(202) 789-2126
Internet: http://www.curenational.org/index1.html

Citizens United for Rehabilitation of Errants (CURE) is a national organization established in 1972 to support criminal justice reform. CURE began in San Antonio, Texas, when a small number of families of prisoners and other concerned individuals went to the Texas legislature in Austin to work against the death penalty. In 1975, CURE formally organized with an annual convention and a constitution, and by 1985, it had expanded to a national organization. CURE has a chapter or organizational affiliate in most states. Although the majority of the members are prisoners, former prisoners, and their families, the membership also includes public officials, clergy, attorneys, educators, and concerned citizens.

CURE aims generally at improving the productivity and civility of inmates. Specific areas of concern may include improving rehabilitative programs; strengthening family and inmate bonds; educating and mobilizing; and ensuring that prisons are used only as institutions of last resort. CURE members are active in fighting against increased use of the death penalty and racism in the application of the death penalty; renewing the Targeted Jobs Tax Credit to pay a portion of the starting salary of a newly employed ex-felon; reinstating ex-prisoners' voting rights in federal elections; improving the availability of military veteran's benefits and services to incarcerated veterans; encouraging prison-based businesses; increasing awareness of the special needs of women prisoners; and promoting enforcement of the Civil Rights of Institutionalized Persons Act. CURE publishes a newsletter and holds a biannual convention in Washington, D.C.

Correctional Association of New York
135 East 15th Street
New York, NY 10003
(212) 254-5700
Fax: (212) 473-2807

Founded in 1844 as the Prison Association of New York, the Correctional Association of New York aims primarily at ensuring a humane, fair, and efficient correctional system. It played a major role in the development of the New York State prison system and has been a driving force behind national prison reform movements for well over a century. In 1846, the association was granted the right to inspect New York state prisons and jails and recommend improvements to policymakers and the public, which gave it a unique watchdog role. In the late nineteenth century the association published the first evidence in support of indeterminate sentencing; thereafter it took the lead in developing the rehabilitation model of punishment. Today the association focuses on prison overcrowding, citizen involvement in the improvement of prisons, policy reform, and community-based prevention approaches to juvenile justice. The Prison Visiting Project, founded in 1989, is concerned with the conditions of incarceration. In 1991 the association started the Women in Prison Project, and in 1997 it inaugurated the Juvenile Justice Project. Almost since the beginning, the association has had a separate division, the Women's Prison Association of New York (see below).

Correctional Education Association
8025 Laurel Lakes Court
Laurel, MD 20707
(301) 206-5100 or (301) 918-1915
Internet: http://sunsite.unc.edu/cea

The Correctional Education Association (CEA) was established in 1946 to assist educators and administrators who provide services to students in prisons, juvenile facilities, jails, and community corrections programs. The CEA is the largest affiliate of the American Correctional Association (see above). Its primary goals are: (1) to increase the effectiveness, expertise, and skills of its members; (2) to create a support network for members; (3) to improve the quality of educational programs within correctional institutions; and (4) to represent the interests of correctional educators with the government, press, and public. The CEA runs offices in nine regions across the country. It sponsors a national conference and hosts a series of training teleconferences on instructional techniques for learning-disabled adults. Members receive a quarterly journal, newsletters, and other publications.

Correctional Health Resources, Inc.
PO Box 80406
Lansing, MI 48908
(800) 600-9313 or (517) 321-9313
Fax: (517) 327-6489
E-mail: chr@corrections.com
Internet: http://www.corrections.com/chr

Correctional Health Resources (CHR) provides prisons, jails, and community-based correctional programs with technical assistance, consultation, and resources pertaining to prison health care. Acting as a broker between health-care workers and correctional facilities, it develops health-care plans to meet the requirements and budgets of specific institutions. CHR staff members conduct needs assessments and assist with the staffing of health-care programs. In addition, the organization provides technical assistance in preparing legal defenses when prisoners sue over health care, develops policy and procedure manuals, and prepares accreditation surveys.

Correctional HIV Consortium
1525 Santa Barbara Street #1
Santa Barbara, CA 93101

(805) 568-1400 or (800) 572-9310
Fax: (805) 564-4381
E-mail: chc@silcom.com
Internet: http://www.silcom.com/~chc/

The Correctional HIV Consortium provides a wide range of programs and services to two principal groups: (1) correctional agencies, institutions, administrators, and medical professionals; and (2) inmates, members of their families and support groups, and those who offer them services. Their website provides information for people in these groups; a commissary for purchasing health-care products; a listing of special events; bibliographical materials; a video lending library; and a national listing of open and secure hospice programs for offenders.

Correctional Industries Association, Inc.
1420 North Charles Street, Suite CH-415
Baltimore, MD 21201-5779
(410) 837-5036
Fax: (410) 837-5039
E-mail: cia@corrections.com
Internet: http://www.corrections.com/industries

The Correctional Industries Association, Inc. (CIA), founded in 1941 as the Penal Industries Association (PIA), promotes the establishment, development, and improvement of prison industries and assists institutions with the employment, training, education, and rehabilitation of inmates. The organization also encourages program development and evaluation. CIA operates as an international, nonprofit professional organization of individuals, agencies, and companies, both public and private. It provides members with training programs, an annual directory and quarterly newsletter, and a clearinghouse for the exchange of ideas and information. CIA administers the Private Sector/Prison Industry Enhancement Certification Program for the U.S. Department of Justice, Bureau of Justice Assistance.

Correctional Medical Services, Inc.
12647 Olive Boulevard
St. Louis, MO 63141-6345
(314) 919-9102 or (800) 325-4809
Internet: http://www.cmsstl.com

Founded in 1979, Correctional Medical Services (CMS) provides managed health care services to prisons and jails. It holds more than 40 percent of all contracts awarded to private-sector providers of correctional health care, servicing more than 283,000 inmates at 346 correctional facilities in 30 states. As of July 1998, CMS was delivering comprehensive health care to all inmates in the correctional systems of Alabama, Arkansas, Idaho, Massachusetts, Michigan, Minnesota, Missouri, New Jersey, New Mexico,and Wyoming. In addition, CMS assists corrections personnel in designing inmate health-care programs. CMS is known for its KEY Program, a substance abuse treatment program for inmates.

Corrections Connection Network
159 Burgin Parkway
Quincy, MA 02194
(617) 471-4445
Fax: (617) 770-3339
E-mail: ednet@corrections.com
Internet: http://www.corrections.com/

The Corrections Connection Network (CCN) is one of the largest on-line resources for news and information about corrections. Operating on an international level, it is home to more than fifteen professional and public correctional organizations. CCN provides a bulletin board for announcements, current events, conferences, news reports, products, research, and publications. Their website provides links to correctional agencies worldwide, including private and public organizations at all levels of government. CCN also offers an on-line forum for practitioners, administrators, and researchers to discuss current issues and problems related to inmate classification, prison gangs, geriatrics, health care, delinquency, litigation, overcrowding, prerelease programs, alternative sanctions, and private placements. In addition, this site provides information on purchasing contracts, on-line product inventories and services, vendors, shopping guides, agency directories, yellow and white pages, e-mail directories, educational networks, career services, a résumé database, classified advertisements, and data on student services.

Corrections Program Office
810 7th Street, NW
Washington, DC 20531
(202) 307-0703
Technical assistance: (800) 848-6325
E-mail: askcpo@ojp.usdoj.gov
Internet: http://www.ojp.usdoj.gov/cpo/

The Corrections Program Office (CPO) was established in 1995 by the Office of Justice Programs to administer and monitor grant programs developed as a result of the Violent Crime Control and Law Enforcement Act of 1994. The CPO manages the Violent Offender Incarceration and Truth-in-Sentencing Incentive Formula Grant Program (VOI/TIS), the Residential Substance Abuse Treatment for State Prisoners Formula Grant Program (RSAT), and the Facilities on Tribal Lands Discretionary Grant Program. Additionally, it continues to administer active grant awards from prior years' appropriations for the Correctional Boot Camp Initiative and the Tuberculosis Prevention, Diagnosis, and Treatment Discretionary Grant Programs. Beyond administering grants, the CPO is an active voice in Washington for both federal and state corrections programs. It disseminates information on federal initiatives on policy and program development related to sentencing, corrections, and corrections-based substance abuse treatment to state corrections institutions. It also assists state policymakers and adult and juvenile correctional administrators in exploring policy issues related to justice, sentencing, and corrections and in assessing the intended and unintended consequences of policy changes. The CPO offers program guides and workshops to help grant applicants acquire the information necessary to apply for funds, and grant recipients to implement the grant programs. It offers a series of conferences, workshops, seminars, and symposia designed to provide a forum for debate and analysis of such issues as sentencing reform, privatization, and violent juvenile offenders. The CPO also offers training and on-site technical assistance to correctional agencies and other grantees.

Crime and Justice Foundation
95 Berkeley Street
Boston, MA 02116
(617) 426-9800
E-mail: candjf@aol.com
Internet: http://members.aol.com/candjf/index.htm

Founded in 1878, the Crime and Justice Foundation is a nonprofit agency committed to correctional reform and progressive change in the administration of justice. The foundation manages adult and juvenile community corrections and criminal mediation programs, directs research, and provides technical support in program development, corrections management, and community-based sanctions.

Drug Treatment Alternative to Prison
Brooklyn Municipal Building
210 Joralemon Street, Room 407
Brooklyn, NY 11201
(718) 250-2231
E-mail: da@brooklynda.org
Internet: http://www.718web.com/brooklynda/dtap.htm

The Drug Treatment Alternative to Prison program (DTAP) was the first prosecution-run program in the country to divert prison-bound felony drug offenders to residential drug treatment. DTAP targets drug-addicted defendants arrested for felony drug offenses who have one or more prior convictions for nonviolent felonies. The DTAP program, an alternative to prosecution and imprisonment, is a 15- to 24-month residential therapeutic program. Offenders have their criminal charges dismissed when they successfully complete the program, and they are then provided with assistance in locating jobs and housing. Those who do not complete the program are brought back to court and prosecuted on the original charges.

Drugs and Crime Data Center and Clearinghouse
Office of National Drug Control Policy
1600 Research Boulevard
Rockville, MD 20850
(800) 666-3332
E-mail: ondcp@ncjrs.org
Internet: http://www.whitehousedrugpolicy.gov

The Drugs and Crime Data Center and Clearinghouse publishes reports and current data on the impact of drugs on the administration of justice, overcrowding in prisons and jails, drug-using offenders in the criminal justice system, drug violations and sentencing, and incarceration rates of drug-law-violating offenders. The principal purpose of the Drugs and Crime Center is to establish objectives, policies, and priorities for the nation's drug control program, the goals of which are to reduce illicit drug use, manufacturing, and trafficking, drug-related crime and violence, and drug-related health problems. Its website provides information on the nation's drug control policies, prevention and treatment strategies, new documents, and scheduled conferences. It also presents drug facts and figures, press releases, commentaries and speeches, and congressional testimony.

Edna McConnell Clark Foundation
250 Park Avenue
New York, NY 10177-0026
(212) 551-9100

The State-Centered Program of the
Edna McConnell Clark Foundation
377 Broadway, 11th Floor
New York, NY 10013
(212) 334-1300
Internet: http://fdncenter.org/grantmaker/emclark/index.html

The Edna McConnell Clark Foundation promotes the development of humane, safe, and affordable criminal sanctions for adult offenders. It works with state officials and policymakers to develop sentencing and correctional policies. The foundation provides funding to states for the development and implementation of reform strategies to improve prison and jail conditions, sentencing and correctional policies and practices, the availability of alternatives to incarceration, and support for policy and program reform. The foundation also supports litigation and educational initiatives to improve conditions in prisons and jails throughout the country.

Families Against Mandatory Minimums
1001 Pennsylvania Avenue, NW
Suite 200 South
Washington, DC 20004
(202) 457-5790
Internet: http://www.famm.org

Families Against Mandatory Minimums (FAMM) is a national organization working to repeal mandatory sentencing laws for nonviolent offenses and to ensure that the punishment fits the crime. Founded in 1991 by judges, attorneys, criminal justice experts, and families of inmates, FAMM today has chapters in twenty-five states. Its 17,000 members are involved in public education, community organizing, working with the media, and legislative activities. FAMM was established to promote rational sentencing policies and to educate the general public, the media, and policymakers about the negative effects of mandatory minimum sentences on the criminal justice system, corrections budgets, conditions of confinement, and individuals. FAMM argues for judicial discretion as a means of distinguishing among defendants and sentencing them according to their culpability. It offers brochures, newsletters, action kits, and background information on sentencing. FAMM operates a 24-hour telephone hotline that provides weekly updates of sentencing-related issues. It also conducts an annual two-day workshop in Washington, D.C., to help people understand the complexities of sentencing reform and learn how to argue for it more persuasively. Participants are taught basic legal concepts, public speaking, how to attract media attention, and how to communicate with legislators and reporters. FAMM's quarterly newsletter, *FAMM-gram*, covers changes in federal and some state sentencing policies as well as legal news, prison news, and media reports.

Family and Corrections Network
32 Oak Grove Road
Palmyra, VA 22963
(804) 589-3036
Fax: (804) 589-6520
E-mail: fcn@fcnetwork.org
Internet: http://www.fcnetwork.org

The Family and Corrections Network (FCN), established in 1983, is an organization of volunteers whose primary concern is to increase general awareness about the needs of and issues associated with families of offenders. The FCN provides information and support to families of offenders, correctional administrators and staff, and concerned citizens. It publishes the *FCN Report* (formerly the *FCN News*), a national publication devoted to issues involving offenders' families. It also publishes working papers on topics such as children of prisoners, parenting programs for prisoners, prison visitations, incarcerated fathers and mothers, and prison marriage. Another publication lists over 300 programs serving families of adult offenders in the United States and Canada. FCN distributes a video, *The Prisoner's Family: A Community Concern*, and sponsors conferences such as the National Leadership Conference on Families of Adult Offenders, the National Conference on the Family and Corrections, and the FCN Strategic Planning Conference. The FCN has established a liaison with the Canadian Correctional Services as well as with correctional agencies throughout the United States, providing consultation and offering presentations on specific issues related to families of offenders.

Fathers Behind Bars
PO Box 86
Niles, MI 49120
(616) 684-5715
E-mail: fathersbehindbars@msn.com
Internet: http://www.amandla.org/osepp/resources/
child_family.html#FBB

Fathers Behind Bars is a reform group run by prisoners for prisoners to enhance visitation between male inmates and their families. The main objective is to assist male inmates with maintaining or reestablishing contact with their families and to encourage family unity. The agency helps set up institutional parent groups for incarcerated fathers, teaches basic parenting skills, and prepares inmates for the role of fatherhood.

Federal Bureau of Prisons
Office of the General Counsel
320 First Street, NW, Room 738
Washington, DC 20534
(202) 514-6655
Internet: http://www.bop.gov

The Federal Bureau of Prisons was established as an outcome of the 1930 act of Congress that directed the development of an integrated system of federal prisons to provide custody and programs for federal offenders. The Bureau's central office in Washington, D.C., provides leadership, draws up long-range plans, formulates policy, and coordinates the national network of federal correctional facilities and community resources. The bureau is divided into six geographical regions, each with a director and staff, that provide technical support and on-site assistance to field locations and institutions. The bureau stipulates that all federal inmates who are able to do so must work and be paid a small wage, a portion of which some prisoners use to make restitution to victims through the Inmate Financial Responsibility Program. Most inmates serve the last few months of their sentence in a community corrections center or halfway house, and many hold jobs in the community while preparing for release. Although the bureau oversees all federal community corrections programs, many of its halfway houses and community corrections programs are privately operated under contract. The Bureau of Prisons also provides up-to-date statistics, through both the Internet and annual publications, on the characteristics of inmates in federal institutions.

International Association of Correctional Officers
1333 S. Wabash, Box 53
Chicago, IL 60605
(312) 996-5401
Internet: http://www.acsp.uic.edu/iaco/May96C.htm

Founded in 1977, the International Association of Correctional Officers promotes efficiency and effectiveness in the management of prisons and jails. It develops standards, trains correctional officers in operational effectiveness, and publishes a quarterly newsletter, *Keeper's Voice.*

International Community Corrections Association
PO Box 1987
La Crosse, WI 54602
(608) 785-0200
Fax: (608) 784-5335
Internet: http://www.cssnet.com/icca

Established in 1964, the International Community Corrections Association (ICCA), formerly the International Halfway House Association, is a private, nonprofit organization dedicated to the enhancement of community-based correctional services. The ICCA promotes the development of community-based residential treatment programs for offenders, alcoholics, drug addicts, and delinquent and dependent youth. Its goals include collecting and disseminating information for the international corrections community; becoming recognized as a leader for community corrections in North America; providing training resources for community agencies and staff; and promoting standards, research, and certification in order to assure effective community corrections.

Legal Services for Prisoners with Children
100 McAllister Street
San Francisco, CA 94102
(415) 255-7036
Fax: (415) 552-3150
E-mail: lspc@igc.org

When Legal Services for Prisoners with Children (LSPC) began in 1978, it was one of the first legal organizations in the country to focus on prisoners and their children. LSPC's central goals are to provide training, technical assistance, and other types of support to legal service offices and prisoners and their families throughout California. LSPC is primarily a policy organization, but it also provides information to prisoners, their children, relatives, and lawyers. LSPC established the Kinship Project to help relatives hold together families at risk of breaking apart because of an incarcerated parent. The Kinship Project regularly organizes workshops and conferences, and it disseminates information through publications and the Internet. Another LSPC project, the Grandparent-Relative Caregivers Advocacy Project, coordinates services and support for relatives who assume a child-care role when a parent is incarcerated. More generally, the LSPC offers legal training and community education workshops; shares information on custody, public benefits, and other services with support groups; and provides technical assistance to legal and social service agencies. Its publications include training manuals; a guide for grandparent-relative caregivers; materials related to the legal and social support of inmates and their families; and a national guide to resources that is available on the Internet.

Mental Health in Corrections Consortium
Ward Parkway, Suite 200
Kansas City, MO 64114
(816) 444-3500
Fax: (816) 444-0330
E-mail: webmaster@mfassoc.com
Internet: http://www.mhcca.org

The Mental Health in Corrections Consortium (MHCC) was established in 1993 to offer resources to providers of mental health and substance abuse services in correctional settings. The MHCC publishes the *Journal of the Mental Health Corrections Consortium,* the official publication of the Association of Criminal Justice Mental Health and Substance Abuse Treatment Professionals.

Mothers Inside Loving Kids (MILK)
Virginia Correctional Center for Women
PO Box 1
Goochland, VA 23063
(804) 784-3582

The MILK Program helps mothers in the Virginia Correctional Center for Women stay in touch with their children. MILK plans four annual all-day contact visits aimed at fostering ties between mothers and children. Mothers in MILK meet regularly in a support group to discuss the difficulties of parenting from behind prison walls. Members plan the quarterly family visits and decide on topics to cover in group discussion. They invite speakers on a variety of topics, including discipline, child development, strategies for maintaining contact with a child's school, and child protective services. Potential members must first complete a parenting course offered at the prison. Women who have accumulated several prison rule infractions or whose crime is related to harming a child generally are excluded. MILK members pay a $1 monthly dues fee and raise funds to pay for family visits.

National Association of Sentencing Advocates
918 F Street, Suite 501
Washington, DC 20004
(202) 628-0871
Fax: (202) 628-1091
E-mail: nasa@sproject.com
Internet: http://www.sproject.com/nasa.htm

The National Association of Sentencing Advocates (NASA) was established in 1992 by a group of sentencing advocates who work with defense counsel on behalf of defendants, inmates, and parolees. It shares the resources of the Sentencing Project (see below), with which it is affiliated. Its goals include providing education and training to the association's membership and promoting effective responses to crime based on principles of fairness, equity, and human dignity. The association publishes a newsletter, *NASA Notes*, and occasional briefing sheets. It holds an annual conference and speaks out on issues of criminal justice and sentencing. Members are available as speakers, expert witnesses, and consultants in criminal justice matters.

National Center on Institutions and Alternatives
3125 Mt. Vernon Avenue
Alexandria, VA 22305
(703) 684-0373
Fax: (703) 684-6037
E-mail: ncia@igc.apc.org
Internet: http://www.ncianet.org/ncia

The National Center on Institutions and Alternatives (NCIA) is a private, nonprofit agency established in 1977 to assist federal, state, and local agencies in coping with prison overcrowding. NCIA will examine the process by which people enter, move through, and exit correctional facilities; investigate alternative sentencing possibilities; develop alternatives to imprisonment for technical violations of probation and parole; and analyze pretrial, early release, community custody, intensive supervision, and electronic monitoring programs and policies. Since 1979, one of NCIA's primary areas of focus has been on sentencing and parole procedures in federal, state, county, and local criminal justice systems across the country. It aims at providing courts with detailed, highly structured sentencing options that will reduce the reliance on incarceration.

National Commission on Correctional Health Care
1300 W. Belmont Avenue
Chicago, IL 60657
(773) 880-1460
Fax: (773) 880-2424
Internet: http://www.corrections.com/ncchc

The National Commission on Correctional Health Care (NCCHC) is a nonprofit organization primarily concerned with improving the quality of medical care in jails, prisons, and juvenile detention facilities. NCCHC offers consultation and technical assistance services; publications; educational conferences and seminars; programs designed to help correctional health systems provide efficient health care; and health service accreditation and professional certification. NCCHC sponsors the National Conference on Correctional Health Care, the largest educational conference in the world devoted to institutional health care. At these conferences speakers address such topics as the treatment of infectious diseases, substance abuse programs, mental health staffing, legal and ethical issues, and cost containment. NCCHC publications include policy bulletins, research reports, and news releases. NCCHC also offers internships at criminal justice agencies.

National Criminal Justice Reference Service
National Institute of Justice
U.S. Department of Justice
Box 6000
Rockville, MD 20850
(800) 851-3420 or (301) 251-5000
E-mail: look@ncjrs.org
Internet: http://www.ncjrs.org

Since 1972, the National Criminal Justice Reference Service (NCJRS) has served as a centralized clearinghouse for the criminal justice community. The NCJRS disseminates information from the National Institute of Justice, the Office of Juvenile Justice and Delinquency Prevention, the Bureau of Justice Assistance, the Bureau of Justice Statistics, the Office of Victims of Crime, and the Office of National Drug Control Policy. It maintains a file of more than 100,000 criminal justice documents, providing customized and topical searches as well as referral services. The NCJRS also distributes documents, many of them without charge. Contact NCJRS to get on its mailing list for free documents in specific subject areas.

The National GAINS Center
Policy Research, Inc.
262 Delaware Avenue
Delmar, NY 12054
(800) 311-4246
Fax: (518) 439-7612
E-mail: gains@prainc.com
Internet: http://www.prainc.com/gains/index.html

The National GAINS Center was established in September 1995 to serve as a national hub for the collection and dissemination of information about mental health and substance abuse services for people who have mental illnesses and are also substance abusers and come into contact with the justice system. The center is a federal partnership between two centers of the Substance Abuse and Mental Health Services Administration (one is the Center for Substance Abuse Treatment, the other the Center for Mental Health Services) and the National Institute of Corrections. It provides technical assistance and program curricula to state and local criminal justice agencies and other organizations that operate programs for people who come into contact with the criminal justice system and have both mental health and substance abuse disorders. The GAINS Center emphasizes the needs of women and juveniles, and it seeks the active involvement of citizens and family members. It organizes forums and workshops while also offering a variety of publications to support the implementation of service strategies designed for its target population.

National Institute of Corrections
320 First Street, NW
Washington, DC 20534
(202) 307-3995
Internet: http://www.nicic.org/inst

A division of the U.S. Department of Justice, the National Institute of Corrections (NIC) provides technical support, training, information, and funding for special projects to state and local correctional agencies. It maintains a database on correctional programs, policies, and standards and publishes an annual report and program plan.

National Prison Hospice Association
PO Box 3769
Boulder, CO 80306-0941
(303) 666-9638
Fax: (303) 665-9437
E-mail: npha-news@npha.org
Internet: http://www.npha.org/abtnpha.html

The National Prison Hospice Association (NPHA) promotes hospice care for terminally ill inmates and those facing the prospect of dying in prison. It provides support and assistance to corrections professionals in the development of patient care procedures and management programs. The NPHA serves as a center for the exchange of information between corrections facilities and hospices about existing and projected programs. The hospice, as defined by the NPHA, is a comfort-oriented unit that allows seriously ill patients to die with dignity and humanity and with as little pain as possible in an environment where they have mental and spiritual support. Since 1995, the NPHA has published a newsletter three times a year. Its website provides a list of current research and literature and a direct link to the National Hospice Organization.

National Prison Project
American Civil Liberties Union Foundation
1875 Connecticut Avenue, NW, Suite 410
Washington, DC 20009
(202) 234-4830

The National Prison Project (NPP), supported by the American Civil Liberties Union Foundation (see above), is one of the nation's leaders in prison reform. Challenging unconstitutional conditions in prisons and jails and litigating prisoners' rights cases, the NPP also develops alternatives to incarceration. It seeks to reduce prison overcrowding, reduce reliance on incarceration as a criminal justice sanction, create constitutional prison conditions, and strengthen prisoners' rights through a program of class-action litigation and public education. The NPP provides expert advice and technical assistance to local community groups and lawyers throughout the country and works to inform and educate the media. Publications include the *National Prison Project Journal,* a quarterly featuring articles, reports, legal analysis, legislative news, and stories on other developments in the field. The *Prisoners' Assistance Directory,* another NPP publication, identifies and describes organizations and agencies providing assistance to prisoners. The NPP's *Status Reports* provide up-to-date overviews of prison litigation by state, and its *Primer for Jail Litigators* offers practical suggestions for litigating jail conditions cases. The *AIDS in Prison Bibliography* lists educational, medical, legal, and correctional resources for coping with AIDS in prison. *AIDS in Prisons: The Facts for Inmates and Officers,* answers commonly asked questions about AIDS in an easy-to-read format, and *TB in Prisons: The Facts for Inmates and Officers* does the same for questions about tuberculosis.

Office of Correctional Education
Division of National Programs
Office of Vocational and Adult Education
U.S. Department of Education
600 Independence Avenue, SW
Switzer Building, Room 4529
Washington, DC 20020
(202) 205-5621
Internet: http://www.ed.gov/offices/OVAE/OCE/

In April 1991, the U.S. Department of Education created a new office to provide national leadership on issues in correctional education. The Office of Correctional Education (OCE) provides technical assistance to states, local schools, and correctional institutions. It coordinates all correctional education programs within the Department of Education and sends an annual report to Congress on the status of correctional education in the United States. Working with state correctional educators, the OCE collects information on the number of individuals who complete vocational education sequences, earn high school degrees or general equivalency diplomas, and earn postsecondary degrees while incarcerated; the OCE then correlates this information with job placement, job retention, and recidivism. The OCE has funded demonstration projects in literacy and vocational education for prisoners. Other demonstration programs involve the screening and testing of inmates for functional literacy and learning disabilities. Demonstration vocational education programs expand or improve on existing vocational education programs in correctional institutions, using curricula that integrate academic with vocational content.

Parents and Children Together, Inc.
PO Box 14828
Fort Worth, TX 76117
(817) 924-7776
E-mail: dkpact@juno.com

Parents and Children Together (PACT) is a nonprofit organization established in 1984 to preserve and strengthen families of incarcerated persons. PACT's primary objective is to prevent the incarceration of future generations by encouraging stronger, healthier families in the present. PACT offers local community network and referral services to families of incarcerated persons and to ex-offenders, and it runs a bimonthly support group. It also provides information to correctional facilities across the country. A volunteer mentor program offers support, friendship, and guidance to prisoners and their families.

Prison Activist Resource Center
Berkeley's Long-Haul Project
PO Box 339
Berkeley, CA 94701
(510) 845-8813
Fax: (510) 845-8816
E-mail: parc@prisonactivist.org
Internet: http://www.prisonactivist.org

The Prison Activist Resource Center (PARC) was founded in 1994 out of the Berkeley's Long-Haul Project, an activist community center and political library. PARC's main goal is to promote progressive social change as a solution to crime and an alternative to mass incarceration. Coordinated and maintained by long-time prison activists and legal workers, PARC aims at exposing prison injustices, advocating prisoners' human and civil rights, promoting nonviolent and humane solutions to prison violence, and providing support to activists who are working toward these goals. PARC has helped defense committees and other prisoner advocates in organizing demonstrations, organizing educational presentations, building reform campaigns, and conducting research. PARC serves as an information clearinghouse and publishes progressive and radical information on prisons and the criminal prosecution system, political prisoners, women in prison, the death penalty, and prison abolition. PARC also catalogues information on organizations working on prison reform and abolition.

Prison Fellowship Ministries
PO Box 17500
Washington, DC 20041-0500
(703) 478-0100

Prison Fellowship Ministries is a nonprofit, volunteer-based organization with the mission of ministering to prisoners, ex-prisoners, victims, and their families and of promoting biblical standards of justice in the criminal justice system. To accomplish this mission, Prison Fellowship recruits, trains, and mobilizes volunteers from a wide variety of backgrounds and denominations to participate in a broad array of in-prison and community ministries. The organization was founded in 1976 by Charles W. Colson, the former Special Counsel to President Richard Nixon, who, after serving time for a Watergate-related offense, became convinced of the need for a ministry for men and women in prison.

The Sentencing Project
918 F Street, NW, Suite 501
Washington, DC 20004
(202) 628-0871
Fax: (202) 628-1091
E-mail: staff@sproject.com
Internet: http://www.sentencingproject.org

The Sentencing Project, incorporated in 1986, is an independent source of information on criminal justice policy reform. It has helped promote defense-based alternative sentencing programs and services in more than twenty states. The Sentencing Project helps public defenders devise constructive options to incarceration. It also seeks to provide judges with a broad range of sentencing options that will make effective use of community resources and supervision. Sponsored by the National Association of Sentencing Advocates (see above), the Sentencing Project also draws upon a pool of national experts to consult with local and state governments on strategies and programs to alleviate jail and prison overcrowding. In the field of criminal justice policy, the Sentencing Project is widely known for its reports and analyses highlighting inequities in the criminal justice system.

Major reports include nationally acclaimed publications such as "Young Black Men and the Criminal Justice System," the "Americans Behind Bars" series on international rates of incarceration, and "Does the Punishment Fit the Crime? Drug Users and Drunk Drivers, Questions of Race and Class." These reports received widespread media coverage, led to congressional and state legislative hearings, and fostered new programs designed to address the issues of racial and economic disparities in sentencing. They have also helped change the way Americans think about crime and punishment. The Sentencing Project has made its staff a resource for reporters, editors, and producers of major media covering criminal justice issues. Staff are frequently interviewed and provide background information to national television and radio networks and major newspapers. In 1992, the Sentencing Project fostered the development of the Campaign for an Effective Crime Policy to give voice to criminal justice leaders who seek change in sentencing and corrections policy. In addition, the Sentencing Project sponsors national conferences.

Stop Prisoner Rape, Inc.
President
333 North Avenue 61 #4
Los Angeles, CA 90042
(213) 257-6164
State Chapter Office
PO Box 632
Fort Bragg, CA 95437
(707) 964-0820
E-mail: information@spr.org
Internet: http://www.spr.org

Stop Prisoner Rape, Inc. (SPR) is a national nonprofit organization established in 1979 as People Organized to Stop Rape of Imprisoned Persons. SPR is dedicated to preventing the rape, sexual slavery, forced prostitution, and sexual harassment in correctional facilities. It provides education and training to correctional workers, free literature, an audio tape called "Becoming a Survivor," counseling, and legal support to inmates. SPR strives to educate prisoners, the public, and corrections professionals and to reach out to survivors both inside and outside the walls. SPR encourages class action suits and works with lawyers for survivors filing damage claims against institutions that have not protected inmates. The organization provides a list of current publications, training manuals, tapes, lectures, and legal materials on the Internet.

U.S. Bureau of Justice Assistance
U.S. Department of Justice
Assistant Attorney General
Office of Justice Programs
633 Indiana Avenue, NW
Washington, DC 20531
(202) 514-6687 or (800) 421-6770
Fax: (202) 307-6394
E-mail: askbja@ojp.usdoj.gov
Internet: http://www.ojp.usdoj.gov/BJA

The Bureau of Justice Assistance (BJA) provides funding, training, evaluation services, technical assistance, and information to states and local communities across the country. Although all areas of criminal justice are considered for funding, the key areas in corrections in which the BJA awards discretionary grants are in improvements in the operation of corrections; prison and jail work and industries; evaluation of correctional options; community corrections; and changes in structured sentencing. The goal of the BJA's evaluation component is to identify programs of proven effectiveness and to disseminate information about these programs so that other jurisdictions throughout the country can replicate them. Successful program evaluations guide the formulation of policy and programs within federal, state, and local criminal justice agencies. The BJA's Technical Assistance and Training Program identifies needs and develops responses to improve management capabilities at both the national and state levels relating to program development and performance. Training and technical assistance is accomplished through special topic workshops, national and regional conferences, and on-site sessions. BJA publications and related documents in criminal justice are maintained in the National Criminal Justice Reference Service (see above).

U.S. Parole Commission
Park Place Building
5550 Friendship Boulevard, Suite 420
Chevy Chase, MD 20815-7286
(301) 492-5990

The U.S. Parole Commission consists of three members appointed by the president of the United States with the consent of the Senate. It is responsible for granting, modifying, and revoking paroles of eligible U.S. prisoners. It is also responsible for the supervision of parolees and prisoners released upon the expiration of their sentences less good time. As a result of sentencing reform acts abolishing parole, the commission is gradually being phased out, to terminate on 1 November 2002.

U.S. Sentencing Commission
One Columbus Circle, NE
Washington, DC 20002-8002
E-mail: pubaffairs@ussc.gov
Internet: http://www.ussc.gov

The U.S. Sentencing Commission is an independent agency in the judicial branch of government. The commission's purpose is to establish sentencing policies and practices for the federal courts, including detailed guidelines for the punishment of offenders convicted of federal crimes. The primary responsibilities of the commission are to develop, monitor, and amend the sentencing guidelines and to provide training, conduct research on sentencing-related issues, and serve as an information resource for Congress, criminal justice practitioners, and the public. The commission is also charged with evaluating the effects of the sentencing guidelines on the criminal justice system, recommending to Congress appropriate modifications of substantive criminal law and sentencing procedures, and establishing a research and development program on sentencing issues. The commission publishes numerous research and special project reports, bulletins, reports to Congress, and news updates.

Women's Prison Association of New York
110 2nd Avenue
New York, NY 10003
(212) 674-1163

Founded in 1844 to provide assistance to women in conflict with the law, the Women's Prison Association of New York was one of the nation's leaders in the crusade to establish separate prisons for women. Directed for many years by Abigail Hopper Gibbons, the Association supported a halfway house for released female inmates. Today the association continues to sponsor transitional programs for women being released from prison, including the Hopper Home Alternative to Incarceration program.

Print
Resources

The literature on American prisons is large and complex. It includes historical studies, reports by all levels of government (federal, state, county, and city) that operate penal institutions, reports by organizations and agencies involved in supervising prisons or providing programs, legal materials such as court investigations of prison conditions, monographs on special topics such as private prisons, prisoners' writings, and academic and professional journals. In addition, the government units in charge of prisons produce numerous statistical reports on such matters as prison population size and rate of increase, inmate health and mortality, and prisoner characteristics (age, race, sex, and so on). For people interested in statistics the most accessible and convenient resource is the *Sourcebook of Criminal Justice Statistics,* published annually by the Bureau of Justice Statistics (BJS), a division of the U.S. Department of Justice. (Information on obtaining a copy of the *Sourcebook* and other federal government publications pertaining to prisons appears below under Bureau of Justice Statistics.)

This chapter is designed to guide readers through this maze of print resources so they can quickly and easily find the best materials for their purposes. In the lists that follow, the emphasis falls on the eight major topic areas addressed in Chapter 2 and on recent publications. The chapter is divided into three parts: (1) books and reference materials; (2) journals, magazines, and newsletters; and (3) government documents and agency publications. Readers interested in additional government information on prisons should contact the National Criminal Justice Reference Service (NCJRS) or the Bureau of Justice Statistics Clearinghouse; contact information on both appears in Chapter 6.

Books and Reference Materials

Abbott, Jack Henry. *In the Belly of the Beast: Letters from Prison.* New York: Vintage Books, 1991 (originally published in 1981). 166 pages.

Jack Abbott, a prisoner serving a long sentence for violence, began writing letters to the novelist Norman Mailer, who decided that Abbott was a gifted artist and helped him gain release on parole. Little time passed, however, before Abbott killed someone and was returned to prison for life. These are his letters to Mailer about prison conditions and his reactions to them. Few prisoners react to confinement as Abbott did (or said he did)—with unrelenting defiance of his keepers, a reaction that resulted in years in solitary. The letters give us a vivid portrait of an extremely angry, violent, and volatile inmate who describes himself as willing to kill other prisoners to maintain his own image and status. Abbott justifies his antagonism toward everything and everybody with the rhetoric of the 1960s and 1970s prisoners' movement.

Abu-Jamal, Mumia, with an introduction by John Edgar Wideman. *Live from Death Row.* Reading, Mass.: Addison-Wesley, 1995. 215 pages.

In 1982 Mumia Abu-Jamal, a radio reporter in Philadelphia, was convicted of the murder of police officer Daniel Faulkner and sentenced to death. While waiting to be executed, Abu-Jamal has led a crusade against racism and political bias in the U.S. criminal justice system. In this book, he presents a scathing account of prison brutalities and humiliations. His essays from death row are vivid, thought-provoking accounts of daily life in prison. Abu-Jamal moves beyond the usual objections to the death penalty to present a firsthand account of waiting to be executed.

Beaumont, Gustave de, and Alexis de Tocqueville. *On the Penitentiary System in the United States and Its Application in France.* New York: Augustus M. Kelley, 1970 (originally published in 1833). 301 pages.

This is a survey of all the state prisons in the United States, conducted in the early 1800s by Beaumont and Tocqueville, Frenchmen who were doing research on which France could base its own plans for punishing offenders. Available in many libraries, this book remains the most vivid source of information on very early American prisons and the conditions inside them. It also contains fascinating statistical data on offenses and sentences and detailed discussions of prison discipline. The introduction by Francis Lieber, an American with an interest in prison reform, includes important discussions of the causes of crime and nature of female criminality.

Blumberg, Mark. *AIDS: The Impact on the Criminal Justice System.* Columbus, Ohio: Merrill, 1990. 243 pages.

This book examines the impact of AIDS on the criminal justice system, including three chapters on AIDS and prisons. One covers issues and controversies regarding the management of AIDS in penal institutions; a second chapter covers AIDS and prisoners' rights law; and a third deals with confidentiality, legal, and labor-relations issues. Although the statistics and legal materials are somewhat dated now, the book provides a thoughtful and thorough analysis of the issues.

Braithwaite, Ronald L., Theodore M. Hammett, and Robert Morris Mayberry. *Prisons and AIDS: A Public Health Challenge.* San Francisco: Jossey-Bass, 1996. 247 pages.

Providing a public-health perspective on the problem of HIV and AIDS in prisons, this book discusses the design and implementation of education and prevention programs. The material is based on research funded by the National Institute of Justice and the Centers for Disease Control and Prevention. The authors describe patterns of HIV/AIDS cases among male and female adult and juvenile inmates and present strategies for developing culturally sensitive HIV/AIDS prevention programs in correctional settings. Case studies from a variety of correctional facilities reveal details on the frequency of sexual contact, drug use, needle sharing, tattooing, and the availability of condom protection. The book suggests policies and strategies for prevention, testing and disclosure, partner notification, research, and special housing.

Braswell, Michael C., Reid H. Montgomery Jr., and Lucien X. Lombardo. *Prison Violence in America,* 2d ed. Cincinnati, Ohio: Anderson, 1994. 426 pages.

This is a collection of essays on violence in American prisons today, written by prison inmates, scholars, and prison administrators who have been exposed to life behind bars. The authors cover such topics as physical and sexual assaults, riots, the effects of prison size and overcrowding, and inmate subcultures. Section I provides reflections on the experience of prison violence, starting with a letter by George Jackson, a California prisoner who was killed during an uprising. Section II, on violence among inmates and prison officers, covers physical and sexual assaults, staff-inflicted brutality, and court decisions on the use of force in prisons. Section III, an overview of prison riots, highlights the history of U.S. prison riots from 1774 to 1991, including the two major riots at New York's Attica Prison and the New Mexico Penitentiary. This section also discusses judicial reform and prison control, concentrating on the impact of the important Texas case, *Ruiz v. Estelle,* on stress and collective violence, and on creating a typology of the causes of prison riots. Section IV covers administrative strategies for regaining control of a prison and the importance of understanding the social climate of prison. This is one of the most comprehensive and thoughtful books on prison violence.

Cummins, Eric. *The Rise and Fall of California's Radical Prison Movement.* Stanford: Stanford University Press, 1994. 319 pages.

Cummins provides historical background on California's radical prison movement from 1950 to 1980, highlighting events at San Quentin State Prison, located in the San Francisco Bay area. Cummins discusses the influence of inmates such as Caryl Chessman, Eldridge Cleaver, and George Jackson and of inmate groups affiliated with the Black Panther Party and the Symbionese Liberation Army. He focuses on the development of an inmate ideology of protest and rebellion and on its impact on the outside world. Cummins also describes the resistance of correctional staff members to the prisoners' movement and their attempts to modify inmate ideology. Covering the trial of the San Quentin Six and the passage of California's 1977 Determinate Sentencing Law, Cummins goes on to write about the creation of the new "maxi-maxi security" prisons. Well-informed and critical of parties on all sides of this debate, this is one of the best studies of the recent history of a state prison system, and in this case, the state prison system in question is one that influences practices throughout the nation.

Currie, Elliott. *Crime and Punishment in America.* New York: Henry Holt & Company, 1998. 208 pages.

Challenging the myths that he feels dominate discussions of crime and punishment in the United States, Currie examines the current era of building many new prisons and warehousing offenders. He outlines objections to the further proliferation of prisons, additional increases in the number of supermax prisons, and harsh treatment of prisoners. Currie then presents alternative approaches to the crime problem, focusing on improved equity and social justice, social supports, and opportunities aimed at the most vulnerable Americans. He also advocates the reintegration of offenders into the community. Criticizing policies such as mandatory sentencing and three-strikes laws, Currie argues that the system needs to turn not to more severe measures but to alternative punishments. He supports his arguments for increasing prison alternatives with data derived from research and pilot programs. In sum, the book demythologizes criminal justice policies that have dominated the national debate over the past two decades.

DeRosia, Victoria R. *Living Inside Prison Walls: Adjustment Behavior.* Westport, Conn.: Praeger, 1998. 206 pages.

In DeRosia's study, a sample of inmates from New York state prisons was sorted into two groups, one consisting of inmates with little social status before prison and the other consisting of inmates who, before incarceration, had earned college degrees and held high-status occupations. DeRosia compares each group on the basis of their ability to adjust to prison and remain out of trouble. Her findings reveal that advantaged offenders exhibit little if any involvement in prison misconduct; they tend to avoid conflict, remain occupied, and exhibit effective coping strategies. The results of her study suggest that advantaged inmates adjust rapidly and more productively to prison life.

Earley, Kevin E. (ed.). *Drug Treatment Behind Bars: Prison-Based Strategies for Change.* Westport, Conn.: Praeger, 1996. 192 pages.

The essays in this collection are written by practitioners in the field of prison-based drug treatment and therapy programs. The book provides a detailed discussion of the effects of drug use on crime in general and on violent crime in particular. It also covers the impact of drugs on recidivism and rates of relapse into addiction. In the past two decades the prison population in the United States has soared beyond prison capacity, an increase fueled largely by increases in the number of people convicted of and imprisoned for drug-related offenses. These offenders include a disproportionate number of recidivists, people who commit crimes over and over again and thus are responsible for a relatively large proportion of criminal activity in our society. However, the data show that most offenders are poor, young, unemployed, uneducated, African American males from dysfunctional families. Contrary to public opinion, many of these offenders are tired of their "revolving door" relationship with the police, courts, and correctional institutions. However, without appropriate social and therapeutic support, there is little hope of altering their behavior. This study is a contribution to the literature examining the extent to which rehabilitation and prison-based drug treatment programs can reduce recidivism, the rate of drug relapse, and violent crime in our society.

Earley, Peter. *The Hot House: Life inside Leavenworth Prison.* New York: Bantam Books, 1992. 383 pages.

Drawing on interviews with inmates and corrections officers, Earley, the first journalist ever granted unlimited access to this federal maximum-security institution, presents an eyewitness account of daily life inside the U.S. Penitentiary at Leavenworth, Kansas. The book offers both officer and prisoner perspectives. Earley provides an account of daily routines, stresses, and problems as well as of the unpredictable, chaotic events that mark an average day in prison.

Flanagan, Timothy J., James W. Marquart, and Kenneth G. Adams (eds.). *Incarcerating Criminals: Prisons and Jails in Social and Organizational Context.* New York: Oxford University Press, 1998. 352 pages.

The authors of the essays in this collection examine the social and institutional environments of U.S. prisons and jails. They discuss the philosophies, theories, and goals of corrections today; management policies and practices; staffing and programming; inmate prisonization; classification and treatment; and security and social control within prisons. They also assess future goals of corrections.

Freedman, Estelle B. *Maternal Justice: Miriam Van Waters and the Female Reform Tradition, 1887–1974.* Chicago: University of Chicago Press, 1996. 458 pages.

This is the authoritative biography of Miriam Van Waters (1887–1974), one of the most influential leaders in women's prison reform and juvenile justice. Van Waters devoted her life to helping women and children in conflict with the law. A feminist, she fought to achieve equal and just treatment of women offenders and to attain respect as a female administrator. In 1932 Van Waters became superintendent of the Massachusetts Reformatory for Women, where she crusaded for progressive rehabilitation methods for incarcerated women and children. Some of her innovative ideas and her tolerance of homosexuality drew a great deal of criticism, and she was temporarily dismissed in 1945. However, strong public support and her unwavering struggle for exoneration led to her reinstatement, and she remained at the reformatory until her retirement in 1957. Van Waters and her generation of activists provide a legacy for contemporary reformers of women's prisons.

Friedman, Lawrence. *Crime and Punishment in American History.* New York: Basic Books, 1993. 577 pages.

Friedman fills gaps in the prior literature by presenting a comprehensive picture of the development of the American criminal justice system from colonial days to the present, locating this development in the context of social, political, legal, and economic issues. He elucidates the making of criminal law and ways in which behaviors come to be defined as criminal. The book covers each of the three major components of the criminal justice system: law enforcement, the courts, and prisons.

Gabel, Katherine, and Denise Johnston. *Children of Incarcerated Parents.* New York: Free Press, 1997. 336 pages.

Gabel and Johnston address the effects of parental incarceration on children, the problems associated with caring for the children of incarcerated parents, and issues associated with loss of parental rights. They find that the age of the child at the time of separation, the length of the separation period, and the degree to which the child is familiar with the substitute caregivers affect the child's experience of long-term trauma and stress when a mother is incarcerated. Many women give birth while incarcerated, and for most inmates separation from the newborn is immediate. Gabel and Johnston describe long-term care nurseries in prisons, assessing the benefits to children and parents. Young children who are separated from their imprisoned mothers may suffer from posttraumatic stress syndrome. Incarcerated mothers sometimes lose track of their children when the children are placed outside of the family. Thus for some families years may pass after the mother's release before reunion occurs. The authors also discuss visitations of children with incarcerated parents, which tend to be limited in frequency and may never occur for those without transportation or the means to travel to a distant prison facility. This book provides guidance to social workers and others working with children of incarcerated parents to meet their needs, thus helping to prevent future delinquency and cross-generational incarceration. The authors provide suggestions for identifying the best time to intervene after trauma and explanations of how direct preventative and early intervention services can help children cope and remain crime-free. Several community-based programs and support structures are presented as means to create alternatives to women's incarceration and thereby reduce the impact and trauma of separation on children.

Gaddis, Thomas E., with an epilogue by Phyllis E. Gaddis. *Birdman of Alcatraz: The Story of Robert Stroud.* Comstock Book Distributors, 1989 (originally published in 1958). 272 pages.

Gaddis recounts the life story of inmate Robert "Birdman" Stroud, a convicted felon who served much of his life sentence at the U.S. Penitentiary on Alcatraz Island in California. Gaddis relates how Stroud overcame the hardships and limitations of years in prison, transforming himself from a brutal illiterate into a man respected throughout the world for his contributions to science. The details of Stroud's prison experience—most of it in solitary confinement—leave the reader with a sense of respect for a man who, despite his life circumstances, was able to develop his potential and become a world famous ornithologist.

Girshick, Lori B. *Soledad Women: Wives of Prisoners Speak Out.* Westport, Conn.: Praeger, 1996. 160 pages.

Girshick examines the impact of incarceration on prisoners' spouses and discusses ways in which spouses can influence the rehabilitation of offenders. Through interviews with the wives of twenty-five inmates from Soledad Prison in California, Girshick focuses on topics such as stigma, coping, finances, children, visitation, prison policies, and rehabilitation. This study shows that spouses are a stabilizing force that contributes to rehabilitation and the prevention of recidivism. This book accentuates the need for the criminal justice system to include spouses and intimate partners of offenders as resources in the fight against crime. Recommendations are made for changing prison policy to reflect the importance of family relationships and encourage the maintenance of family ties.

Glaser, Daniel. *Preparing Convicts for Law-Abiding Lives: The Pioneering Penology of Richard A. McGee.* Albany, N.Y.: State University of New York Press, 1995. 224 pages.

Glaser evaluates the work of McGee, a former director of the California prison system who promoted rehabilitation and improved the management of inmates. Although McGee's principles and policies are out of favor today, he was a leader for more than thirty years in developing rehabilitation programs, expanding drug treatment services, instituting conjugal visits, and encouraging the assessment of programs to determine their effectiveness. The book draws on interviews with McGee and others who worked closely with him. His efforts reached beyond the California correctional system, influencing reform at the national level. McGee helped to make prison work a nonpolitical career service. He also improved inmate academic and vocational education, divided large prisons into autonomous smaller units, fostered prisoner contacts with their families, and encouraged new types of counseling. Furthermore, he developed more intensive supervision and assistance for both parolees and probationers. Perhaps most important, he insisted on evaluation of research in correctional institutions, including assessment of practices by controlled experiments.

Harden, Judy, and Marcia Hill (eds.). *Breaking the Rules: Women in Prison and Feminist Therapy.* Binghamton, N.Y.: Haworth Press, 1998. 255 pages.

Harden and Hill bring together essays contributed by experts in the fields of psychology, criminology, sociology, women's studies, and counseling. Their collaborative strategies and feminist perspective challenge the quality and type of prison programs and services available to female offenders. The book describes the experiences of women in prison, the impact of prison on female survivors of childhood sexual abuse, motherhood and mothers' programs in prison, and the influence of race and ethnicity on mothering and the care of prisoners' children. In addition, it deals with restorative justice in the treatment of female adolescent offenders, the histories of abuse of women who have murdered their abusive partners, treatment approaches for women, and the lack of treatment for addicted women prisoners. It also examines vocational and educational services for women in prison and a prison boot camp program. The authors lay out the major issues and offer solutions. Examples of several prison programs designed specifically with women in mind show how participants learn to connect with themselves, with others in the group, with their families, and with their communities. The book also describes programs that focus on coming to terms with the past, building a future, and developing individual strengths. This book provides information useful to scholars, therapists, public policymakers, and prison workers interested in finding treatment options that can help women with problems such as drug abuse, domestic violence, poverty, and prostitution rather than punishing them.

Harris, Jean. *Stranger in Two Worlds.* New York: Macmillan, 1986. 388 pages.

In 1981, Harris was convicted of murder and sentenced to prison for fifteen years to life. Her case was one of the media sensations of the 1980s. Here she presents her own story of her life before her conviction and during her imprisonment at New York's Bedford Hills Correctional Facility for Women. She describes her long relationship with Herman Tarnower and the events that led up to his death in March 1980. Harris also reminisces about her more than thirty-six years as a teacher and headmistress of an elite private girls' school. She describes her own criminal trial dispassionately. The most moving parts of this book are the chapters describing Harris's experiences in prison and presenting excerpts from her prison diary. She spent most of her prison time helping other women and working in the prison nursery. She taught parenting classes to young mothers and gave them moral support. Harris played a major role in the development of the Children's Center, a program for children to visit their mothers daily at the prison and spend time rebuilding their relationships. Host families participating in this program volunteer to house children of incarcerated women for a week and transport the children to the prison each day. Harris closes the book with thoughts about child care and the future of our children. She stresses her concerns about the fate of women who have spent time in prison and their children, along with the need to prepare female offenders better for survival in the outside world. In sum, this autobiography by a convicted female murderer gives us views of her unusual life prior to and after the crime.

Hassine, Victor. *Life Without Parole: Living in Prison Today,* edited by Thomas J. Bernard and Richard McCleary. Los Angeles: Roxbury, 1996. 158 pages.

Hassine, a convicted murderer sentenced in 1981 to prison for life without parole, provides an insightful look at life in an American prison. Most of the material is based on his experience as an inmate at the State Correctional Institution at Graterford, Pennsylvania. He describes the process of adapting to prison life, prison subcultures, and convict slang. He presents detailed accounts of living conditions, security issues, violence, politics, and the underground prison economy. Hassine also summarizes interviews with fellow inmates. As he narrates his experiences, Bernard and McCleary, scholars in the field of criminal justice, provide editorial notes to support and clarify the material presented.

Hawkes, Mary Q. *Excellent Effect: The Edna Mahan Story.* Laurel, Md.: American Correctional Association, 1994. 243 pages.

Hawkes recounts the life story of one of the most influential superintendents in U.S. prison history, Edna Mahan. Mahan served as superintendent of the New Jersey Reformatory for Women for forty years. Her commitment to rehabilitation and her willingness to experiment with innovative treatment approaches made her a leader not only in the field of women's prisons but also in corrections as a whole. Drawing on archival materials, interviews, and her own memories of working with Mahan, Hawkes simultaneously provides a biography of Mahan, a history of the New Jersey Reformatory, and an overview of women's evolving role in U.S. corrections.

Irwin, John, and James Austin. *It's About Time: America's Imprisonment Binge*, 2d ed. Belmont, Calif.: Wadsworth, 1997. 182 pages.

Irwin and Austin offer a critique of the U.S. prison system, up-to-date statistics, and a historical overview of the growth of the prison system. It is a concise, easy-to-read text that provides facts, explains issues, questions current policy, and challenges the primacy of prisons in our response to the crime problem.

Jackson, George. *Soledad Brother: The Prison Letters of George Jackson.* New York: Bantam Books, 1994 (originally published in 1970). 250 pages.

George Jackson, convicted in the 1960s of robbery and given one of California's then-common open-ended sentences, became a revolutionary in prison, self-educated by the works of Marx, Fanon, Mao, and Che Guevara. Through his prison letters to family, friends, and his lawyer, he presents a firsthand, brutal appraisal of the U.S. prison system. Jackson died in 1971 at California's San Quentin Prison in the course of what was apparently an attempt to break out. His book has become a symbol of both the Black Power movement and the prisoners' rights movement of the 1970s.

Jacobs, James B. *Stateville: The Penitentiary in Mass Society.* Chicago: University of Chicago Press, 1977. 281 pages.

One of the classics of the prison literature, this book presents a biography of a specific prison: Stateville, a large state institution outside Chicago. Opened in 1925, Stateville is one of the few penal institutions built in accordance with Jeremy Bentham's panopticon model of the circular prison, in which a guard in the center of the circle can (at least in theory) observe all the prisoners in the perimeter cells. For many years Stateville was administered by Warden Joseph Ragen, a tough, old-school manager who dominated both inmates and staff and ran his institution in an authoritarian manner. Although the book profiles only one prison, it sets that institution's history in social context, thus providing an overview of U.S. prisons in general in the early and mid–twentieth century. During that period prisons moved from being closed, tightly managed, and isolated institutions on the margins of society to being more open, accessible institutions in which Ragen-type dominance was no longer possible. Jacobs traces the rise of the prisoners' rights movement, the increasing fluidity between streets and prison as gangs became an important segment of the inmate population, the unionization of the guard force, and other factors that have changed the nature of incarceration and prison management in the course of the twentieth century.

James, Adrian, A. Keith Bottomley, Alison Liebling, and Emma Clare. *Privatizing Prisons: Rhetoric and Reality.* Thousand Oaks, Calif.: Sage Publications, 1997. 208 pages.

The authors explore theoretical, practical, and ethical issues associated with the privatization of prisons, a trend in which government bodies responsible for prisons increasingly turn to private companies for help with programs, food and health services, and in some cases complete management of a penal institution. Though their primary focus is on the United Kingdom's privatization experience, the authors provide a comparative discussion of private-sector involvement in the United Kingdom, North America, Europe, and Australia.

Johnson, Robert. *Death Work: A Study of the Modern Execution Process.* Pacific Grove, Calif.: Brooks-Cole, 1990. 174 pages.

This study begins by putting executions in historical perspective, and proceeds to detail executions in the twentieth century and describe life on death row. A section titled "In Cold Blood" outlines the work of the modern execution team and describes an actual execution and its aftermath. In the conclusion Johnson reviews moral considerations raised by the death penalty.

Johnson, Robert. *Hard Time: Understanding and Reforming the Prison,* 2d ed. Belmont, Calif.: Wadsworth, 1996. 336 pages.

Johnson, a criminal justice professor, examines the historical and philosophical context of incarceration in the United States. He provides material on life in contemporary maximum-security prisons for male inmates. Presenting statistics and research findings, Johnson also discusses the realities of prison life, the management and social control of inmates, and the role of rehabilitation in prison operations. Although Johnson continues to support the goal of rehabilitation, he suggests that improved strategies and better treatment models are required actually to achieve this goal. This readable book offers a thorough and thoughtful introduction to prison life and controversies about prison management.

Liberatore, Paul. *The Road to Hell: The True Story of George Jackson and Stephen Bingham and the San Quentin Massacre.* Emeryville, Calif.: Grove-Atlantic, 1996. 270 pages.

Liberatore, a journalist, provides a compelling and fast-paced account of the 1971 San Quentin massacre that involved George Jackson, the Black Panther leader and author of the prison memoir *Soledad Brother,* and his lawyer, Stephen Bingham, a radical New Leftist. Liberatore traces the relationship of these two men and examines the civil rights and antiwar struggles of the 1960s as a way of clarifying how American politics may have influenced prisons and the behavior that led up to the San Quentin massacre. Jackson set off the disturbance that ultimately resulted in his own death as well as the death of three prison guards and two other inmates. Bingham seems to have provided Jackson with the gun used in the disturbance. Liberatore presents character profiles of each man and shows the vast contrast between Jackson, a working-class black man convicted of a $70 robbery, and Bingham, a white Yale-educated lawyer from a prominent New England family. The latter half of the book presents a detailed account of Bingham's exile in Europe after the shootings and his return to the United States to face trial in 1983; it is a stunning and emotional presentation of the final events in a deadly sequence.

Lombardo, Lucien X. 1989. *Guards Imprisoned: Correctional Officers at Work,* 2d ed. Cincinnati, Ohio: Anderson, 1996. 250 pages.

Lombardo, a former teacher at Auburn Prison in New York State and now a professor of criminal justice, provides an in-depth examination of the working life of correctional officers, as they perceive and experience it, in a maximum-security prison for men. This study is based on extensive interviews with correctional officers, observational research, and the author's own experience of working inside a prison. Lombardo explores the role of the officer in the life of the prison community and the factors that shape the officer's role. This study offers a personal and human examination of life behind bars as seen through the eyes of the prison officer. It views officers as people rather than as stereotypical disciplinarians and custodians, and, surprisingly, it finds that this is a view often shared by inmates.

Marquart, James W., and Jonathan R. Sorenson (eds.). *Correctional Contexts: Contemporary and Classical Readings.* Los Angeles: Roxbury, 1997. 492 pages.

This collection of essays presents an overview of the major issues and developments in American corrections. Readings from some of the key contributors to the field such as Brockway, Clemmer, Foucault, Lombardo, Martinson, Rothman, and Sykes are included. The compendium reflects on historical change and addresses central controversies in contemporary corrections.

Martin, Steve J., and Sheldon Ekland-Olson. *Texas Prisons: The Walls Came Tumbling Down.* Austin: Texas Monthly Press, 1987. 289 pages.

This is a fascinating account of brutality and prison reform in Texas leading up to the 1980 *Ruiz v. Estelle* decision that found that the state's prisons were operating unconstitutionally. Wayne J. Estelle, the head of the prison system at the time, was widely respected for running a safe, if tough, prison system. Beneath the surface, however, it was one of the most brutal systems in the nation, especially because of the lack of oversight and the state's method of saving money by appointing the roughest inmates to maintain order in the cell blocks (the infamous "building tender" system). Inmates complained to a federal court, and after a titanic battle, during which the state apparently had some prisoner-witnesses killed, the court outlawed the building tender system and demanded a host of reforms. This is one of the most sobering books on the subject of prisoner discipline, prison management, and court-based prison reform.

McConnell, Elizabeth Huffmaster, and Laura J. Moriarty. *American Prisons: An Annotated Bibliography.* Westport, Conn.: Greenwood Press, 1998. 344 pages.

This is a comprehensive and up-to-date bibliography of publications on U.S. prisons. Searches may be conducted by author's last name and by subject area. Listings include annotations for landmark cases related to corrections.

McShane, Marilyn D., and Franklin P. Williams. *Encyclopedia of American Prisons.* New York: Garland, 1996. 560 pages.

This encyclopedia offers a comprehensive overview of corrections in the United States in more than 160 essays covering prison history, operations, problems, and social and legal issues. The volume opens with a brief history of U.S. prisons from 1773 to 1993, and essays follow in alphabetical order by topic. Although the organization and treatment of the topics within each essay vary, most articles contain some historical discussion to frame the issue, explanations of important developments and trends in the topic, and a bibliography for further reading. Biographies of significant individuals in prison history are included, as are histories of famous prisons and extended explanations of selected terms encountered in prison studies. Entries on current concerns such as crowding, elderly inmates, diversity, mental illness, and health care issues help the reader to gain a general understanding of the issues confronting corrections today. They also provide direction for future research and assessment. This encyclopedia is an objective, reliable, and authoritative source of current information about U.S. penal institutions.

Morris, Norval, and David J. Rothman (eds.). *The Oxford History of the Prison: The Practice of Punishment in Western Society.* New York: Oxford University Press, 1995. 512 pages.

Two distinguished scholars trace the emergence and evolution of the prison from biblical times to the present, in the process also painting a portrait of the social world of prisoners over the centuries. The book includes more than 100 illustrations, sixteen of them color plates. Eight historical essays and six articles on particular topics specific to issues of imprisonment, such as juvenile detention, Australian prison colonies, women in prison over the ages, development of the local jail, and political prisoners, provide an overview of prisons in the United States, Great Britain, and to a lesser extent, Continental Europe. Although this volume provides a historical and contemporary perspective on how criminals were punished through the ages, it focuses primarily on the rise of the prison in England and the United States. Particularly useful are its extensive chapter bibliographies.

Morris, Roger. *The Devil's Butcher Shop: The New Mexico Prison Uprising.* Albuquerque: University of New Mexico Press, 1988 (originally published in 1983). 168 pages.

This may be the best book written about a prison riot. It is certainly the best of the many books about the New Mexico Penitentiary riot of 1980, the most brutal disturbance in U.S. prison history. Morris, a journalist, skillfully places the events in their social and historical contexts. He documents the long series of administrative missteps and the public indifference that led up to the violence. He also takes us step by step through the events of the riot, from the overpowering of the guards to the mutilation of inmates in protective segregation, and at the end, he reminds us that the responsibility for maintaining decent penal institutions lies with voters.

New York State Special Commission on Attica. *Attica: The Official Report.* New York: Bantam Books, 1972. 533 pages.

This is the detailed and riveting report of the investigation of the 1971 Attica Prison uprising that left forty-three people dead, most of them killed (and eighty others wounded) during the fifteen minutes it took the State Police to retake the prison. This is the definitive report on one of the nation's worst prison disturbances. It is also a deeply disturbing documentation of the racism that pervaded New York's prison system at the time of the uprising and that was one of its central causes.

O'Shea, Kathleen A. *Women and the Death Penalty in the United States, 1900–1998.* Westport, Conn.: Praeger, 1998. 424 pages.

Examining women and the death penalty in the United States from 1900 to 1998, the author provides information on the legal foundations of capital punishment and methods of execution for each of the states that authorize the death penalty. Adding a personal dimension, O'Shea incorporates stories from interviews with women who have since been executed or who are currently on death row. This book offers a gender perspective on the recurring sociopolitical and moral issues associated with execution.

Palmer, Ted. *A Profile of Correctional Effectiveness and New Directions for Research.* Albany, N.Y.: State University of New York Press, 1994. 339 pages.

Palmer provides an updated analysis of the large body of research on the effectiveness of correctional control, treatment, and rehabilitation. Raising important issues, he discusses contemporary methods for understanding why and how certain programs work.

Pisciotta, Alexander W. *Benevolent Repression: Social Control and the American Reformatory-Prison Movement.* New York: New York University Press, 1996. 197 pages.

Pisciotta presents a unique history of the adult reformatory movement between 1876 and 1920, focusing on the establishment of a system of rehabilitative prisons for young men. Drawing upon previously unexamined sources from over a half dozen states as well as on seven inmate case histories and a decade of research, Pisciotta describes the reformatory philosophy of humane, constructive, and charitable treatment. However, he also invalidates the myth that American reformatories represented progress in the treatment of criminals and youthful offenders. Pisciotta demonstrates the disparity between the reformatory philosophy and actual practices. He concludes that the reformatory movement became an active agent for social control of the lower classes. A close examination of New York's Elmira Reformatory finds that prisoners under Superintendent Zebulon Brockway (the "father of American corrections") were in fact whipped, restricted to bread and water during months of solitary confinement, and brutally subjected to a wide range of other physical and psychological abuses. Escapes, riots, violence, drug use, suicide, arson, and rape were commonplace in reformatories. Reflecting the racism and sexism of the general social order, the new penology legitimized the repression of the lower classes. This study fills an important gap in the historical literature of penal history and reform.

Pollack, Joycelyn M. *Counseling Women in Prison.* Thousand Oaks, Calif.: Sage Publications, 1998. 219 pages.

Pollock presents an overview of the female offender, women's prisons, and clinical treatment approaches for women. She provides an understanding of criminological theory as it pertains to female offending and discusses sociological factors, the prison environment, background characteristics of the female offender, classification, family and cultural issues, drug abuse, and prison programs designed specifically for female offenders.

Rafter, Nicole Hahn. *Creating Born Criminals.* Urbana, Ill.: University of Illinois Press, 1997. 320 pages.

This is a social history of the impact of biological theories of crime on the prison system. Dealing simultaneously with the history of residential "schools" for persons with mental retardation and with prisons, Rafter shows how, in the mid–nineteenth century, public sentiment began to shift toward the opinion that persons with mental retardation are inherently criminalistic.

When eugenicists (reformers intent on improving the human race through better "breeding") took up this theme of inborn criminality, the result was a movement for life incarceration of mentally retarded criminals, to prevent them from producing more of their kind. Rafter reveals the impact of eugenic criminology on the prison system through the establishment of eugenic prisons with up-to-life sentences and, in some cases, through sterilization of inmates. She also discusses the implications of eugenic criminology and eugenic prisons for biological theories of crime today.

Rafter, Nicole Hahn. *Partial Justice: Women, Prisons, and Social Control,* 2d ed. New Brunswick, N.J.: Transaction Publishers, 1990. 290 pages.

This is the only history of women's prisons to cover the entire United States. Starting with the treatment of women in early and mid–nineteenth century men's prisons, Rafter shows how even treatment that was similar on the surface resulted in harsher conditions for the women, because of their much smaller numbers in these institutions and strong social sentiment against female criminals. Aware of these problems and anxious to rescue their less fortunate "sisters," late-nineteenth-century middle-class feminists founded a new kind of prison, the reformatory, designed solely for women and staffed entirely by other women. Rafter traces the reformatory movement as it spread throughout the United States and then died out about 1930. Subsequent chapters discuss the other main model of women's prison, the custodial model; race and racism in state prisons for women; and the development of the women's prison system since 1935. A final chapter on the "parity movement" describes how feminists and others are responding today to the perennial problem of sex discrimination in prisons.

Reiman, Jeffrey H. *The Rich Get Richer and the Poor Get Prison: Ideology, Class, and Criminal Justice,* 5th ed. Needham Heights, Mass.: Allyn & Bacon, 1997. 288 pages.

Reiman takes a hard look at the notion of social dangerousness, arguing that white collar crime is our biggest threat to life and limb and that it is far more costly than street crime. This is one of the most readable and thought-provoking works on the role of prisons in society today.

Rideau, Wilbert, and Ron Wikberg (eds.). *Life Sentences: Rage and Survival Behind Bars.* New York: Time Books, 1992. 342 pages.

This firsthand account by prisoners reprints columns that originally appeared in *The Angolite,* the newspaper of the Louisiana State Penitentiary at Angola. In addition to presenting riveting pictures of prison life from inmates' viewpoints, the book is also useful as an account of life in a specifically *Southern* state prison, where, historically, routines differed considerably from those of Northern prisons. The frequently cited chapter titled "The Sexual Jungle" gives a graphic account of the nature and meaning of prison rape. Another chapter describes life on death row, and a third focuses on dying from natural causes in prison. One of the editors, Rideau, is one of the most famous prisoners in the United States. A long-term editor of *The Angolite,* he has since moved on to working in radio and film, despite his life sentence at one of the harshest prisons in the United States.

Shichor, David. *Punishment for Profit: Private Prisons/Public Concerns.* Thousand Oaks, Calif.: Sage Publishing, 1995. 293 pages.

Shichor addresses the economic, legal, managerial, philosophical, theoretical, and quality-control issues involved in the operation of private prisons, contrasting their merits with those of traditional, public prisons. Focusing on public policy, Shichor provides valuable empirical data on private prison programs and operations and assesses program effectiveness. This is the most thorough recent contribution to the literature on prison privatization, and it offers comprehensive references for additional resources on this topic.

Sullivan, Larry E. *The Prison Reform Movement: Forlorn Hope.* Boston: Twayne, 1990. 200 pages.

Sullivan, a historian, became interested in prison reform in the 1970s, when he was the librarian at the Maryland State Penitentiary, at that time the second oldest maximum security prison still in use in the United States. He examines the various philosophies that support differing goals of punishment, focusing on rehabilitation and the implementation of prison treatment programs. Sullivan questions the validity of rehabilitation, pointing to high recidivism rates, and argues that the primary function of incarceration is punishment.

Useem, Bert, Camille G. Camp, and George M. Camp. *Resolution of Prison Riots: Strategies and Policies.* New York: Oxford University Press, 1996. 232 pages.

This book addresses the causes of prison riots and presents strategies for avoiding serious violent outbreaks. Better prison policies, improvements in administration and communications, and more sophisticated control strategies can help prison managers avoid future incidents. This study examines the developments that led to eight major American prison riots, the events that occurred during the riots, and the aftermath of the riots. Extensive details on each riot provide the reader with an inside view of actual events and the process of regaining organizational control. The case studies are used to explore issues related to conflict management, negotiations, the use of force, and strategies of administrative organization. The research analyzes the options for ending a prison riot while minimizing the amount of damage and costs.

Walens, Susann. *War Stories: An Oral History of Life Behind Bars.* Westport, Conn.: Praeger, 1997. 200 pages.

Walens introduces the life experiences of fifteen men in a maximum-security prison. She enables us to hear the voices of prisoners as they express their thoughts about the roots of crime and the efficiency of the criminal justice system. The stories told by these prisoners force readers to question the easy categories usually used to determine guilt and innocence. Some of the men arouse our indignation, and others compel us to question the workings of the criminal justice system. A few illustrate the ignorance and prejudice that can lie behind the desire to "lock 'em up and throw away the key." The book brings readers close to men who are sometimes simultaneously perpetrators and victims of criminal behavior.

Watterson, Kathryn. *Women in Prison: Inside the Concrete Womb,* rev. ed. Boston: Northeastern University Press, 1996. 402 pages.

This is a reprint of a book originally published by Watterson in the early 1970s, with a new preface by Meda Chesney-Lind, a well-known feminist criminologist. The text discusses such matters as fitting the punishment to the crime, the profile of the woman who ends up in prison, the nature of incarceration in a women's institution, and forced dependency on prison. Incorporating hundreds of interviews with both female inmates and correctional officers, Watterson is able to profile the criminal activities and summarize the personal experiences of women serving time. The trauma of separation from their children, the process of building prison relationships, the effects of excessive security, and the stress of returning to society upon release, are all described in this detailed study, which characterizes the internal culture and living environment typical of women's prisons as a "concrete womb." The author finds that the system often treats females more harshly than males who committed the same or similar crimes and that it often fails to deliver adequate medical care, mental health services, and other treatment programs.

Williams, Vergil L. *Dictionary of American Penology*, rev. ed. Westport, Conn.: Greenwood, 1996. 504 pages.

This dictionary gives concise information on a broad variety of topics in American penology. Each entry is followed by references and cross-references to clarify technical terminology. Entries cover such topics as administrative structures, adult and adolescent institutional populations, and budgets and provides information on programs, state and federal prison system addresses, prison-reform organizations, statistics, trends, and new concepts.

Williford, Miriam (ed.). *Higher Education in Prison: A Contradiction in Terms?* Phoenix, Ariz.: Oryx Press, 1996. 194 pages.

Williford's book presents the results of studies of more than 300 continuing education programs that provide courses to more than 50,000 inmates around the country each year. Contributors discuss the different course offerings and programs that service this student population. They suggest that courses directed toward inmates should include more than the basic course material. Inmate courses should also focus on life issues, personal improvement, goal fulfillment, and acquiring the educational and vocational credentials and life skills necessary for achieving success in the community upon release.

Wright, Richard A. *In Defense of Prisons*. Westport, Conn.: Greenwood, 1993. 216 pages.

Reviewing the topics of punishment, incapacitation, imprisonment, and crime deterrence, Wright offers a comprehensive examination of the effectiveness of prisons. He provides evidence that supports conventional imprisonment policies, and he offers sentencing recommendations that may maximize the effectiveness of prisons as agents of social control. Wright defends prisons, which he views as an important social institution. His research shows that prisons are moderately effective in achieving specific and general deterrence and collective and selective incapacitation. This book is useful for its presentation of the research literature and for raising important issues related to prison reform.

Zehr, Howard. *Doing Life: Reflections on Men and Women Serving Life Sentences.* Intercourse, Pa.: Good Books, 1996. 124 pages.

Zehr, director of the Mennonite Central Committee's U.S. Office on Crime and Justice, actively promotes victim/offender reconciliation programs and a form of restorative justice focused on offender accountability. His book provides both a narrative and materials based on more than sixty interviews with men and women serving life sentences in the Pennsylvania prison system. The inmates discuss the impact of their crimes and reflect on their experiences, feelings, loneliness, and coping strategies.

Zimmer, Lynn E. *Women Guarding Men.* Chicago: University of Chicago Press, 1986. 264 pages.

More than a book about prisons, Zimmer's work is a study of social change. It examines the struggles of the earliest female correction officers, who entered a world that others believed should be closed to women. This study embodies feminist perspectives on women's occupational opportunities as it follows women breaking into the all-male world of the men's maximum-security prison. Chapters are based on interviews with female and male guards, inmates, and prison administrators. Zimmer documents the daily reality of female officers fighting discrimination and hostility from male officers and inmates. The book also documents the results of women's entry into the subculture of male officers. This book has become one of the classics in the literature on the sociology of work and on women in criminal justice occupations.

Journals, Magazines, and Newsletters

The Angolite
Louisiana State Penitentiary
Angola, LA 70712
Bimonthly. $24.00.

This news magazine, published by and for the inmates of the Louisiana State Penitentiary at Angola, is the most lively and informative prison journal in the United States. It highlights current issues, recent and upcoming events, and aspects of daily life at the penitentiary and presents convict opinions on such topics as parole, prison accreditation, and habitual offender laws.

Correctional Law Reporter
Civic Research Institute
4490 U.S. Route 27, PO Box 585
Kingston, NJ 08528
(609) 683-4450
Fax: (609) 683-7291
Bimonthly. $142.00.

This journal is devoted to helping administrators manage their facilities, staff, and inmate populations more effectively. Articles address legal issues in correctional programming, supervised release, probation, and parole.

Corrections Compendium
American Correctional Association
Tel: (800) 222-5646, ext. 1879
Monthly. $75.00.

A monthly newsletter published by the American Correctional Association, the compendium compiles information from fifty-two U.S. and thirteen Canadian correctional systems. It provides feature articles, updates on legal issues, current news, and statistical summaries on a state-by-state basis. Articles are concerned with prisons, jails, probation and parole, juvenile justice systems, community-based corrections, and private correctional services.

Corrections Today
American Correctional Association Publications
4380 Forbes Boulevard
Lanham, MD 20706

(301) 918-1800
Seven issues per year. ACA Professional I member: $35.00; ACA Professional II member: $75.00.

This magazine covers contemporary corrections, practitioner issues, and controversies related to policy and professional development. (From 1954 to 1979 it was called *American Journal of Correction.*)

Earth Bridge
Earthbridge People of the Red Tail Sunny Chobeka-sepe
PO Box 1872
Jeff City, MO 65102
Biannual. No cost.

This is a newsletter by and for Native American prisoners and their outside supporters.

Federal Prisons Journal
U.S. Department of Justice, Federal Bureau of Prisons
320 First Street, NW, Room 738
Washington, DC 20534
(202) 514-6655
Internet: http://www.bop.gov
Quarterly. No cost.

This journal features articles on management issues and policies related to the federal prison system.

International Journal of Offender Therapy
and Comparative Criminology
Sage Publications, Inc.
2455 Teller Road
Thousand Oaks, CA 91320-2218
(805) 499-9774
Quarterly. Individual: $45.00; institutional: $169.20.

This journal provides a forum for the advancement of research in offender treatment across a wide range of disciplines. It offers therapists, counselors, researchers, policymakers, and other professionals reports on relevant research conducted around the world.

Journal of Correctional Health Care
National Commission of Correctional Health Care
1300 W. Belmont St.
Chicago, IL 60657

(773) 880-1460
Fax: (773) 880-2424
Biannual. $30.00.

This journal, formerly known as the *Journal of Prison and Jail Health Care,* addresses issues and current research at the juncture of medicine, law, corrections, and ethics. It provides a forum for professionals involved in the provision of health care in prisons and jails.

Journal of Offender Rehabilitation
Haworth Press
10 Alice Street
Binghamton, NY 13904
(607) 722-5857
Fax: (607) 722-6362
Quarterly. $60.

This journal, formerly known as the *Journal of Offender Counseling, Services, and Rehabilitation* (1979–1990), focuses on current treatment modalities and on research related to the rehabilitation of criminal offenders.

National Prison Project Journal
National Prison Project
ACLU Foundation
1875 Connecticut Avenue, NW, #410
Washington, DC 20009
(202) 234-4830
Quarterly. $30.00.

A publication of the American Civil Liberties Union, this journal contains valuable information on current prisoners' rights litigation and recent case law pertaining to prisoners' rights.

Overcrowded Times
Castine Research Corporation
PO Box 110
Castine, ME 04421
(207) 326-9521
Fax: (207) 326-9528
Bimonthly. Individual: $35; institutional: $75.

This journal presents the most recent information on sentencing, state policies for dealing with prison overcrowding, and innovations in community corrections. Recent issues have covered current research and policies regarding boot camps, electronic monitoring, house arrest, day fines, intensive supervision, day reporting, victim-offender mediation, and sentencing reform.

The Prison Journal
Sage Publications, Inc.
2455 Teller Street
Thousand Oaks, CA 91320-2218
(805) 499-9774
Quarterly. Individual, $53.00; institutional, $135.00.

This journal, the official publication of the Pennsylvania Prison Society, provides an international forum for research on and policy discussions of incarceration and alternative sanctions. It reports on current research projects and on advances in theory, policy, and practice. Articles cover state-of-the-art programs, policy debates, and evaluation surveys. The journal offers a diversity of perspectives across a range of disciplines, and its coverage is international in scope.

Prison Law Monitor
Institution Educational Services
1806 T Street, NW
Washington, DC 20009
Quarterly. $25.00.

This journal discusses current legislation and litigation pertaining to prisoners and correctional policy. Recent issues have featured articles on case law and on current legal and policy issues related to prisoners' rights, correctional law and practice, and prisoners' legal status.

Punishment and Society:
The International Journal of Penology
Sage Publications
Thousand Oaks, CA 91320-2218
E-mail: journal@sagepub.com
Quarterly. Individual: $28.00; institutional: $100.00.

This new journal, which started publication in July 1999, aims at providing an international, interdisciplinary forum for research and scholarship dealing with punishment, penal institutions, penal theory, and penal control. It will also cover philosophical, cultural, and historical aspects of punishment. Articles will represent a range of disciplinary perspectives including criminology, penology, the sociology of punishment, history, law, and philosophy. The journal plans to include book reviews, symposia, and debates as well as coverage of recent developments.

Sexual Abuse: A Journal of Research and Treatment
Association for the Treatment of Sexual Abusers
10700 SW Beaverton-Hillsdale Highway, Suite 26
Beaverton, OR 97005-3035
Quarterly. Individual: $40.00; institutional: $100.00.

This publication, formerly the *Annals of Sex Research,* is the official journal of the Association for the Treatment of Sexual Abusers. It a forum for contemporary research on both clinical and theoretical aspects of sexual abuse. It also covers assessment and treatment of the sexual offender, the effects of sexual abuse on victims and families, and the causes of sexual offending. It aims at a readership of clinicians and academics, including psychologists, psychiatrists, social workers, therapists/counselors, corrections officers, and allied professionals.

Government Documents and Agency Publications

American Correctional Association. *Directory of Juvenile and Adult Correctional Departments, Institutions, Agencies, and Paroling Authorities.* Laurel, Md.: American Correctional Association, 1998. 783 pages.

This annual publication contains information on more than 4,000 U.S. and Canadian state and federal penal institutions. The directory offers both a facilities locator and a personnel locator. Historical background, security level, capacity, population, and details on current trends, budgets, and anticipated costs for each facility are provided. Also included for each institution are addresses, fax and telephone numbers, and a list of programs and services offered. The manual also offers summaries of such areas as expenditures and budgets, populations, programs and services, and personnel. This is the best source of current profiles of individual institutions and of all the institutions in particular jurisdictions.

American Correctional Association. *Vital Statistics in Corrections, 1998.* Laurel, Md.: American Correctional Association, 1999. 100 pages.

This is an up-to-date volume of statistical information on facility administration and management, staff, budgets, training, programming, offender populations, and aftercare services. Published annually, this handbook includes graphs, tables, and charts.

Bloom, Barbara, and David Steinhart. *Why Punish the Children? A Reappraisal of the Children of Incarcerated Mothers in America.* San Francisco: National Council on Crime and Delinquency, 1992. 87 pages.

This policy analysis is addresses a by-product of the increasing rates of female incarceration: the growth of an invisible class of children (infants, toddlers, and teenagers) with mothers behind bars. The authors discuss the powerlessness of government agencies to attend to the needs of children, mothers, and alternate caregivers and the need for a renewed commitment to serve this population. They describe deficiencies in the systems that handle custody matters and services for children and their incarcerated parents.

Bureau of Justice Statistics Publications. What follows is a partial listing of BJS publications pertaining to prisons. The easiest way to order these documents is through the Internet: http://www.ojp.usdoj.gov/bjs/pubalp2.htm. In what follows, the order number of each document appears after its title.

Capital Punishment 1997. NCJ 172881.

Census of State and Federal Correctional Facilities, 1995. NCJ 166582.

Challenging the Conditions of Prisons and Jails: A Report on Section 1983 Litigation. NCJ 151652.

Comparing Federal and State Prison Inmates, 1991. NCJ 145864.

Correctional Populations in the United States, 1995. NCJ 163916 (Executive Summary: NCJ 163917).

National Corrections Reporting Program, 1992. NCJ 145862. *Prisoners in 1997.* NCJ 170014.

Prisoner Petitions in the Federal Courts, 1980–96. NCJ 164615.

Sourcebook of Criminal Justice Statistics, 1997. NCJ 171147.

Survey of State Prison Inmates, 1991. NCJ 136949.

Violent Offenders in State Prison: Sentences and Time Served—State Inmates, 1992–94. NCJ 154632.
Women in Prison. NCJ 145321.

Cahalan, Margaret Werner, and Lee Anne Parsons. *Historical Corrections Statistics in the United States, 1850–1984.* U.S. Department of Justice, Bureau of Justice Statistics, 1986. NCJ 102529.

This report, which can be found in many libraries, provides summary tables and commentary on government-published corrections statistics for the period of 1850 (when such reporting began) to 1984. It provides data on institutional populations, capital punishment, state and federal prison systems, jails, institutions for juvenile delinquents, probation, and parole. This is a particularly valuable resource for anyone interested in the history of incarceration in the United States.

Correctional Association of New York. *Rehabilitation That Works: Improving and Expanding Shock Incarceration and Similar Programs in New York State.* New York: Correctional Association of New York, 1996.

This report examines prison and community-based programs designed to rehabilitate inmates and implemented in New York State in recent years.

Faiver, Kenneth L. *Health Care Management Issues for Corrections.* Laurel, Md.: American Correctional Association, 1998. 285 pages.

In this overview of correctional health-care services and practices throughout the United States, Faiver presents a guide for building a working relationship between correctional staff and health-care professionals. Practical concerns, policy issues, and current trends are discussed, and the trends in correctional health-care services are outlined in the context of the large variations among correctional populations and the varying needs of different types of inmates. The book emphasizes, as matters of particular concern, the mental health care needs of inmates, ethical issues, the quality of institutional health care, access to health care in correctional settings, and the trend toward privatizing health-care services in penal facilities.

Hayes, Lindsay M. *Prison Suicide: An Overview and Guide to Prevention.* Washington, D.C.: National Center on Institutions and Alternatives, 1995. 107 pages.

This publication discusses the magnitude of the problem of suicide in prison and presents results of a survey of all fifty state departments of correction, plus the prison department of the District of Columbia and the Federal Bureau of Prisons regarding their suicide policies and procedures. It also reviews the literature available on the subject, national and state standards for prison suicide prevention, and the involvement of courts in this matter. In addition, it describes effective prison suicide prevention programs in operation at two state prisons and at federal institutions.

Human Rights Watch Women's Rights Project. *All Too Familiar: Sexual Abuse of Women in U.S. State Prisons.* New York: Human Rights Watch, 1996. 347 pages.

This study documents the sexual abuse of women in U.S. prisons. Being a female inmate in a U.S. penal institution can be a terrifying experience. If one is sexually abused, one cannot escape an abuser. Grievance or investigatory procedures, where they exist, often do not work, and correctional employees continue to engage in abuse because they believe they can get away with it. Few people outside prison walls are aware of the problem, and those who do know about it do little or nothing to address it. *All Too Familiar* gives historical background on the issue and reviews pertinent national and international law. It sets forth details on the problem in six jurisdictions. An appendix sets forth standard minimum rules for the treatment of prisoners, and the first chapter summarizes the project's recommendation to the federal government.

Maruschak, Laura. *HIV in Prisons and Jails, 1995.* Bureau of Justice Statistics, Washington, D.C.: U.S. Department of Justice, 1997. (Annual bulletin.) 12 pages.

This bulletin, like its predecessors, provides information on the number of HIV-positive and active AIDS cases among prisoners held in each state and the federal prison system. For prisons, the report provides data on the number of AIDS-related deaths, HIV testing policies, differences between women and men in the number of AIDS cases, and comparisons with AIDS rates in the general population.

Morash, Merry, Timothy S. Bynum, and Barbara A. Koons. *Women Offenders: Programming Needs and Promising Approaches.* Washington, D.C.: National Institute of Justice, 1998. 11 pages.

The authors address the gender-specific treatment needs of female offenders. They present the results of a survey of state-level correctional administrators, jail administrators, and program administrators to determine these special needs. The survey elicited the respondents' perceptions of assessment, screening, management, and programming issues regarding female offenders. On the basis of the survey results, the authors report on innovative programs that address the disproportionate numbers of victims of sexual and physical abuse in women's prisons as well as female prisoners' addiction to drugs and alcohol, mental illnesses, child care responsibilities, and difficulties in finding employment prior to incarceration. The results presented in this report provide an important first step in improving treatment and in assessing female offenders' programs and services.

Morton, JoAnn (ed.). *Complex Challenges, Collaborative Solutions: Programming for Adult and Juvenile Female Offenders.* Laurel, Md.: American Correctional Association, 1998. 325 pages.

Issues associated with adult and juvenile female offenders and their treatment needs are discussed throughout this edited volume. Experts in the field of female corrections present readings on current problems and controversies. Model community and institutional treatment programs are outlined along with information on their impact on reducing female offending and preventing juveniles from moving into adult crime.

National Institute of Corrections. *Prison Medical Care: Special Needs Populations and Cost Control.* Washington, D.C.: National Institute of Corrections Information Center, 1997. 15 pages.

This report summarizes approaches used by state corrections agencies to care for elderly, terminally ill, and chronically ill inmates. It also discusses agencies' involvement in controlling overall costs for prison medical services through telemedicine, inmate fees, automation, managed care, and contracted medical services.

Nonprint Resources

Had this chapter been written twenty years ago, its main section, which covers films, would have been easily subdivided into documentary films on the one hand and fictional films on the other. Moreover, most of what was available in the way of prison-related fictional films would have been excluded on the ground that they were not sufficiently modeled on reality to be instructive on prisons or prison life. Over the past twenty years, however, the lines between fact and fiction, documentary and drama, have blurred, so that it is no longer so easy to distinguish between documentary films about (for instance) death row and fictional films that use paid actors and staged events to deal with the same topic.

This point about the partial merger of documentaries and fictional films can be illustrated with filmed versions of the Attica Prison riot of 1971, an event that riveted the nation for a full week and left forty-three dead. Because of the heavy involvement of the press in the negotiations between the prisoners and state officials, Attica was a well-filmed event. Especially dramatic is footage taken from the perspective of national guardsmen on the wall, just before they started firing into the yard where the prisoners and hostages were gathered. Such footage was turned into a documentary shortly after the riot. However, it is now difficult to locate a copy of this original film, and the original is in some ways less effective than the made-for-television recreation of Attica events listed below. Although the made-for-television version adheres closely to the historical events, its cameras also depict scenes that were off-limits to cameramen during the actual riot. Moreover, the actual prisoners' appearances—their afro haircuts and bell-bottom pants, for example—tend to distract today's viewers from the events themselves. Thus in some ways, the made-for-television film is more effective than the original footage.

Another example of the tendency toward merger of documentary and fiction films can be found in *Dead Man Walking,* the 1995 film starring Susan Sarandon and Sean Penn. As a commercial Hollywood movie, this is the sort of film that twenty years ago would not have been considered suitable for serious students of the American prison. Yet it closely follows actual events in the life of a real person, Sister Helen Prejean, who befriended a rapist-killer on death row at the Louisiana State Penitentiary. Although *Dead Man Walking* fictionalizes actual events, it does not prettify them, and it offers an accurate, close-up view of death row to which most viewers would not otherwise have access.

Thus the following list includes a range of film types, from the purely documentary to fictional movies based on actual events. (However, there are no entries for purely fictional films such as *The Shawshank Redemption,* which was derived from a Stephen King novel and, although entertaining, does not present an accurate picture of prison life.) The films listed here were selected on the basis of a single, overriding criterion: the degree to which they provide an accurate view of some aspect of incarceration today. Most people never see the inside of a prison, and those who do usually see only a small segment of prison life. Thus the following list aims at giving readers close-up views of daily activities and unusual events in American prisons.

In addition to listing films, this chapter also provides information on another type of nonprint resource on American prisons: Internet sites. This section is much shorter, because Chapters 6 and 7 have already covered a great deal of ground on using the Internet for information on prison operations. However, its purpose, like that of the section on films, is to guide readers to materials that will increase their understanding of the American prison system.

Films

Against the Wall

Type:	VHS, color
Length:	110 minutes
Date:	1994
Cost:	Purchase $12.99, rental $4.50
Source:	Reel, Inc.

2655 Shattuck Avenue
Berkeley, CA 94704
(888) 707-7335
Internet: http://www.reel.com

This video, made for HBO TV, is based on the true story of the uprising at Attica Prison in 1971. It presents details of the days leading up to the uprising, the four long days of negotiations, and the deadly outcome. Exposing poor management practices and lack of communication among administrators, staff, and inmates, the film explores difficult issues of control. This video is of particular use for investigating the problems that may lead to a riot and for demonstrating the trauma and loss that can result from a major riot and hostage situation. It is also useful for developing training strategies and riot prevention plans.

Aileen Wuornos: The Selling of a Serial Killer

Type:	VHS, color
Length:	87 minutes
Date:	1992
Cost:	Purchase $19.95 (item #53-823)
Source:	Movies Unlimited

3015 Darnell Road
Philadelphia, PA 19154-3295
(800) 4-MOVIES
E-mail: movies@moviesunlimited.com

This documentary focuses on the death-row inmate known as "America's first female serial killer." Director Nick Broomfield traveled to Florida to interview Wuornos, a former prostitute who confessed to killing seven male customers. He includes footage of negotiations with the prison officials who repeatedly thwart his efforts to meet with Wuornos as well as scenes with Wuornos herself, whom he eventually succeeds in interviewing. Broomfield also interviews others involved in her story—a former lover who testified against Wuornos, evidently to avoid being charged as her partner-in-crime; a self-proclaimed Christian who "adopted" Wuornos in order to profit from her story; one of Wuornos's customers; and so on. The result is a many-layered tale with multiple views of the woman and her crimes.

Alcatraz: Escaping America's Toughest Prison
Type: VHS, color
Length: 50 minutes
Date: 1993
Cost: Purchase $29.95 (item #120-VD8)
Source: American Correctional Association

8025 Laurel Lakes Court
Laurel, MD 20707
(800) 222-5646
Fax: (301) 918-1886
E-mail: aca@corrections.com
Internet: http://www.corrections.com/aca

The U.S. Penitentiary on Alcatraz Island, located off the coast of San Francisco and once considered escape-proof, was for decades the ultimate prison for America's most notorious federal criminals. This video, made for the TV series *American Justice,* describes how inmates have attempted to break out of Alcatraz and other maximum security facilities located around the country. In interviews, prisoners, correctional officers, and prison administrators discuss some of the most complex and ingenious escape plans that inmates developed, often working over a very long time and with a great deal of resourcefulness and insight. Some of the most secure prisons have proved vulnerable to escape plans. The video characterizes the type of relationships and the power struggle between escapees and other inmates and prison staff. Viewers are exposed to the internal world of prisons, their informal rules, values, and subcultures. It is also useful for showing how a facility's vulnerability may affect inmates, staff, and the local community.

American Me
Type: VHS, color
Length: 125 minutes
Date: 1992
Cost: Purchase $16.99
Source: Reel, Inc.
Produced by: Universal City Studios

2655 Shattuck Avenue
Berkeley, CA 94704
(888) 707-7335
Internet: http://www.reel.com

This fictionalized version of a true story centers on the figure of Santana, a Mexican-American street gang leader and drug king-pin. The film reflects on Santana's experiences while locked inside Folsom Prison for eighteen years, offering a vivid portrayal of prison life, culture, and the prisonization experience. It depicts the ruthlessness of prison life and the inevitable changes produced in men who spend their lives inside. Highlighting Santana's criminal education in both juvenile and adult prisons, the film shows how Santana continues to rule over all the drug-and-murder activities behind bars. When released from prison, Santana intends to lead a peaceful, crime-free life. Nevertheless, he is too brutalized by a lifetime in prison to build a conventional lifestyle and returns to his old habits. His short release from prison is limited to drug dens and a few square blocks of the old neighborhood. Throughout, the video illustrates prison culture and the familial nature of gang relationships. Members of the gang drift in and out of prison, dealing drugs, murdering those who oppose them, and protecting one another from the police and other gangs. After spending more than half of his life behind bars, Santana experiences a violent but inevitable death when members of a rival prison gang stab him outside his cell.

The American Prison: A Video History
Type:	VHS, color
Length:	30 minutes
Date:	1990
Cost:	Purchase $83.50 (item #415 P7)
Source:	American Correctional Association

8025 Laurel Lakes Court
Laurel, MD 20707
(800) 222-5646
Fax: (301) 918-1886
E-mail: aca@corrections.com
Internet: http://www.corrections.com/aca

This pictorial commentary on the evolution of American prisons looks at the architecture of early and contemporary prisons and examines philosophies, attitudes, and events that have shaped the American prison. It also explores methods of inmate management and examines how the prison system has been affected by prison reformers, politics, and technological advances. Based on the American Correctional Association publication *The American Prison: From the Beginning,* the film uses photographs and prints collected and archived by the ACA. It is particularly useful for explaining the origins of our prison system.

Attica

Type:	VHS, color
Length:	97 minutes
Date:	1980
Cost:	Rental $3.50 (check your local store)
Source:	Blockbuster Headquarters
Produced by:	ABC Circle Films

Renaissance Tower
1201 Elm Street
Dallas, TX 75270
(800) 800-6767
Fax: (214) 854-4848
Internet: http://www.Blockbuster.com

This made-for-television documentary is a probing recreation of the tragic events of the Attica Prison riot of 9 September 1971. It provides an inside look at a prison uprising that resulted in a deadly conflict between inmates, administrators, correctional staff, and law enforcement personnel. The film highlights problems associated with prison overcrowding and the breakdown of security in a prison. It demonstrates how poor staff training, a faulty riot control plan, and the administration's failure to take proper precautions can lead to a prison takeover. Inmates are shown demanding better food and living conditions while using makeshift weapons to hold thirty-eight guards hostage. Administrators, politicians, and law enforcement personnel are shown struggling to devise a riot control plan and establish a leadership role while chaos reigns. The negotiation process begins immediately, revealing the continuous and steady shifting between agreement and conflict. Four days into the crisis, the uprising ends in a bloodbath as state troopers fire on prisoners, killing hostages in the process. The termination of the riot by law enforcement agents was one of the worst attacks on civilians in U.S. history. The film is based on the eyewitness reporting of *New York Times* reporter Tom Wicker, who was one of the negotiators during the standoff.

Boot Camps in Corrections
Type: VHS, color
Length: 20 minutes
Date: 1995
Cost: Purchase $99.95 (item #289-VD8)
Source: American Correctional Association

8025 Laurel Lakes Court
Laurel, MD 20707
(800) 222-5646
Fax: (301) 918-1886
E-mail: aca@corrections.com
Internet: http://www.corrections.com/aca

This documentary takes viewers through several "model" boot camps, revealing the layout, security structure, and training approach of the boot camp program. A brief introduction to the basic philosophy, goals, and purpose of boot camps is presented. Boot camps are an alternative to long-term incarceration for young first-time offenders. Boot camp participants often serve a brief portion of their sentence in prison, later accepting assignment to a boot camp for the purpose of developing discipline and respect for authority. The program is similar to military basic training in that it includes rigorous physical conditioning, discipline, education, and job training. The video shows physical training drills, hard labor projects, disciplinary sessions, classroom training, and staff-inmate encounters. It discusses the objectives of boot camp programs while explaining who is eligible and how they succeed in the program.

Brubaker
Type: VHS, color
Length: 131 minutes
Date: 1980
Cost: Purchase $8.49 (check your local store)
Source: Blockbuster Headquarters
Produced by: 20th Century Fox

Renaissance Tower
1201 Elm Street
Dallas, TX 75270
(800) 800-6767
Fax: (214) 854-4848
Internet: http://www.Blockbuster.com

Brubaker is based on the true story of Tom Murton, a reform-minded warden at the Arkansas State Prison during the 1960s.

Played by the actor Robert Redford, Brubaker discovers that prisoners are living in conditions of filth and violence. The officers, like the former warden, are engaged in an illicit alliance with contractors, with all taking money meant to be spent on food and equipment for inmates. Brubaker fights a one-man battle to clean up a corrupt prison. To learn firsthand of his prisoners' living conditions, Brubaker initially has himself arrested and thrown into his own prison. Later, he finds the bodies of missing inmates buried on part of the prison farm. Although violence and deceit pervade the movie, it ends on a triumphant note, with the inmates acknowledging Brubaker's fight on their behalf even as he is removed from his position. This film is valuable for its vivid and accurate portrayal of conditions at one of America's most brutal prisons.

Burden of Justice: Alternatives to Prison Overcrowding
Type: VHS, color
Length: 28 minutes
Date: 1991
Cost: Purchase $95 (item #155-INT)
Source: American Correctional Association

8025 Laurel Lakes Court
Laurel, MD 20707
(800) 222-5646
Fax: (301) 918-1886
E-mail: aca@corrections.com
Internet: http://www.corrections.com/aca

This documentary, narrated by Hal Holbrook, takes an in-depth look at how Alabama is coping with prison overcrowding in its sixteen correctional institutions and one juvenile center. The state's correctional system is similar in capacity to that of other states with similar incarceration rates. One major effect of prison overcrowding is to reduce the proportion of inmates in rehabilitation programs. Faced with limited resources and budgetary constraints, Alabama's judges, prosecutors, and police are seeking ways to punish nonviolent criminals without sending them to prison. At least eleven community-based facilities are operating throughout the state as alternatives to prison, and several community-based programs are examined in this video. Also discussed are the basic philosophies, goals, and strategies of community-based alternatives to prison.

CCI: Case Study of a Southern Prison

Type:	VHS, black and white
Length:	30 minutes
Date:	1993
Cost:	Purchase $129, rental $75 (item #BBK7031)
Source:	Films for the Humanities and Sciences

PO Box 2053
Princeton, NJ 08543-2053
(800) 257-5126
Fax: (609) 275-3767
Internet: http://www.films.com

This video presents live footage of the Central Correctional Institution in South Carolina. The overall focus is on the problem of the growing underclass, their limited opportunities, and their poor prospects for rehabilitation in prison. The film explores the success and failure rates of rehabilitation methods and programs. Interviews with inmates and staff provide an inside look at the problems of racism and violence that pervade prison life. Those interviewed express their feelings of despair and anger at their dismal prison conditions and limited access to treatment programs.

Correcting Our Elders

Type:	VHS, color
Length:	26 minutes
Date:	1992
Cost:	Purchase $85 (item #469-VD8)
Source:	American Correctional Association

8025 Laurel Lakes Court
Laurel, MD 20707
(800) 222-5646
Fax: (301) 918-1886
E-mail: aca@corrections.com
Internet: http://www.corrections.com/aca

This educational video discusses the challenges of managing the growing population of older inmates, outlining their special security needs and health concerns. Longer prison sentences and greater use of life-without-parole sentences have increased the elderly population in prison. Aging inmates have more difficulty handling physical ailments and the stress associated with incarceration. Recommendations are made for medical and mental health services and for pre- and postrelease support.

Correctional Perspectives: Inmates
Type: VHS, color
Length: 24 minutes
Date: 1996
Cost: Purchase $120 (item #482-T98)
Source: American Correctional Association

8025 Laurel Lakes Court
Laurel, MD 20707
(800) 222-5646
Fax: (301) 918-1886
E-mail: aca@corrections.com
Internet: http://www.corrections.com/aca

This video offers a look at the inside of a prison from an inmate's perspective. Three major topics are discussed by the inmates who are interviewed, including inmate care, custody, and correctional programming. This video offers a firsthand examination of ways in which correctional staff can improve their ability to manage offenders by better understanding how inmates see their prison world. This material is particularly useful for educating students, academics, researchers, and practitioners about the prison experience and the internal world of prisons.

Crime and Punishment in America
Type: VHS, color
Length: 120 minutes
Date: 1997
Cost: Purchase $109 (item #GU783)
Source: Insight Media
Produced by: KCET TV, Los Angeles, CA

2162 Broadway
New York, NY 10024
(212) 721-6316 or (800) 233-9910
Fax: (212) 799-5309
Internet: http://www.insight-media.com

This PBS news special focuses on both the historical and contemporary definition of criminal behavior and on the evolution of the varying approaches to punishment. The film explains how the definition of what constitutes crime continually changes over time on the basis of society's reaction and sensitivity to crime. In addition, it explains how the goals of punishment are influenced by the immediate definition of criminal behavior and by the public's fears of crime and perceptions of criminals. Live footage of street-crime activities and prison interiors is interspersed with taped testimony from law enforcement personnel, prosecutors, judges, prison wardens, historians, reformers, and citizens.

Crimes and Punishments: A History

Type:	VHS, color
Length:	30 minutes
Date:	1993
Cost:	Purchase $129, rental $75 (item #BBK6868)
Source:	Films for the Humanities and Sciences

PO Box 2053
Princeton, NJ 08543-2053
(800) 257-5126
Fax: (609) 275-3767
Internet: http://www.films.com

This documentary offers a history of criminal punishment from the medieval era to the present. It uses old lithographs to illustrate the brutal punishments of the past and to show how the move toward prison construction was influenced by more humane attitudes toward punishment. Interviews with prison officials describe the challenges involved in running large prisons such as the Central Correctional Institution in South Carolina. The film also features interviews with inmates and correctional officers, providing impressions of daily life in prison and information on the effectiveness of rehabilitation programs.

Cruel and Unusual

Type:	VHS, color
Length:	50 minutes
Date:	1995
Cost:	Purchase $99 (item #GT557)
Source:	Insight Media

2162 Broadway
New York, NY 10024
(212) 721-6316 or (800) 233-9910
Fax: (212) 799-5309
Internet: http://www.insight-media.com

This video examines philosophical issues raised by the treatment of the most dangerous prisoners in the United States. It profiles cases of punishment that have been called cruel and unusual on the basis of the Eighth Amendment of the U.S. Constitution. To exemplify cruel and unusual punishments, the video portrays the dungeons of the U.S. Penitentiary at Alcatraz, beatings by the guards, and horrible deaths during botched executions. It offers an informative but harsh look at how the U.S. prison system punishes, controls, and protects others from those considered beyond the scope of rehabilitation. It encourages discussion of the question: When does punishment exceed the crime?

Dead Man Walking

Type:	VHS, color
Length:	122 minutes
Date:	1995
Cost:	Purchase $12.99
Source:	Reel, Inc.
Produced by:	Gramercy Pictures

2655 Shattuck Avenue
Berkeley, CA 94704
(888) 707-7335
Internet: http://www.reel.com

This powerful, thought-provoking, factual drama presents both sides of the volatile subject of capital punishment. Based on the autobiography of Sister Helen Prejean, a Roman Catholic nun and spiritual adviser to death row prisoners, the film concentrates on her relationship with a Louisiana inmate named Matthew Poncelet. It is her mission to help the convicts find some peace and quietly accept responsibility for their crimes before they die. A fervent opponent of the death penalty, Sister Prejean is nonetheless a pragmatic soul, able to see both sides of a very difficult issue. She gets involved in the prison system after receiving a letter from brutal killer Matthew, asking her to become his "spiritual adviser." Something in the letter touches her and she travels to the Louisiana State Penitentiary at Angola to meet with him on death row. When they first meet, Poncelet swears that he is innocent. He blames the rape-murder on his crime partner and the fact that they had been drinking and drugging that night. Much of the film is centered on the intense conversations between the nun, portrayed by Susan Sarandon, and the prisoner, played by Sean Penn. As part of her job, Sister Helen must visit the victims' parents to help them deal with their rage and invite their forgiveness. What makes this film unique is that it takes no sides; the people involved are realistically presented, and the viewer is left to sort out his or her own feelings on the issue.

Defending Our Lives
Type: VHS, color
Length: 42 minutes (30-minute version also available)
Date: 1993
Cost: Purchase $160, rental $55
Source: Cambridge Documentary Films, Inc.
Produced by: Margaret Lazarus, Renna Wunderlich,
               and Stacey Kabat

PO Box 390385
Cambridge, MA 02139-0004
(617) 484-3993
Fax: (617) 484-0754
Internet: http://www1.shore.net/~cdf/defend.html

The winner of an Academy Award for Best Documentary Film, this film was made by advocates of battered women and features four women imprisoned at the Massachusetts Correctional Institution, Framingham, for killing their batterers in self-defense. At the time that they were sentenced to long terms in prison, Massachusetts did not allow women the defense of self-defense against a batterer except in circumstances of immediate self-protection. As those circumstances do not always pertain in battering relationships (victims are more likely to wait until they have some kind of an advantage and can fight back effectively), victims were in effect punished for crimes initiated by others. As a result of the work of women depicted in this film, the state did change its rules to allow such victims of partner-abuse a legal defense. In the film, the speakers dramatically tell their horrifying stories of rapes, beatings, and torture at the hands of their husbands and boyfriends.

Doing Time
Type: VHS, color
Length: 56 minutes
Date: 1990
Cost: Purchase $179 (item #GT446)
Source: Insight Media

2162 Broadway
New York, NY 10024
(212) 721-6316 or (800) 233-9910
Fax: (212) 799-5309
Internet: http://www.insight-media.com

This winner of the Emmy Award examines conditions at the New Mexico Penitentiary in 1990. Through interviews with prisoners, the video captures the stories of the real people serving time in a maximum-security prison. It also tells the stories of men who have experienced a successful release from prison and return to the community, and of offenders who have failed upon release and returned to prison. This video is a ten-year follow-up of a 1980 video that visited the New Mexico Penitentiary just two months before the institution's major uprising, an event that became the bloodiest prison riot in U.S. history. Interviews in this follow-up video are conducted with inmates and ex-inmates who lived through the riot.

Drug Abuse Treatment in Prison: A New Way Out
Type: VHS, color
Length: 24 minutes
Date: 1995
Cost: Purchase $12.50 (item #VHS72)
Source: National Clearinghouse for Alcohol and Drug
             Information (NCADI)

PO Box 2345
Rockville, MD 20847-2345
(800) 729-6686
Fax: (301) 468-6433
Internet: http://www.health.org/

This National Institute for Drug Abuse video presents two treatment approaches that have been effective for men and women in state and federal prisons. The video discusses the philosophies behind drug treatment for offenders and describes the goals and program components of these two gender-specific programs.

The Execution Protocol
Type: VHS, color
Length: 83 minutes
Date: 1992
Cost: Information not available
Source: First Run/Icarus Films
Produced by: Worldview Pictures and West End Film Production

153 Waverly Place
New York, NY 10014
(212) 727-1711
Fax: (212) 989-7649
E-mail: info@frif.com
Internet: http://www.frif.com

This remarkable documentary by Stephen Trombley includes interviews with death row prisoners, with government and prison officials, and with all participants in capital punishment, including the inventor of the lethal injection machine. Filmed at a Missouri prison built to hold only prisoners sentenced to natural life or execution, the documentary shows what daily life is like at such an institution. Viewers are taken on a tour of the institution by an inmate who is awaiting execution. (Incidentally, viewers also thereby gain an inside view of security operations in one of the new, high-technology prisons.) We learn how inmates relieve tensions and how they occupy themselves during an execution. Most chilling of all are scenes where officials review the "protocols" or routines for executions so that all will go smoothly.

The Executioners

Type:	VHS, color
Length:	100 minutes
Date:	1995
Cost:	Purchase $29.95 (item #118-VD8)
Source:	American Correctional Association

8025 Laurel Lakes Court
Laurel, MD 20707
(800) 222-5646
Fax: (301) 918-1886
E-mail: aca@corrections.com
Internet: http://www.corrections.com/aca

This video explores the origins and evolution of capital punishment from ancient times to the twentieth century. From Hammurabi's law to modern executions by lethal injection, capital punishment has been practiced by almost every society in the world. The video examines various sides of the issue of capital punishment, with debates conducted by actual crime victims, lawyers, judges, family members, and executioners.

The Farm: Angola U.S.A.

Type:	VHS, Color
Length:	100 minutes
Date:	1998
Cost:	Purchase $20.99
Source:	Reel, Inc.
Produced by:	A & E, *Investigative Reports*

2655 Shattuck Avenue

Berkeley, CA 94704
(888) 707-7335
Internet: http://www.reel.com

This documentary has received several national film awards and a 1998 Oscar nomination for best documentary feature film. Wilbert Rideau, a prisoner at the Louisiana State Penitentiary at Angola for the past 38 years, codirected the film. *The Farm* is a grim portrayal of life and death inside the walls of Angola. The filmmakers lead viewers through an emotional journey that explores a year in the life of six male inmates incarcerated at Angola. Angola is Louisiana's largest maximum security facility, housing more than 5,000 inmates on a former slave plantation. As both codirector and intimate participant in the interviews of the six inmates, their victims, and prison officials, Rideau's own experience helps to provide a truthful vision of life inside prison. Viewers are shown how the harsh realities of life at Angola are intertwined with each man's experience, lost dreams, passionate admissions of remorse, and sense of mortality. The six men include a wife-killer, rapist, armed robber, drug dealer, and two murderers. This impassioned film leaves a lasting impression on both the seasoned professionals in the field and the amateur.

From One Prison
Type: VHS, color
Length: 70 minutes
Date: 1996
Cost: Purchase $225, rental $70
Source: University of California Extension
Produced by: Carol Jacobsen

Center for Media and Independent Learning
2000 Center Street, 4th floor
Berkeley, CA 94704
(510) 642-0460
Fax: (510) 643-9271
Internet: http://www-cmil.unex.berkeley.edu/media

From One Prison is a documentary focusing on the lives of four female inmates serving life or long-term sentences for killing abusive men in self-defense. The women are serving their sentences in a Michigan prison, where most of the video is filmed. They reflect on their prison experiences, discussing the issues of sexual harassment and prison rape, overcrowded living conditions, poor medical care, unhealthy food, and their relationships with their family members and children. They relate their histories of abuse, their criminal defenses, and the failings of the criminal justice system when it comes to cases of this type.

The Growth of Incarceration in the U.S.:
Where Are All the Prisoners Coming From?

Type: VHS, color
Length: 60 minutes
Date: 1998
Cost: Purchase $19 (NCJ 172853)
Source: National Criminal Justice Reference Service

PO Box 6000
Rockville, MD 20849-6000
(800) 851-3420
Fax: (212) 799-5309
Internet: http://www.ncjrs.gov

This documentary research video presents Alfred Blumstein, of Carnegie Mellon University, and Allen Beck, the Bureau of Justice Statistics, discussing their research on the expansion of prison populations, its causes, and policy considerations for the future. They also engage in a question-and-answer discussion with an audience.

Hard Time

Type: VHS, color
Length: 27 minutes
Date: 1980
Cost: Purchase $119 (item #26U741)
Source: Insight Media

2162 Broadway
New York, NY 10024
(212) 721-6316 or (800) 233-9910
Fax: (212) 799-5309
Internet: http://www.insight-media.com

This video was filmed inside the Stateville Prison at Joliet, Illinois, giving viewers a firsthand look at the conditions in this prison. Stateville is a maximum-security facility with the reputation of being one of America's "toughest" prisons, housing some of Chicago's most notorious offenders. The video addresses issues raised by poor conditions and dangerous and unsafe prison environments that produce criminal activities inside prison and offenders who return to society angrier and tougher than when they went in.

Let the Doors Be Made of Iron: 19th-Century Prison Reform

Type:	VHS, color
Length:	23 minutes
Date:	1987
Cost:	Purchase $129, rental $75 (item #BBK6867)
Source:	Films for the Humanities and Sciences

PO Box 2053
Princeton, NJ 08543-2053
(800) 257-5126
Fax: (609) 275-3767
Internet: http://www.films.com

This film uses old lithographs and photographs to trace the fascinating history of the first full-scale penitentiary, Eastern State Penitentiary in Philadelphia, opened in the early nineteenth century. The Quakers who helped found this penitentiary viewed it as a more humane and effective alternative to corrupt jails and physical punishments. The penitentiary's fortresslike design, separate cells, and system of labor became the correctional model for prisons worldwide. The film presents important events in the penitentiary's history, including the arrival of its first prisoner in 1829. The film provides insight on the early experimentation with more humane treatment, long-term confinement, and rehabilitation of criminals at one of the world's most famous penal institutions. Today Eastern State Penitentiary is a museum, and it can be toured on certain days from May through October.

Life after Prison: Success on the Outside

Type:	VHS, color
Length:	30 minutes
Date:	1998
Cost:	Purchase $139 (item #GU837)
Source:	Insight Media

2162 Broadway
New York, NY 10024
(212) 721-6316 or (800) 233-9910
Fax: (212) 799-5309
Internet: http://www.insight-media.com

This film presents taped interviews with former inmates relating their experiences on being released from prison. Several interviews are with men who have broken with their past criminal behaviors and successfully returned to the community. Other interviews are with men who, unable to break the cycle of a criminal lifestyle, have been rearrested and returned to prison. Commentaries from parole officers provide an understanding of why some people fail when released whereas others are able to move away from a criminal lifestyle. The program stresses the importance of having solid ties in the community such as employment and family support, and it includes information on building inmates' skills before release and helping them find employment in a local community.

Lock-Up: The Prisoners of Rikers Island
Type: VHS, color
Length: 75 minutes
Date: 1994
Cost: Purchase $149, rental $75 (item #BBK6286)
Source: Films for the Humanities and Sciences
Produced by: HBO

PO Box 2053
Princeton, NJ 08543-2053
(800) 257-5126
Fax: (609) 275-3767
Internet: http://www.films.com

This HBO television special provides a unique inside look at how prisoners live and how officials try to maintain order at New York City's Rikers Island Jail, a massive holding facility for those awaiting trial or sentencing to a permanent prison facility. If someone is arrested in New York City and cannot make bail, he or she will be transported to Rikers Island, the nation's largest jail complex, through which more than 140,000 people pass each year. The film profiles the typical Rikers Island inmate, who is a poor, undereducated member of a minority group and arrested for a drug-related crime. It also shows everyday jail activities, including such disconcerting scenes as a cell block strip search by corrections officers, the story of an AIDS-infected drug user who was born in prison and will most likely die there, a trip to the holding cells for "disorganized and paranoid" prisoners, and the anguish of women who will see their children born in jail.

Men, Women, and Respect: Stopping Sexual Harassment in Correctional Facilities
Type: VHS, color
Length: 20 minutes
Date: 1993

Cost: Purchase $99 (item #224-VD8)
Source: American Correctional Association

8025 Laurel Lakes Court
Laurel, MD 20707
(800) 222-5646
Fax: (301) 918-1886
E-mail: aca@corrections.com
Internet: http://www.corrections.com/aca

This training video explores how sexual harassment within prisons affects the harasser, the victim, and the prison administration. It defines sexual harassment and explains why cases of this type often go unreported. A study guide accompanies this video.

Prison Stories: Women on the Inside
Type: VHS, color
Length: 94 minutes
Date: 1991
Cost: Information not available
Source: Reel, Inc.
Produced by: Prism Enterprises

2655 Shattuck Avenue
Berkeley, CA 94704
(888) 707-7335
Internet: http://www.reel.com

This made-for-television film is a fictional anthology of the stories of three women in prison. Vividly portraying the harsh realities of prison life, the segments are directed by three well-known women directors and star strong actors such as Annabella Sciorra. The first story is about lifelong friends who must test their friendship while serving time together; one of them is pregnant and needs protection from a gang. The second story is about a woman who attempts to keep her young nephew from following in his mother's footsteps and leading a life of crime. In the third story, an abused wife in prison for murdering her husband is afraid to leave the security of life behind bars to renew her relationship with her daughter.

Prisoner on the Run
Type: VHS, color
Length: 54 minutes
Date: 1996
Cost: Purchase $89.95 (item #AZA4036)

Source: Films for the Humanities and Sciences

PO Box 2053
Princeton, NJ 08543-2053
(800) 257-5126
Fax: (609) 275-3767
Internet: http://www.films.com

This documentary about the escape of a forty-three-year-old man confined to prison since committing murder at the age of fifteen examines the prison experience from a prisoner's perspective. It addresses questions regarding the harshness of his life sentence, details of his offense, and the degree to which this sympathetic man is a danger to society.

Quiet Rage: The Stanford Prison Experiment
Type: VHS, color
Length: 50 minutes
Date: 1990
Cost: Purchase $149 (item #GT408)
Source: Insight Media

2162 Broadway
New York, NY 10024
(212) 721-6316 or (800) 233-9910
Fax: (212) 799-5309
Internet: http://www.insight-media.com

This is a documentary of the famous research experiment in which a California professor, Philip Zimbardo, created a mock prison as a means to investigate the psychological effects of incarceration. Zimbardo randomly assigned students to play the role of either prisoners or correctional officers. The video covers their experiences, taking viewers through the various stages of the actual experiment. Because of the mounting cruelty of the student guards and the psychological deterioration of the student prisoners, the experiment had to be terminated after only six days. Postexperiment interviews are conducted with both student prisoners and guards.

Security Levels in Correctional Facilities
Type: VHS, color
Length: 23 minutes
Date: 1997
Cost: Purchase $120 (item #629-S7)
Source: American Correctional Association

8025 Laurel Lakes Court
Laurel, MD 20707
(800) 222-5646
Fax: (301) 918-1886
E-mail: aca@corrections.com
Internet: http://www.corrections.com/aca

This video discusses the three security levels found in correctional institutions—maximum, medium, and minimum—and examines how they help institutions meet their goals. Interviews with administrative personnel and correctional staff show how the physical aspects of security affect daily working and living experiences. Areas explored include classification, cell constraints, restriction of movement, external perimeter control, the presence or absence of guard towers, external patrols, the number of detection devices, the security of housing areas, monitoring strategies, and staffing.

Shakedown at Santa Fe
Type: VHS, color
Length: 58 minutes
Date: 1988
Cost: Information not available
Source: PBS Video
Produced by: Produced for the Documentary Consortium
               by WGBH

1320 Bradock Place
Alexandria, VA 22314-1698
(703) 739-5000
fax: (703) 739-0775
Internet: http://www.shop.pbs.org

One of the best of all prison documentaries, this video, originally produced for *Frontline*, discusses the mistreatment of prisoners at the New Mexico Penitentiary in the days leading up to the violent riot of February 1980. It also interviews prisoners who lived through the disturbance, guards who worked at the institution at the time, and current prisoners in protective segregation. One riveting sequence focuses on the woman who currently heads the guard force at this maximum-security institution for male offenders, showing how she commands respect from both prisoners and other officers. Another sequence tours a new unit, built since the riot. The interviews bring viewers face-to-face with tough issues of prisoners' rights versus administrative control.

The Thin Blue Line

Type:	VHS, Beta, color
Length:	Information not available
Date:	1988
Cost:	Purchase $19.98
Source:	HBO

http://www.hbohomevideo.com

One of the most influential docudramas of recent years, *The Thin Blue Line* concerns the true story of the shooting of a police officer in Dallas County, Texas, in 1977. It focuses on Randall Adams, the drifter who was mistakenly convicted of the crime and sentenced to death. The filmmaker, Errol Morris, interviews Adams in prison and, through these conversations and other interviews, reconstructs the crime and its aftermath. Thanks to the film's new information on the identity of the actual killer, Adams was eventually released from death row. The film covers the entire spectrum of criminal justice, from arrest procedures through imposition of the death penalty, showing viewers how justice can miscarry so drastically. This film won the Edgar Allen Poe Award in 1988 for Best Screenplay.

Through the Wire

Type:	VHS, color
Length:	68 minutes
Date:	1990
Cost:	Information not available
Source:	Cinema Guild
Produced by:	Produced and directed by Nina Rosenblum; production company: Daedalus Productions Inc.

1697 Broadway, Suite 506
New York, NY 10019
(212) 246-5522
Internet: http://www.cinemaguild.com/home.html

This documentary deals with three political prisoners being held in a specially constructed unit at a federal prison in Lexington, Kentucky. The prisoners feel they are being subjected to an experiment in sensory deprivation, a belief the film confirms through dramatic footage of the women's daily routines. The film also relates the stories of their crimes, and it interviews families and friends, demonstrating that the prisoners acted on the highest principles when they committed their offenses. As a result of this film, the special unit was eventually shut down and the women transferred elsewhere. *Through the Wire* takes us into a type of prison where few outsiders have ever visited, revealing secretive practices of the Federal Bureau of Prisons.

Titicut Follies

Type:	VHS, color
Length:	84 minutes
Date:	Originally released in 1967 as a motion picture
Cost:	Purchase $500, rental $150
Source:	Zipporah Films
Produced by:	Frederick Wiseman

One Richdale Avenue, Unit #4
Cambridge, MA 02140
(617) 576-3603
Fax: (617) 864-8006
E-mail: info@zipporah.com
Internet: http://www.zipporah.com/index.html

This documentary film was made at Massachusetts Correctional Institution, Bridgewater, the prison for the state's criminally insane prisoners. Its remarkable footage shows scenes from the daily life of inmates and their guards, including shots of a talent show ("Titicut Follies") that they stage together. It leaves viewers with no doubt that any prisoner sent here will only become more ill, not because of malice but because of horrifying neglect and "treatment" by incompetent staff. This is one of the most famous documentaries ever made of prison life, and perhaps the only one made inside a prison mental hospital.

Voices from Inside

Type:	VHS, color
Length:	60 minutes
Date:	Information not available
Cost:	Purchase $250, rental $75
Source:	New Day Film Library

22D Hollywood Avenue
Hohokus, NJ 07423
(201) 652-6590
Fax: (201) 652-1973
Internet address: http://www.newday.com

This documentary video follows a German-born theater artist into a federal women's prison where she encourages a racially mixed circle of women to find their own voices through poetry and creative expression. The women tell their life stories and share their experience of prison life.

Why Not Wilbert Rideau?
Type: VHS, color
Length: Information not available
Date: Information not available
Cost: Purchase $25.95
Source: Prentice Hall, Inc.
Produced by: ABC News

One Lake Street
Upper Saddle River, NJ 07458
(800) 526-0485

Barbara Walters and Hugh Downs narrate this story (originally broadcast as a *20/20* television special) of convicted murderer Wilbert Rideau, who shot and stabbed three hostages while robbing a bank in Louisiana. One hostage died. Today Rideau is considered the most rehabilitated prisoner in America. Although many have petitioned for his release, including three pardon boards and many prison officials, he remains incarcerated at the Louisiana State Penitentiary at Angola. He spends a great deal of time traveling around the state speaking to students to help persuade them from committing crimes. This video addresses questions about the goals of rehabilitation, the length of prison sentences, the decision to execute versus life in prison, and the point at which a person should be deemed fit to return to society.

Women Doing Time
Type: VHS, color
Length: 48 minutes
Date: 1992
Cost: Purchase $149 (item #GT222)
Source: Insight Media

2162 Broadway
New York, NY 10024
(212) 721-6316 or (800) 233-9910
Fax: (212) 799-5309
Internet: http://www.insight-media.com

This *48 Hours* television news special was filmed in the New York Bedford Hills Correctional Facility for Women, one of the oldest women's prisons in the country. It examines the lives of women in prison, profiling their offenses and sentences. The film focuses on relationships of women with their children, investigating what happens to children left on the outside and to their imprisoned mothers.

Young Criminals, Adult Punishment
Type: VHS, color
Length: 23 minutes
Date: 1996
Cost: Purchase $129, rental $75 (item #BHP7658)
Source: Films for the Humanities and Sciences

PO Box 2053
Princeton, NJ 08543-2053
(800) 257-5126
Fax: (609) 275-3767
Internet: http://www.films.com

This ABC news program examines criminal justice approaches to violent juvenile offenders. As crimes committed by youngsters become progressively more violent, the criminal justice system must decide whether the harsh sentences given to adult criminals, including capital punishment, should also apply to violent young offenders. This news story interviews young, violent offenders, their families, attorneys, prosecutors, and law enforcement officials, presenting various perceptions of the issues and possible solutions to violence among youths. Herbert Hoelter of the National Criminal Justice Commission discusses the various state laws governing juvenile punishment. He suggests rehabilitation for kids who commit violent crimes but do not fall into the category of "super-predators"; the latter may never benefit from rehabilitation.

Internet Addresses

Note: See Chapters 6 and 7 for other Internet addresses.

Global Bibliography of Prison Systems
Philip L. Reichel
Department of Sociology
University of Northern Colorado
501 20th Street
Greeley, CO 80639
(970) 351-2107
Fax: (970) 351-1527

E-mail: plreich@unco.edu
Internet: http://www.ifs.univie.ac.at/~uncjin/gbops/gbops.htm

The primary goal for developing this bibliographical website was to provide practitioners, scholars, and students with a comprehensive source for identifying information written about international prison systems. Most of the material included in the bibliography dates from 1985 or earlier, and unless otherwise noted, materials are submitted in the language of their original publication. The development of the bibliography is an ongoing project, with items added as material becomes available.

Prison Law Page
A. Erickson
PO Box 2111
San Anselmo, CA 94974.
Internet: http://www.wco.com/~aerick/

The Prison Law Page is a site that focuses on issues associated with prison reform, the judicial process, restorative justice, anti–death penalty work, and sentencing. Although this site targets California prisons, most of its material is relevant to other states as well. Information is available from current publications, archives, lists of prison rules, a prison dictionary, newspapers, inmate writings, and announcements by prison-related organizations.

Prisons.com
PO Box 1283
Forestdale, MA 02644
(508) 362-1037 or (508) 477-3631
Fax: (508) 375-4039
E-mail: warden@prisons.com
Internet: http://www.prisons.com/

The prisons.com (PCOM) website is a worldwide Internet resource for the corrections industry. It provides a vast amount of information on current news, research, events, funding, products, programs, technology, and employment opportunities. PCOM announces opportunities for funded research, providing the application and submission forms. It also presents exhibits on current activities and upcoming events; provides a headline news service for national stories related to prisons; and offers links to other criminal justice websites and a directory of correctional organizations and industries. Areas of information recently added to this site include a listing of law publications; a correctional health reference; an e-mail forum and discussion groups for debating prison issues with other professionals; and descriptions of computer equipment for use in prisons.

Sourcebook of Criminal Justice Statistics
Bureau of Justice Statistics Clearinghouse
E-mail: asksb@cnsunix.albany.edu
Internet: http://www.albany.edu/sourcebook

As noted in Chapter 7, the *Sourcebook* brings together data about all aspects of criminal justice in the United States. Chapter 7 gave information on ordering hard copies; here we offer Internet information. Available at this site are more than 600 tables and 4 figures from over 100 sources that are updated annually. Although the *Sourcebook* is an annual publication, its compilation is an ongoing process. The website continually provides updates of tables and new data sources; its updates reflect new data as they will appear in the next edition. The viewer is alerted to updates by flags that appear next to titles in the table and figure list. In addition, the What's New page announces changes as they occur and new data sources available on the Web. Information is provided on how to order reports, how to contact the editors, questions about data coverage and reliability, reporting periods, table and figure preparation, and symbols used in the tables. Viewers can access information of interest by browsing the contents, table and figure list, and index or by searching with keywords, and viewers may look at individual tables displayed in separate files or download an entire section to a personal computer file.

State Departments of Correction—Links
The Corrections Connection Network
159 Burgin Parkway
Quincy, MA 02194
(617) 471-4445
Fax: (617) 770-3339
E-mail: ednet@corrections.com
Internet: http://www.corrections.com/state.html#state

This site provides a complete listing of and direct linkage to all state department of correction sites and related state agency sites. Websites for state departments of correction provide direct access to the agency. Most state correctional sites include detailed information about their history, mission, philosophies, goals, and budgets, and administrative services. Most also offer state and local statistics on prison and jail populations and on offenses. Further information can be found on crimes, sentencing, prison reform activities, newsworthy events, programs and services, recent legislation, and prison industries. In most cases site visitors will also find a directory of facilities, administrators, staff and services, funded projects, current research, and employment opportunities.

Glossary

Auburn system   An approach to prison architecture, management, and discipline used in the earliest penitentiaries. Under the Auburn system, prisoners lived and slept in single cells but were brought together during the day to labor silently in workshops. The term derives from New York's Auburn Penitentiary, the first institution to implement this system. Often contrasted with the **Pennsylvania system,** the Auburn system was favored in the United States because it was more economical. It is also known as the *congregate system* of prisoner discipline because it enables convicts to congregate or gather together in workshops during the day.

building tender system   A method of prison management used in Texas until prohibited by the 1980 federal district court decision in *Ruiz v. Estelle.* Building tenders or "BTs" were tough, violent inmates appointed by prison officials to "tend" other prisoners. The BT system saved the cost of hiring guards to perform the same work, and it kept inmates terrorized into submission. However, it operated with great brutality and meant that the most hardened criminals had license to rape and beat other prisoners in their cell blocks. The system was strongly but unsuccessfully defended by George Beto and his protégé, W. J. Estelle, directors of the Texas Department of Corrections.

congregate system   See **Auburn system.**

definite sentences   Prison sentences that consist of only one number such as "ten years." Also known as "flat," "fixed," or "determinate" sentences, these were the first type used to commit convicts to U.S. prisons. In the late nineteenth century, definite sentences were replaced by **indeterminate sentences.** Recently, however, definite sentences have again become popular with legislatures seeking **"truth in sentencing."**

determinate sentences   See **definite sentences.**

deterrence   A theory of punishment according to which we punish people in order to prevent future crimes. Theorists distinguish between *specific deterrence,* in which an offender is punished to discourage him or her from committing further crimes, and *general deterrence,* in which an offender is punished to discourage others from committing crimes. Deterrence was an important rationale behind the construction of the first U.S. prisons. It is associated with the name of Cesare Beccaria, the Italian political theorist who first articulated the theory.

discretion   Authority to make choices in the disposition of offenders. For most of U.S. prison history, judges had the authority to make discretionary decisions, meaning that they could choose to sentence an offender to probation or to prison and that they could set the length of sentence on the basis of individual factors. In recent years there has been a movement to curtail judicial discretion on the grounds that it leads to unfairness and excessive leniency.

eugenics movement   A social movement, ca. 1870–1925, that endorsed the **medical model** of crime control and totally open-ended or **indefinite sentences.** Eugenicists believed that criminals commit crimes because they have inferior "germ plasm" (genes), and that therefore the way to prevent future crimes is to prevent criminals from reproducing. Most U.S. eugenicists supported indefinite sentences as the best method of keeping "inferiors" in prison and hence from reproducing.

felony   A serious crime (cf. **misdemeanor**). Felonies are offenses for which the potential punishment is one year or more of incarceration. While misdemeanants typically are sent to jails, felons are held in prisons.

good-time   Sentence reduction in return for a prisoner's good behavior. For example, a good-time law might provide that a prisoner can earn a reduction in time served by one day for every five days of good behavior. Good-time laws, which were enacted almost as soon as states built prisons, proved useful in encouraging prisoner compliance and relieving overcrowding. Under definite sentencing, good-time is subtracted from the term (e.g., ten years) specified by the judge. Under indeterminate sentencing, good-time often is subtracted from the minimum time to be served; thus with good-time, a prisoner sentenced to an indeterminate sentence of five to eight years might gain release in four years.

hands-off doctrine   A judicial policy of noninterference in prison administration. This policy prevailed until the 1960s, when the prisoners' rights movement began. Before the 1960s, judges believed that they should not intervene in prison management because of the separation of powers among the branches of government; they belonged to the judiciary branch, whereas prison officials were employed by the executive branch. The effect of this doctrine was to deny prisoners constitutional rights.

indefinite sentences Completely open-ended sentences; sentences with no maximum term beyond which the prisoner may not be held. Sentences of this type were endorsed by the 1870 National Congress on Penitentiary and Reformatory Discipline as well as by reformers active in the Progressive movement and the **eugenics movement.** Indefinite sentences have rarely been enacted, however, because they clash with the **principle of proportionality,** according to which the punishment should fit the crime. Indefinite sentences should not be confused with sentences of "natural life" or "life without parole," which are used to punish offenders convicted of murder and other very serious crimes. Those who advocate indefinite sentencing argue that it should apply to all offenders, irrespective of the gravity of their offense; prisoners should be released only when they have reformed.

indeterminate sentences Sentences with minimum and maximum terms, such as a sentence of five to eight years. Introduced about 1870, indeterminate sentences replaced the older **definite sentences.** Under indeterminate sentencing, well-behaved prisoners can be released early on **parole.** The get-tough sentiment that set in about 1970 has led some states to reject indeterminate sentencing and return to sentences of the definite or determinate type.

jail A local penal institution run by a county, city, or town. In contrast to prisons, jails usually hold people awaiting trial and convicted offenders sentenced to one year or less of incarceration.

mandatory sentences Sentences that are prescribed by the legislature or Congress and leave the judge no discretion to adjust the punishment to fit the particular offender. For example, Massachusetts has a mandatory gun law according to which anyone caught carrying an unregistered handgun must be sentenced to one year in jail.

medical model A theory of crime according to which people who break the law are sick, physically or mentally; also an approach to punishment that advocates keeping criminals in prison until they are "cured." Widely accepted in the late nineteenth and early twentieth centuries, today the medical model of crime control is less popular.

misdemeanor A minor offense (cf. **felony**); an offense for which the maximum punishment does not exceed one year of incarceration. Misdemeanants (those found guilty of misdemeanors) usually serve their time in jails, not prisons.

mitigating and aggravating circumstances Circumstances that may reduce or increase sentence length. A mitigating factor might be present if a partner in a bank robbery never entered the bank but rather sat outside as driver of the getaway car. An aggravating factor might occur if a bank robber not only brandished a gun but also fired it inside the bank.

New York system See **Auburn system.**

panopticon A circular type of prison designed by the English philosopher and jurist Jeremy Bentham. In this design, cells are built into the outer wall of a circular building, and a guard tower is placed in the center. Thus, in theory, a single guard can maintain surveillance over the entire prison population at once. Bentham designed the tower so that the guard within it could not be seen by the prisoners.

parity movement A movement that seeks a solution to the persistent problem of inferior treatment of female prisoners. According to advocates of parity, the solution to unequal care does not lie in trying to provide women prisoners with care identical to that available to men prisoners. Instead the solution lies in providing programs that are just as adequate as those available to men but designed with women's particular treatment needs in mind.

parole Early release from prison in return for good behavior. This method of encouraging prisoner reformation was introduced about 1870 as part of the movement to rehabilitate offenders. An aspect of **indeterminate sentences,** parole involves three sorts of participants: the prisoner who is released early on parole (the "parolee"); the parole board that grants this early release; and the parole officer who supervises the parolee. Parole is a form of conditional release—the parolee can be returned to prison if she or he violates the conditions of parole. In reaction against indeterminate sentencing, some states have recently abolished parole and reinstated **definite sentences.**

penitentiary A type of prison characterized by thick perimeter walls, cells blocks, strict routines, and harsh discipline.

Pennsylvania system An approach to prison architecture, management, and discipline in which prisoners are held in solitary confinement for the entire length of their sentences. Associated with the Eastern State Penitentiary in Philadelphia, the Pennsylvania system was one of two competing early types of penitentiary. It is sometimes referred to as the *segregate system* of prison discipline because its prisoners were segregated entirely from one another, in contrast to the congregate system practiced in the competing model, the **Auburn system.** The Pennsylvania system was admired by Europeans but seldom adopted in this country, as it was more costly than the Auburn system, requiring workbenches and running water in every cell and a separate exercise yard for each prisoner.

penology The study and practice of prison management and prisoner rehabilitation. A "penologist" is one who specializes in these areas.

principle of least eligibility The notion that prisoners should have less access to social benefits than law-abiding citizens. In recent years this principle has led to a scaling-back of prisoner rehabilitation programs. Today the public tends to feel strongly that criminals should not have better access than ordinary taxpayers to luxuries such as free legal education and free use of recreation equipment.

principle of proportionality The principle that punishment should fit the crime. According to this principle, a serious offense should be punished with a more severe sentence than a minor offense. Sometimes contrasted with the idea that the punishment should fit the offender, the principle of proportionality made its way into American jurisprudence partly through *On Crimes and Punishments* (1764), a book by the Italian theorist Cesare Beccaria.

prisonization   The state or condition of having become so accustomed to prison that one can no longer function in the free world.

recidivism   The phenomenon of return to criminal behavior. Recidivists are offenders who, after being punished for one crime, commit another.

segregate system   See **Pennsylvania system.**

trusty   A prisoner who is given authority to manage other prisoners. (Plural: trusties.)

"truth in sentencing"   A slogan used to support the belief that a sentence should mean what it says, so that if someone is sentenced to ten to thirteen years in prison, that person should not be released before serving at least ten years. The phrase has become part of the get-tough movement that started about 1970 and has resulted in much harsher sentencing and larger prison populations.

Index

Note: t. indicates table.

Nicole Hahn Rafter is chair of the Division on Women and Crime of the American Society of Criminology and chair of the Crime, Law, and Deviance section of the American Sociological Association. In addition to books, she has written more than sixty articles, book chapters, and reviews on criminal justice.

Debra L. Stanley is an assistant professor at Central Connecticut State University. She is currently working with a major research project focusing on female offenders with substance abuse, violence, and mental health problems.